A FAMILY

SARA B. STEIN

DOLLHOUSE

A FAMILY DOLLHOUSE
An Introduction to Crafts in Miniature

Text and Drawings by Sara B. Stein
Photographs by Jon Naso

A STUDIO BOOK
· THE VIKING PRESS ·
NEW YORK

For Alix

Photographs by Jon Naso

The dollhouse was made from the author's plans
by Mario Cappabianca.
Several items shown in the room views,
such as the table and ceramic crocks in the kitchen,
were purchased from professional craftspeople.
Other furnishings, such as the rolltop desk and the
Indian baskets, are antiques.

First published in 1979 by The Viking Press
625 Madison Avenue, New York, N.Y. 10022
Published simultaneously in Canada by
Penguin Books Canada Limited

Library of Congress Cataloging in Publication Data
Stein, Sara Bonnett.
A family dollhouse.
(A Studio book)
1. Dollhouses. 2. Doll furniture.
3. Miniature craft. I. Title.
TT173.3.S73   745.59'23   78-27396
ISBN 0-670-30614-2

Text and black-and-white illustrations printed in
the United States of America
Color illustrations printed in Japan

 created by Media Projects Incorporated

❧ Contents ❧

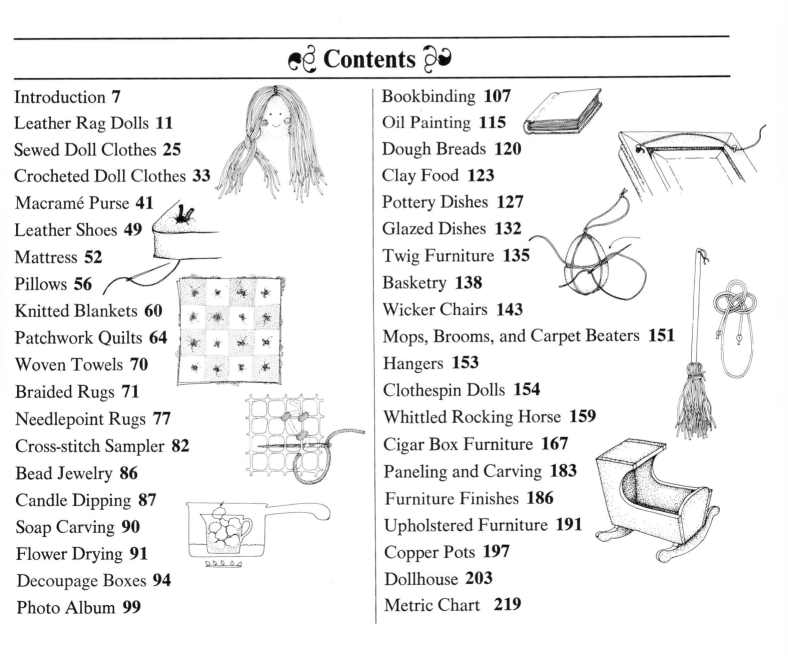

❧ Introduction ❧

Our family dollhouse is eight years old. When it was newly built and freshly furnished from the store, we made the mistake of placing it against the wall opposite our bed. There, as the eleven o'clock news chattered catastrophe, the dollhouse whispered reproach. The floors were bare. The cupboards were barer. The bathtub was ugly. The cradle was clunky. And everything looked like everybody else's. Today, eight years later, only the stove remains—and it has got to go.

The furnishings now, the colors, patterns, and arrangements, were all conceived in bed, long after the news was over. If this reminds you of another form of conception, you are right. There is a similarity between offsprings of the mind and of the body. A dollhouse, like a child, has the personality to direct its own fulfillment.

This dollhouse is peculiar. The bathroom, which lacks a toilet, is also a closet. The dolls, who are all children, eat in the kitchen and sleep together in a double bed. There is a fireplace in the bedroom, but there is no parlor; a ladder leads to a secret room, but there are no stairs. A bear runs the store, where he keeps a plaid blanket under the counter along with his cashbox filled with money and a pearl-handled revolver. Two frogs inhabit the hidden room above the store. They sleep in a hammock at night and play checkers all day. Curiouser and curiouser.

But this is what happens when you keep a dollhouse where you can see it from your bed and hear its whispers. Of course, the rest of the family has a loud voice, too. Before the dollhouse was so much as designed, there was a chorus of demands: a secret room, a trapdoor, a store, an attic. Hardly was the house painted and papered before the frogs moved in. They were followed by bears, one of whom has since been eaten by our dog. The dolls were the last to move in.

The occupants had voices, too, and demands: to sleep in a hammock, to eat a lot, to have a fire in the bedroom, to rock in a rocking chair, to hide under a counter. Between the dolls, bears, frogs, children, and the very walls themselves, the house both discarded and accumulated itself like a bird in molt. Out went the ugly bathtub, in came the antique rolltop desk. Out went the clunky cradle, in came petit point floor pillows. At the point when this book flew into my head—in bed, of course—the house already had furniture and a hammock for the frogs, the counter and ladder for the bear, food, pillows, mattress, and rugs for the dolls, and the corner cupboard, paintings, mantlepiece, and claw-and-ball-foot bathtub.

Since then a new voice, that of an editor with a deadline, has been added. The result is all the other projects that cram the dollhouse and tumble from its drawers, making thirty-seven in all.

It has been an amazing experience. I have learned arcane crafts like bookbinding, and frustrating ones like metalworking. I have learned the homey arts of candle dipping and rug braiding. My four sons have carved spoons, woven doormats, built furniture, and painted dolls. My husband made boxes for the store. And all of them, as my working day stretched to twelve hours and my working week to seven days, were indulgent.

At times exhilaration overtook me. If I wished, couldn't I make a big basket, a real pair of moccasins, my own candles and copper pots? And then I would bring myself back down to earth. Of course I could. People always have. These things never have been made by magic, but by ordinary people using their hands, tools they devised, schemes they invented lying awake in bed at night. These are home crafts.

But readers deserve to know whether or not I am especially talented or experienced before they try to make the things I have made. The answer is yes and so-so. Yes, I am a good designer and have designed professionally. Yes, I can draw okay so long as it is not people and does not require straight lines or accurate measurements. I have a spectacularly good sense of color. I have some sense of how things are put together unless they are machines or motors. My hands usually do as they are told. When I was a girl, my mother taught me to sew, and my ambition to become a boy forced me to carry a pocketknife. I don't think I ever used it. In school I made clay ashtrays and birds' nests with eggs in them. I met my husband in the only art class I ever took, in which he was the best student and I was the worst. I learned to saw wood with a coping saw when my children broke all the glass ornaments on the Christmas tree. The wood ornaments had to be painted, too, so I have some experience there. I do needlepoint in the evening. That's it. Almost everything in this book I have had to learn from scratch. Almost everything I made looked lousy the first time and had to be made again. You are already a step ahead: you have this book to learn from.

Everything we have made is a toy, not a model. The distinction is important, because both the house and all that's in it may disappoint the expert miniaturist, though it will delight the novice. Nothing is correct. The furniture looks vaguely old, but it is of no period. It is not to scale, either, and was made without benefit of ruler. The house is tinged with Colonial saltbox. And the store—though only an eccentric with a hankering for cheese, mops, and dried flowers would shop there—looks like New England, too. But then there's the more-or-less Victorian mantel and the pragmatic wicker chairs. The rocking horse, my sister says, is Rubensesque—a reference to its large behind. The food is all too big, and the bathtub is too small. It's enough to make you laugh.

That's as it should be. After all, a dollhouse is not to make you stand, hands behind your back, jaw dropped in awe, but to make you smile, reach out, and play. You will not be disappointed here. Pull back the patchwork quilt; sure enough there are the sheets. And yes, under the sheets is a real mattress, complete with string tufting. There are extra quilts and blankets stored in the drawers below the house, just as there are all sorts of clothes hung on real hangers in the closet/bath, plenty of extra food, and surprises like combs and pocketknives, cookie cutters, Easter eggs, and real silver jewelry stored in drawers and cupboards.

You can sweep the floors with the brooms, wash the dishes in the copper sink, set the table, write in the book, paste snapshots in the album, dress the dolls for bed. The furniture is there to rearrange—and there's lots more of it in the storage drawers. The sitting room can be made over into a nursery, the bathroom into an attic, the store into a dining room, the bedroom into a parlor.

You are not likely to break anything as you play, because everything is made to be played with. The wood is thick, the clothes have snaps, drawers open, soap lathers, and candles burn. Except for perishables like apples and avocados, there is no fakery in any of the objects in our family dollhouse. Drawer knobs are carved of wood, not faked with beads. The candles are hand-dipped. Wicker chairs are woven of cane, not glued from pre-woven sheets. Books are stitched in signatures and bound in leather, not approximated by covering a book-shaped block of wood. Clothes are made like yours and mine so they can be taken on and off, washed and dried, pressed and hung on hangers (which are made of wood and wire like real ones, too). The sink and bathtub are ceramic, not plastic. The mantelpiece is stone. Even the loaves of bread are baked from dough and sprinkled with caraway, sesame, and poppy seeds. Our dog finds them real enough to eat.

The translation of these "real" crafts to miniature form has not been difficult. Most of the tools are to be found in hardware stores, and you may already have many of them. Sources are given for the few uncommon ones. Techniques had to be simplified to make them manageable in some cases, but for the most part they hardly differ from those required for full-scale crafts. Materials are a greater problem than either tools or techniques. You will find that a mail-order source is given for those materials you may have trouble finding in local stores. People who shop in large cities may prefer to use the local Yellow Pages. More serious than this inconvenience is expense. Many of the materials needed can be bought only in far larger quantities than you need for making tiny objects. We have suggested scrounging scraps from acquaintances who use such materials for their own hobbies, or using substitutes.

The projects in *A Family Dollhouse* range from the cinchy through the tedious to the really frustrating. The easiest ones we have suggested for children, and we have offered simplified versions of even some of the harder ones. It's much more fun if everyone can contribute, and children can surprise you. Aram, ten years old and our youngest child, turned out to be more interested, persistent, inventive, and nimble-fingered than his older brothers. Where I found a craft particularly hard on eyes, fingers, or patience, I have been honest in saying so.

Where design is the crucial issue, I have suggested both sources for copying and techniques for reducing or enlarging the size of the design you choose. (Those who cannot bear my casualness concerning scale might buy an architects' scale to make computations easier. This six-inch-long affair allows you to measure for the miniature directly, without arithmetic. The usual miniaturist's scale is 1 inch equals 1 foot.) But it is my obstinate belief that if the world before today was replete with exquisite quilt designers, cabinetmakers, and basket weavers —the "folk" of folk art—the percentage of talented people cannot have changed so suddenly. Before you drown in the "I can't draw" syndrome, give your own designs a try.

Disregarding perfect scale contributes to the pleasure of the work technically, aesthetically, and emotionally. Technically, it is much easier to paint a larger apple than a smaller one, and certainly easier to avoid measuring a blob of wet clay with an architects' scale. Aesthetically, the fruit looks all the more luscious for the exaggeration. Emotionally, when the apple turns out to be an outrage, you can treat it with a guiltless giggle.

Let accidents happen, too. Our washbowl accidentally became hexagonal when it refused to become round. The dinner set became multicolored when I couldn't choose between glazes. There are many mistakes in the crocheted coat, but they don't show. When something does bother you, do it over. I threw five baskets out before I figured out how to make a decent one.

If I have any secret to offer you, it is the one most nearly impossible to put into words. Our family dollhouse looks old. It makes people think of museums and the antique dollhouses they have seen in them. It fills them with nostalgia. It makes them think of books they had as children, of quaint cottages and abodes beneath the roots of trees. The secret can't be the mixed metaphors of style and size, the odd assortment of occupants, the details of the artifacts, or even the eccentricities of my own family's fantasies. The secret is color. This house is dull red and brown, ochre, tan, and ivory. There is a bit of blue, lavender, pink, and bluish green. There is nothing bright or strident, only subdued and blending. The color makes the house look old, removed, peaceful, plentiful. We come upon a child there sometimes, gazing, longing, moving in in his mind, wandering from room to room, opening a drawer, closing a shutter, putting a doll to bed. We hear him talk of his children, our grandchildren, who will play there. And when we go to bed at night, and when the news is over, I muse upon the future of the house, the pickles and the crocks it needs, the curtains at the dormer and the potty under the bed, the cradle in the nursery, the mixing bowls and candlesticks—all in soft earth colors, blended into the texture of the house as though they grew there, as old now as they will be when grandchildren read what we have written in the book and discover the pictures in the album.

Of course that stove has got to go.

Leather Rag Dolls

One of the first things I can recall making as a child was a rag doll named Miranda. Impatient then as now with raveling seams, I made her from a chamois polishing cloth, which was then standard equipment for any household. These miniature rag dolls are made of different leather, but to my delight I find that chamois is still available in auto supply and hardware stores for car owners addicted to polishing. The light, thin, soft leather is still ideal for stitching together tiny dolls of even rather intricate contours. These two dolls are named Hanna and Thaddeus, after two of the many children I would have had if this were still the good old days when people thought of children by the dozen. Had there been a real Hanna, she might have gotten the dollhouse where her tiny substitute lives. But as it turned out, I acquired it for myself after the repetitive birth of four sons.

Sources

Notions departments or needlework stores for sewing items
Art supply store for sable brush and paint
Hardware or auto supply store for chamois

Materials

Paper for pattern
Optional: Felt for working out your own pattern
Chamois or other thin, soft leather
Thread
Polyester stuffing
No. 8 crochet yarn in hair color (or similar weight knitting or needlepoint yarn)
White glue
Oil or acrylic paints for painting face

Tools

Embroidery scissors
Thimble
No. 10 "sharp" needle
Embroidery needle
Knitting needle
Fine-line ball-point pen
No. 3 pencil
Size 0 sable brush

Step by Step

Making the pattern. The actual pattern given here makes a doll about 5 inches high, which, allowing for both scale and the average size of people in Colonial times, is about right for a "little lady." The pattern is designed to give thickness from back to front in the head and body while keeping the face flat. It avoids the frequent problem of sagging neck, and allows the feet to stick forward and the arms and legs to bend at knees, elbows, hips, and shoulders for easier dressing and for more natural sitting postures. The doll does not stand up. Once you have made one doll—either a finished one of leather or an experimental one of felt—you may wish to change the shapes of the pieces to achieve somewhat different contours.

Trace each piece in the drawing here onto paper for your first pattern. Use felt to experiment with patterns of your own.

Tracing the pattern onto leather. Most leather, even chamois, has a right and a wrong side. The right side is the smoother one; the wrong side is rough or furry. Leather seldom comes in uniform thickness. Sometimes you can feel places that would be too thick for you to stitch easily, or places so thin they might tear. With chamois, you can hold the cloth up to a window and see the too-thin places where light shines through. Before you begin to trace your pattern, mark with a ball-point pen on the wrong side the areas within which the leather is uniform and neither too thick nor too thin. Then turn the leather over and check to be sure there are no blemishes within this area on the right side.

On the wrong side, and within the marked areas, trace the pattern pieces with a fine-line ball-point pen. Trace the front piece once. Trace the back piece once, then flip the pattern over and trace it again. Trace each leg piece once, flip the pattern, and trace again. Trace around the arm piece twice, flip the pattern, and trace it twice more.

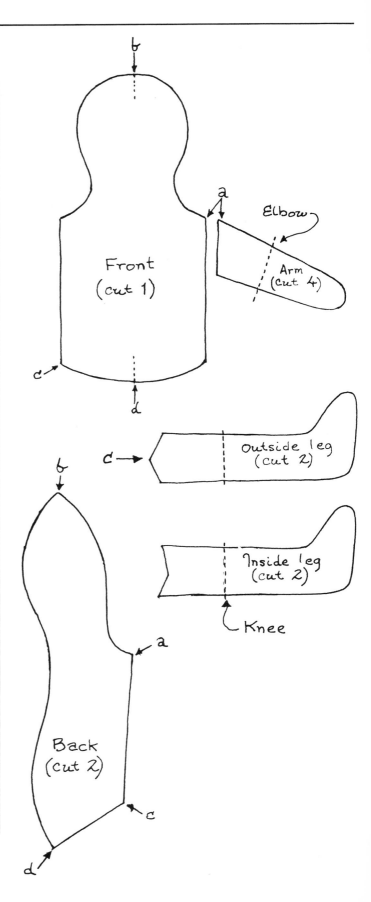

Making the arms and legs. Arms and legs must be finished before the body can be completed. Lay the pattern pieces on top of one another. The arm pieces will exactly match. But the two pieces that make each leg are different from each other: the outside of each leg is notched upward at the top; the inside is notched downward.

Hold the two pieces to be stitched wrong sides together for sewing. Use a No. 10 "sharp" needle, a single strand of ordinary sewing thread, and a thimble. Start the thread by bringing the needle out from the inside of one piece; secure it by overcasting twice through both pieces of leather before continuing. End a thread by taking several small overcasting stitches in place, bringing the thread to the inside on the last stitch. Stitch the pieces together with small overcasting stitches taken as close to the edge of the seam as possible. Check the alignment of the pieces frequently, as they tend to creep out of line as you stitch. Stitch around both arms and legs, leaving the top seams open for stuffing.

Stuff the arms and legs up to the dotted line indicated on the pattern (you can gauge this just by holding the piece next to the pattern). Use very small bits of stuffing and push them in firmly with a knitting needle. Stitch the arms across the elbows with a running stitch at the dotted line. Before stitching across the knee, flatten the leg so that the back and front seams are touching one another inside. The feet are now facing forward, the knee bends properly, and the notched tops line up with one another. Stitch across the knee with a running stitch.

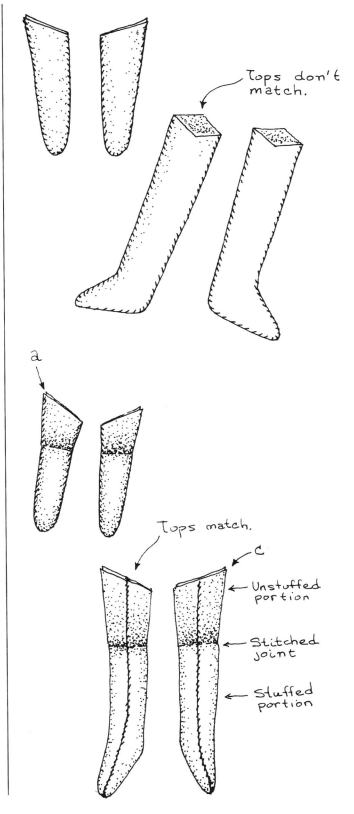

Making the body. Stitch the center seam of the two back pieces together from *b* to *d* as you did the arms. End your thread.

Hold the back and front wrong sides together with the shoulders lined up. Sandwich the left arm in position between the back and front. It should project only about ⅛ inch into the body, lining up at the shoulder point *a*. Start the thread just under the armpit and secure it there. Then use a running stitch to sew through both layers of the arm and the front and back piece of the body. Secure the thread with a couple of stitches in place at the shoulder, then continue on around the neck and head with an overcasting stitch, being sure to match up the center seam of the back with the center line *b* at the top of the head. Continue to the opposite shoulder, insert the second arm and sew it in place through all four layers of leather with a running stitch. Continue down the side, overcasting, to the hip. Line up the right leg at *c* and sew it in as you did the arms. Continue across the crotch, overcasting, then sew in the left leg. Overcast a few stitches up the left side and end your thread.

Through the opening on the left side of the doll, stuff the body. Begin with the head and neck, using small bits of stuffing and pushing them firmly into place with the knitting needle. Knead the body as you stuff to help distribute the stuffing evenly. The head and body should feel plump and firm. When the stuffing has been completed, overcast the opening.

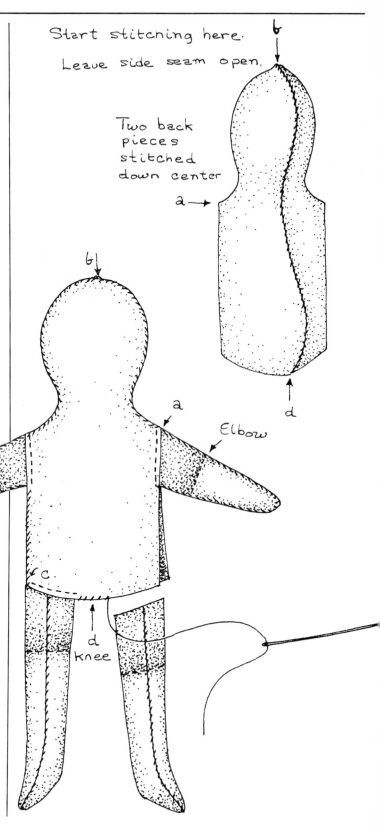

Making the wig. This wig is made right on the doll's head. Cut a piece of shirt cardboard 4½ inches wide. Wind crochet cotton of the color you wish around and around the cardboard. You will need at least 100 full winds if you are using No. 8 crochet yarn. Cut through all the yarn along one edge and lay the strands out flat on a table. Divide them into groups of five so you can pick them up easily as you sew them in place.

Insert an embroidery needle threaded with a single strand of ordinary thread from the top of the head out just below the seam at the top of the forehead. Secure it with two tiny stitches in place. Using a backstitch and working from the forehead down the center seam to just above the neck, catch each group of five strands of yarn into each stitch. Continue until the head is covered.

At this point the strands will be held in place only loosely. To secure them better, thread an embroidery needle with the same yarn you are using for the hair. Knot the end. Bring the needle from beneath the hair up to the nape of the neck where the hair begins, and working up to where the hair ends at the forehead, take small chain stitches (page 58). The needle should enter the head itself at each stitch and not just go around the hair. Finish the thread with several small stitches in place under the wig where the stitches will not show.

Four steps in making a wig.
1. Wind the yarn around cardboard and cut it to get strands of equal length.
2. Backstitch the strands to the doll's head along the center back seam, catching five strands of yarn in each stitch.
3. Chain-stitch with the same yarn you used for the hair to cover the backstitching and to hold the strands in place more securely. The row of chain stitches becomes the part.
4. Braid the hair over each shoulder and tie the braids at the bottom.

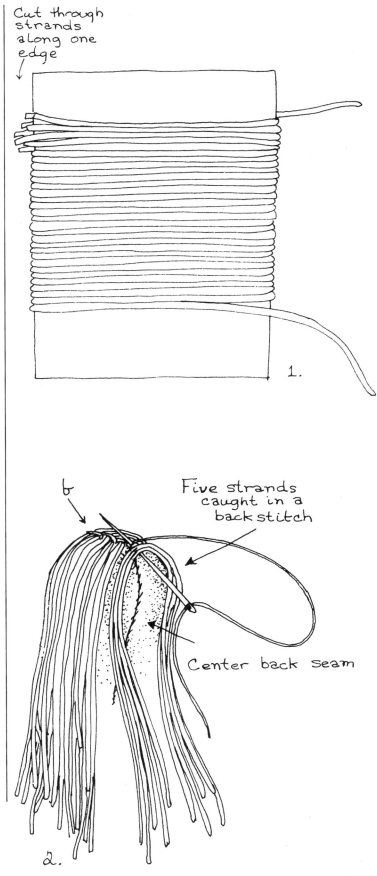

Cut through strands along one edge

1.

b

Five strands caught in a back stitch

Center back seam

2.

Straighten the strands of hair out so they are not crossing one another. Bring all the hair on both sides toward the front, and braid the strands together. Tie the ends of the braids with a strand of the crochet yarn when they are as long as you wish them. A bit of white glue rubbed along the tie with a toothpick will keep it from slipping. Cut the strands to about ½ inch below the ties.

Painting the face. Oil paints thinned slightly with turpentine or acrylic paints thinned with water can be used to paint the face. Both are waterproof when dry. Mark the features lightly on the face with a hard pencil. Use a Size 0 or smaller round sable artist's brush to paint over your marks. In the case of oil paint, allow it to dry for a week before anyone touches the face. Acrylics dry in an hour or less.

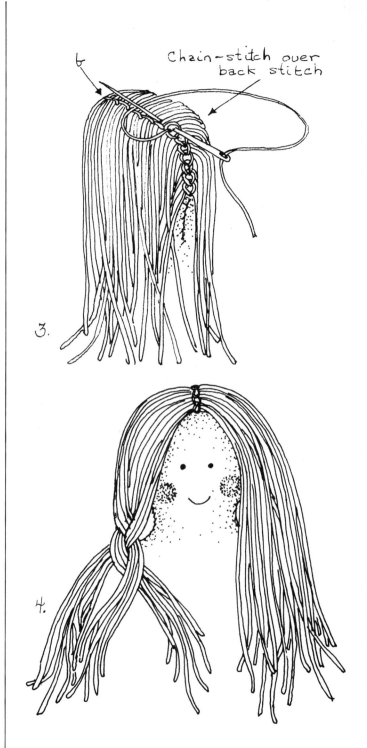

Chain-stitch over back stitch

3.

4.

Two details of the kitchen

Examples of faux marble and wood grains

The kitchen

The store

The bedroom

The sitting room

The nursery and bath

❧ Sewed Doll Clothes ☙

The construction methods used in the clothes shown here are simplified versions of real garments. To simplify any further would result in frayed edges or a makeshift look. Because of this, these clothes are among the hardest projects in this book, and you should probably attempt them only if you have had some experience in sewing full-size clothing. The example used for Step by Step is as close as I could come to a good learning project for the inexperienced, and even it requires a good deal of time and patience.

On the positive side, these clothes are of better quality than any you can buy, and can, of course, be made in styles of your choice. It is possible to use all sorts of fabrics, but the beginner is best off with a hundred percent cotton fabric of fine texture, such as a lawn or broadcloth shirting (from a used shirt). Mixtures of cotton and polyester refuse to crease—and when you can't crease a tiny sleeve hem the frustration is enormous.

It is impossible to give actual patterns here because dolls differ in size and shape. The method given here for making your own patterns is straightforward and can be adapted to many designs. One afterthought: if you are a beginner, there's no better way to learn than to buy a "very easy" pattern for yourself, and while the experience of putting a full-size dress together is still fresh in your memory, give it a try in miniature.

Boys' clothing is more difficult than girls'. Besides the measurements detailed in Step by Step, you will also need to locate the crotch. Worse, you will have to make an extra measurement for a rear end if your doll has one. Mine does, decidedly, and his pants tend to come out either baggy or snug, but never quite right. Shirts are, of course, only shorter versions of dresses, though you may feel a collar is necessary. The photograph shows patterns for overalls and shirt with collar, and the finished garments.

Each dress shown here differs in some respect from the basic pattern. The peasant dress, although made from the same number of pieces, was designed with a wider bodice and neckline to give fullness when the drawstring is tied at the neck. The apron that can be worn over it is also designed to be a sleeveless sun dress. The white dress has a yoke and a gathered skirt. The flowered print dress has set-in sleeves.

To make these more complicated patterns, it's a good idea to consult sewing books or "very easy" full-size patterns from dresses you or your friends have made. Both these sources will help you understand how to shape a sleeve or neckline, construct a yoke, line a bodice, or gather a skirt. A repertoire of three sleeves, three necklines, and three dress constructions is plenty for a large doll wardrobe.

Materials

⅛-inch graph paper
Heavy tracing paper or translucent bond paper
Fine cotton fabric
Thread to match fabric
Snaps or hooks
Optional: Rickrack, lace, or ribbon trim

Tools

Doll for reference
Tape measure
Pencil
Fine (accountant's point) ball-point pen
No. 10 "sharp" needle
Thimble
Scissors
Iron and ironing board

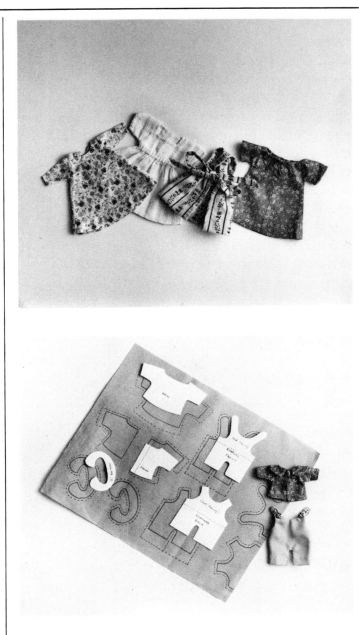

Step by Step

Measuring your doll. Any pattern you make will be based on your doll's body measurements. Make the following measurements, using a tape measure:

>   Width of chest at arm level
>   Width of back at arm level
>   Width of neck front at neckline
>   Width of neck back at neckline
>   Length of arm from shoulder to wrist
>   Length of body from shoulder to ankle
>   Length of body from shoulder to waist

Drawing a grid. Use these measurements to lay out the simple grids representing front and back of the doll, shown on page 27. On ⅛-inch graph paper draw lines as shown to indicate chest width, neck width, length of body from shoulder to ankle, and length of body from shoulder to waist. The center line will help you check that these lines and the later pattern lines are symmetrical. The arm length is not represented on the grids. Notice that the back and front measurements are not at all the same. The back and front pieces of a clothing pattern are rarely the same, either. Draw the lines first in pencil, then darken them with a ball-point pen.

Making the pattern. The dress design used as an example here has three main pattern pieces, plus a facing that is sewed inside the neckline. There are no separate sleeve, collar, or bodice pieces.

1. Make the pattern for the front of the dress first. Lay heavy tracing paper or other translucent paper over the front grid. Tape it so it doesn't slip. Draw a neckline over the grid ¼ inch wider than the neck width. A round neck is the easiest shape. All the lines that follow should be on one side of the grid only. Which side doesn't matter.

2. Place the doll within the drawing with her neck at the neckline. Note the angle at which her arms fall from her shoulders. On one side, make a line from the neck edge to her wrist at the natural slant. If the set of your doll's arms offers no guidance, a good rule is to make the slant just halfway between a true diagonal and a horizontal.

3. Using your arm-length measurement, mark the sleeve length on one side only and draw the end of that sleeve.

4. Using the waistline as a guide, draw the curve of the underarm above it. How far above depends on the structure of your doll. For a rough check, lay the doll on the pattern again and see where her underarm falls.

5. Draw a slanted line down along the side of the dress from the underarm. The greater the slant, the fuller the dress will be, but the harder it will be to keep the underarm seam from puckering.

6. Draw a slight curve from the center of the hemline to the edge of the dress. Hold the doll in place again to check the length.

For ease of photography, the pattern was drawn right on the grid instead of on tracing paper. If tracing paper is used, the grids can be kept for making other clothing patterns. The paper you use should be sturdy enough for you to trace around its edges to transfer the pattern onto cloth.

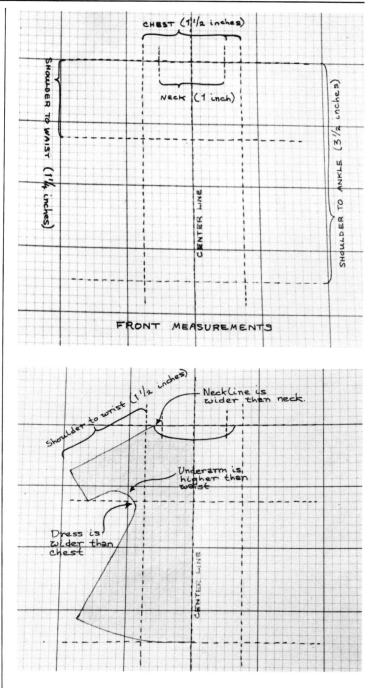

7. Draw a line to indicate the center of the pattern. Fold the whole pattern in half along the center line and cut it out. This is the best way to assure that your pattern is symmetrical.

8. Now place the paper pattern on your doll and bend the paper around her to check critical dimensions. Do the sleeves go at least halfway around her arms? Do the underarms fall in the right place? Is the neck too large or too small? Before continuing, correct anything that is not right by drawing the pattern again, cutting it out, trying it on, and checking.

9. To make a pattern for the back, use the back grid, which represents the back measurements. Draw the back neckline ¼ inch larger than the width of the neck back.

10. Fold the cutout front pattern in half. Place it over the back grid, lining up the neckline edge on one side. Be sure the folded center line is parallel with the center line of the back grid. Now trace around the sleeve, underarm, and side of the front half of the dress.

11. Draw a smooth curve from the center line of the hem to the edge of the dress.

12. Cut out the back pattern. Check it against the front pattern again. The shoulder and arm seams, underarm and side seams should be the same, regardless of the fact that the back might be narrower or wider than the front. The necklines will not line up, and though the length of the hem is the same at the side seams, the curves will be different.

13. The neck opening of this dress is in the back at a center seam. Cut your back pattern in half along the center line. You now have three main pattern pieces.

Top: When the half pattern is folded on the center line and cut out, the resulting finished pattern is perfectly symmetrical.

Bottom: The front pattern is used to trace the shoulder, underarm, and side seams in the back pattern. Notice that the center line of the back grid is parallel to the center fold of the front piece, but is a distance away. The back piece is going to be wider than the front.

14. The only other pattern piece needed is the neckline facing. Place the front and back patterns together along the shoulder seams. Trace around the entire inside curve of the neck, continuing your line for ½ inch down the neck opening. Remove the back and front pattern pieces. Draw a second curved line parallel to and ½ inch from the inside neckline you have already traced. This ½-inch-wide curved piece is the neck facing. Cut out the piece.

Tracing the pattern on fabric. Press the fabric and lay it out on a table wrong side up. One at a time, lay the front and back pattern pieces along the straight grain of the fabric and trace around the outline with a fine ball-point pen. Be sure to leave at least an inch of space between each of the pattern pieces. Lay the facing piece diagonally on the fabric as shown. Trace around it, too. These solid traced lines are your stitching lines.

Lay the pieces with shoulder seams matched to trace the curve of the neck facing.

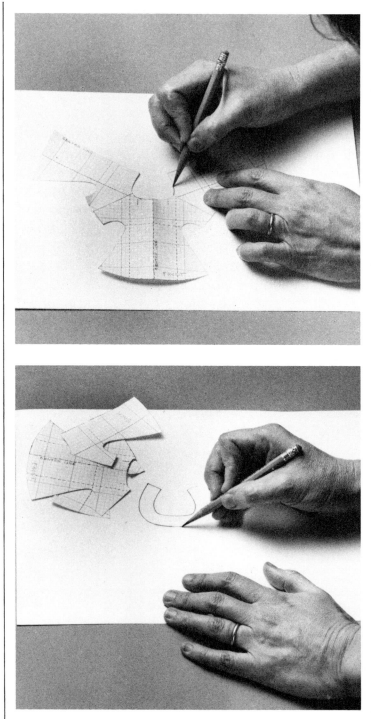

Next to each edge that will be a seam, draw a dotted line ¼ inch or less away. Next to each edge that will be a hem draw a dotted line ½ inch away. These dotted lines are cutting lines.

Cut out all the pattern pieces along the dotted lines.

Stitching the pieces together. When you stitch one piece to another, their right sides are always facing one another. Line them up carefully. Stitch along the solid line, using small stitches. Use a fine needle and a single thread. To begin and end the thread, take several tiny stitches in one place rather than make a knot. When a seam is finished, press it open before stitching the next seam. Trim curved seams to ⅛ inch and clip carefully toward your stitches to prevent the seam from puckering when it is turned.

The order in which seams are stitched differs according to the construction of the garment. This is the order for this dress:

1. Stitch front to back pieces along each shoulder seam. Press open.

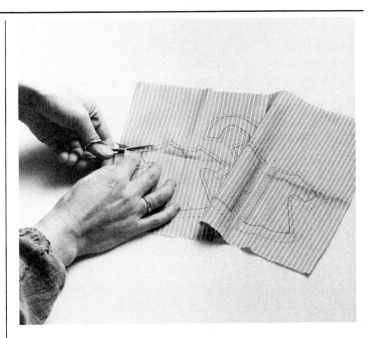

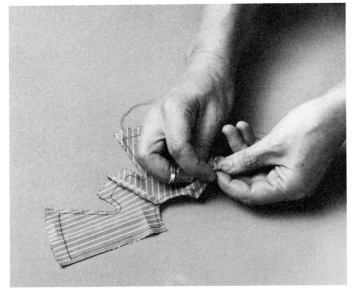

Pattern pieces have been traced onto the wrong side of the fabric. The solid line is the stitching line. The dotted line is the cutting line.

2. Stitch the neck facing to the neck edge. Begin your stitching at the bottom of the neck opening as shown and end it at the same point on the other side of the neck. Trim, clip, turn, and press.

3. Stitch the center back seam, ending where the neck opening begins. Press open.

4. Stitch the side seams from the end of the sleeve, around the underarm, to the bottom edge of the dress. Trim the underarm seam, clip, press entire seam open.

Hemming the dress. Before hemming either the bottom edge or the sleeves, turn the dress right side out and try it on your doll. With a soft pencil, mark a hemline at the bottom edge and at the bottom of both sleeves. You may want to pin the hems up to check for length and evenness.

Crease along the hemline with your fingers and press if necessary.

There are two ways to finish hems on these small garments. If your cloth is very fine, you can turn the raw edge under ⅛ inch, then turn it again to the right depth and secure the hem with a slanting overcasting stitch. If this double turning is too difficult or the results clumsy, trim the cloth back farther, turn in ⅛ inch, and cross-stitch in place. The stitches are sufficient to prevent the raw edge from fraying.

When sleeves are too narrow to get your fingers into them, try slipping the sleeve over a pencil while you stitch the hem.

Top right: Note where the stitching begins. When the facing is turned, the finished edge at center back will be the neck opening.

Bottom right: Two ways of doing hems. The first is neater but bulkier. The second is easy to do and has no bulk. Look carefully at the sequence to see how to do this cross-stitch. It is confusing at first, but easy to do with practice.

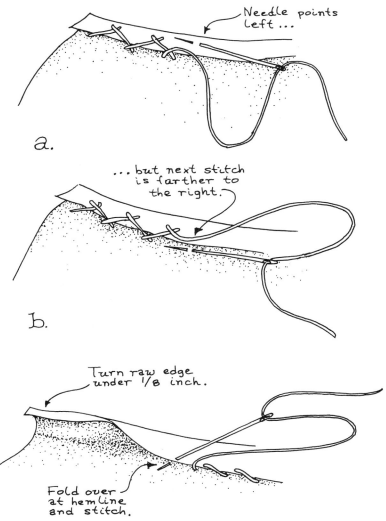

a. *Needle points left ...*

b. *... but next stitch is farther to the right.*

Turn raw edge under ⅛ inch.

Fold over at hemline and stitch.

Fastening and trimming the dress. The neck opening on this dress can be fastened with a hook and eye if the neck is quite snug, or with a snap if it fits loosely. Narrow lace, ribbon trim, or rickrack can be added at the wrist, neck, or hem. A sash of the dress fabric can be made as shown here.

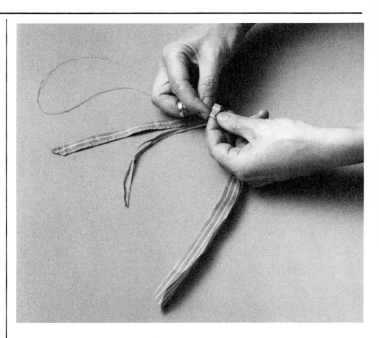

A sash is made by stitching a long tube with slanted ends. Leave about 1½ inches open in the middle for turning. Turn the right side in with the help of a knitting needle. Turn in the remaining seams at the opening and blindstitch.

🐾 Crocheted Doll Clothes 🐾

This dressy coat is the second thing I've ever crocheted, the first being the usual granny-square afghan. It took half a day of mistakes and a full twelve hours on the right track. The hardest part seemed to me to be keeping the same number of stitches in each row, which leads me to believe I should have conquered potholders before frustrating myself to this extent. If you are already an experienced crocheter, you will have no difficulty in following the instructions for how to shape a garment based on the measurements and a pattern. If you have never crocheted before, learn the basics given here in large scale before attempting in miniature. Then try those potholders. An intermediate stage between potholders and clothing might well include a bedspread or curtains made with more open—and therefore faster—stitches than the ones used here. You will find lacy stitches and afghan squares of many kinds in the book suggested in Sources.

The Basics

Although we have done our best with these drawings of the four stitches you will need to crochet the coat illustrated, this is not an easy way to learn to crochet. Go to a friend or to a knitting store and ask to be taught. Neither words nor drawings are as helpful as a demonstration.

The stitches given here are chain, slip stitch, single crochet, and double crochet. They are used both by themselves and as components of more decorative stitches. Chain is used as the first row on which other rows are built; it is also used as a way to increase by as many stitches as you wish at the end of a row. Slip stitch looks like chain. It is used to form a chain along the edge of a piece so you can start crocheting in another direction. Single crochet is a short stitch. Double crochet is a taller stitch.

The instructions are not just for taking a single stitch, but for making a row of stitches. Unless they are followed carefully, you will find you are accidentally decreasing from row to row.

Hold the crochet hook in your right hand as you would a pencil. Hold the work in your left hand between thumb and middle finger. The thread goes from the work, over your forefinger, down inside your other fingers, and out of your hand between your ring finger and your pinkie.

To decrease a stitch on purpose, skip one stitch in the row below. To increase a stitch, take two stitches in the same stitch of the row below. You can also decrease by simply stopping a row short, leaving the remaining stitches unworked. Similarly, you can increase by chaining extra stitches at the end of a row.

To end a piece of yarn, cut it five inches from your work and pull the end through the loop on your hook. Pull it tight to secure it. Ends left hanging in a piece can be threaded to an embroidery needle, pulled through five or six stitches of the fabric, and cut off.

Practice these four stitches and the two ways of increasing and decreasing with a large hook and heavy yarn at first. Then go to the size crochet hook and cotton suggested here, but try a potholder-size object. Only when you can crochet with some comfort and assurance should you try to make a garment.

These illustrations are accurate in the immediate area where the stitch is being taken. Beyond that the drawings falter, through inability rather than ill intent.

Slip knot. Form a loop on the crochet hook, reach the hook under, then over the yarn to grab onto it, pull the yarn through the loop on your hook to form a new loop. Pull on the end of the yarn to tighten the knot. The act of reaching under and over the yarn to grab hold of it is called "yarn over hook."

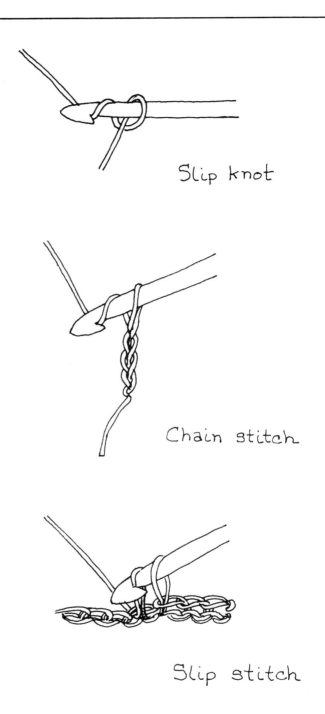

Slip knot

Chain stitch

Slip stitch

Chain stitch. With the first loop on the hook, yarn over hook, and pull the yarn through the loop on the hook to form a new loop. The new loop is a stitch. Repeat until the chain has the desired number of stitches.

Slip stitch. Insert the hook under the top loop of the chain (or of the first stitch in the row below), yarn over hook, pull the yarn through both the stitch and the loop on your hook. Repeat to end of row.

Single crochet. To begin a row of single crochet, chain one stitch. Then skip the first stitch in the row below, taking the first single crochet in the next stitch. The chain stitch counts as one single crochet. At the end of each row, work the last stitch by inserting the hook under the chain that formed the beginning of the row below.

Insert the hook into the stitch, yarn over hook, pull a loop through the stitch. Yarn over hook again, and draw the yarn through both loops on your hook. Repeat to end of row. When starting the next row, don't forget to chain one, then skip a stitch before starting the single crochet stitches.

Double crochet. To begin a row of double crochet, chain three stitches and skip the first stitch in the row below, taking the first double crochet in the next stitch. The three chain stitches count as one double crochet. At the end of each row, work the last stitch by inserting the hook under the chain that formed the beginning of the row below.

Yarn over hook, insert the hook into the stitch, pull a loop through the stitch. Yarn over hook again, pull the yarn through two loops on your hook. Yarn over hook another time, and pull the yarn through the remaining two loops on your hook. Repeat to end of row. When starting the next row, don't forget to chain three, then skip a stitch before starting the double crochet stitches.

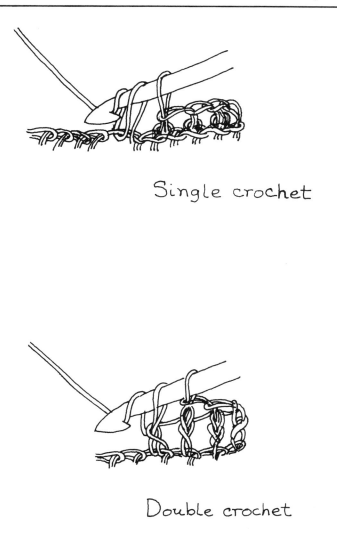

Single crochet

Double crochet

Sources

For instruction and many pattern stitches: *Mon Tricot Knitting Dictionary,* available at yarn stores.

Crochet patterns for Barbie Doll–size clothing (these might be helpful in understanding construction and getting ideas for dollhouse-size clothing): Reference departments of magazines such as *McCall's, Family Circle,* and *Woman's Day* will look up what they have published on doll clothes and send either tear sheets or duplicated copies. Send written request describing what you are looking for. The service is free.

For crochet yarn: The very fine gauge suggested here may not be easy to find. If you can't locate a store that stocks DMC yarns, use the heavier American brands that are widely available. Use the correspondingly larger hook the salesperson can suggest.

Materials

DMC crochet yarn, 20-gauge

Tools

No. 8 crochet hook*
Embroidery needle
Small scissors
Tape measure

---

* There are least three different systems of denoting sizes of crochet hooks. In the system used for this book, the larger the number, the smaller the hook. This hook is very small.

Step by Step

Making a stitch gauge. With the yarn and hook you intend to use, chain 20. Work 6 rows of double crochet (it is easier to count than single crochet). End yarn. Lay the piece flat on a table but don't stretch it. Lay a tape measure across a row. Count the number of double crochet stitches that fall within one inch. This number is your stitch gauge. It tells you how many stitches there are for each inch across a row. The number will be used to figure out how many stitches you will need to get the proper width across the back, neck, or skirt of a garment. It will not be helpful in estimating how many rows you need to get sleeve or skirt length because the height of each row depends on the height of the stitch or pattern you are using.

Making a pattern. Making a pattern for a crocheted garment is similar to making a pattern for sewed clothing (see page 27). Make the same measurements of your doll and draw the same grid. Compare the dress patterns to see how the pattern for this crocheted coat is simpler. Crocheted work is stretchier than fabric, so a little license can be taken for the sake of simplicity. The crochet pattern does not indicate the number or kinds of stitches. Rather, it is used as a reference on which one can lay the work as it progresses to check that it is about the right size and shape and to estimate when and by how much to increase or decrease. The doll herself (or himself) should also be kept handy for reference.

This was the method used to make the coat. The specific instructions and the graphic method of showing the bodice row by row was worked out only after the fact, although an experienced crocheter could probably design a garment in this way.

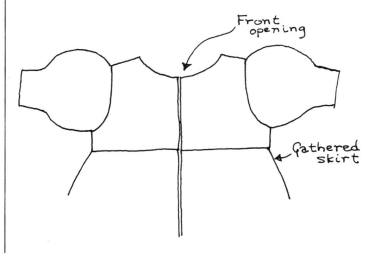

Starting the garment. A crocheted garment can be all in one piece, or it can be sewed together from separate pieces, such as the front and back of the bodice, the skirt, and the sleeves. Working in a single piece is preferable for small items, as the seams are hard to join neatly. This one was worked from the back of the bodice just under the armhole up to the neck, then down the shoulder to the front bodice, again just under the armhole. The next rows of stitches were continuous from one front edge, under the armhole, around the back, under the other armhole and on to the other front edge, so that the bodice was attached under the armholes. At the waist the number of stitches was increased to start the gathered skirt. The sleeves were added when the skirt was finished. Last, the edge of the neckline, the front, and the hem were decorated with fancy stitches. It is easy to work this way with crochet because a section can be finished and the yarn ended, yet you can go back and pick up stitches along any edge to continue crocheting.

To follow the strategy used here, use your doll's back* measurement and your stitch gauge to figure out the number of stitches you will need on the foundation chain that starts at the back below the armholes. For example, my doll measures two inches across the back. My stitch gauge was: 10 stitches equals 1 inch. I chained 20 stitches to start the back bodice of the coat.

Working the bodice out as you go along. Single-crochet two rows just so you can see what you are doing. Lay your work on your pattern to estimate whether or not you should now begin to decrease for the armhole. Continue to check against the curve of the armhole on your drawing until you have reached the shoulder. Double-check against the doll, too. Proceed in this fashion, continually holding your work against the pattern or the doll to check that it is the size and shape you wish. In the case of the coat, one

side of the front must be worked separately from the other. Where sides must match, it's a good idea to jot down details of what you are doing on the first side so you can duplicate them on the opposite side. If you make a mistake, rip out your work and pick it up from before the error.

When both the front and the back of the bodice are completed, you are ready to connect them at the sides and proceed to the waistline. Start the next row across the bottom of one side of the front bodice, add a couple of chain stitches under the armhole, proceed across the bottom of the back bodice, add the same number of chain stitches under the other armhole, and continue across the other side of the front bodice. Add as many more rows as you need to get to the waist, checking against your pattern to determine the length.

Figuring out a pattern for the skirt. The skirt in this coat is the easiest kind: a gathered skirt that is simply formed by taking two stitches in every one stitch of the row below at the waistline. From then on, each succeeding row has the same number of stitches, which is double the number at the waist. A shaped skirt is much more difficult, as not only must you increase in an orderly manner so the skirt flares evenly, but the hemline must be curved as well (see the dress pattern on page 27). Such a design, though it could be worked out similarly to the bodice by making a drawing to use as a reference, would not lend itself to the pattern stitches that can fancy up a gathered or straight skirt. If you are shaping a skirt, stick to a small, unobtrusive stitch that will not emphasize the decreases that form the curve of the hemline.

The pattern in the coat's skirt was achieved by working rows in double crochet interspersed with a very easy stitch called the granit stitch.

Using the pattern you wish, continue crocheting the skirt until the garment is the length indicated on your grid. End the yarn.

---

* If your garment opens in the back instead of the front, you would start with the front of the bodice.

Figuring out the sleeves. Sleeves are added by picking up stitches around the armholes and crocheting in rounds instead of rows. Crocheting in rounds results in a different texture from crocheting in rows, because the work is not turned from front to back. The crocheting proceeds at right angles to the bodice. To figure out how many stitches you will need to pick up, add the number of rows of single crochet from bottom to top of the armhole, multiply by 2 (for both sides of the armhole), and add the number of chain stitches you made to form the underarm. In the coat there were 8 rows of single crochet on each side of the armhole, plus 4 chain stitches under the armhole. Twenty stitches were picked up to start the sleeve.

To pick up the stitches, start at the underarm and slip-stitch in each chain, then in the end of each row until you are back where you started. This is Round 1.

If the sleeve is to be tailored, you can proceed to take as many rounds as you need to get the desired sleeve length. To get a puff sleeve, increase the number of stitches in Round 2. This coat sleeve was increased by an additional 6 stitches along the shoulder. The 26 stitches were maintained for the next 6 rounds. The 26 stitches were reduced to 16 by missing every 4th stitch in the next 2 rounds to make the cuff of the sleeve the narrowest portion.

Trimming the edges. Trimming can be either in the same or in a contrasting color. Start by slip-stitching around the entire edge. (Slip-stitch 1 stitch for each row of single crochet, 2 stitches for each row of double crochet along the front edge and at the shoulders. Slip-stitch 1 stitch in each stitch along the front and back of the neck, and along the hem. When turning a corner, slip-stitch 2 stitches in the same stitch below.) On this base of slip stitch (which functions as a chain), add the edging stitches suggested here or others of your choice.

Coat Pattern

Bodice back and one side of front. Make a foundation chain of 20 sts.

Rows 1 and 2: Single crochet (20 sts).

Row 3: Decrease 1 st at beginning and end of row, single crochet rest of row (18 sts).

Row 4: Single crochet (18 sts).

Row 5: Decrease 1 st at beginning and end of row, single crochet rest of row (16 sts).

Row 6: Single crochet (16 sts).

Row 7: Single crochet first 4 sts, leave rest of row unworked (4 sts).

Row 8: Single crochet 3 sts, leave last st unworked (3 sts).

Row 9: Single crochet (3 sts).

Row 10: Single crochet across row, increase 1 st at end of row (4 sts).

Row 11: Single crochet across row, chain 4 at end of row (8 sts).

Row 12: Single crochet (8 sts).

Row 13: Increase 1 st at beginning of row, single crochet across rest of row (9 sts).

Row 14: Single crochet (9 sts).

Row 15: Increase 1 st at beginning of row, single crochet across rest of row (10 sts).

Row 16: Single crochet (10 sts). End yarn.

Other side of front bodice. Starting at the outside edge of the opposite shoulder, single crochet 4 (same as Row 7) and continue to shape other side of front bodice by repeating Rows 8 to 16 of the bodice instructions.

Waist

Row 1: Single crochet across the 10 sts of one side of bodice, chain 4, single crochet across the 20 sts of the back, chain 4, single crochet across the 10 sts of the other side of the front bodice (48 sts).

Rows 2 and 3: Single crochet (48 sts).

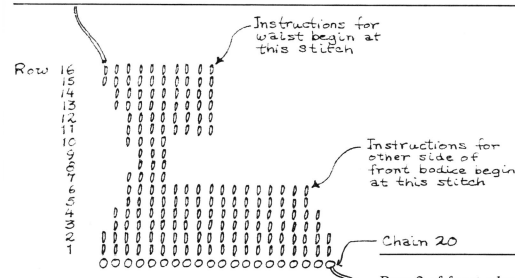

Row 16 ... (graph)
Instructions for waist begin at this stitch

Instructions for other side of front bodice begin at this stitch

Chain 20

Graphed stitch pattern for coat. This drawing shows the exact number of rows and stitches in the back bodice and one side of the front. The other side of the front bodice is started by picking up stitches at the unworked shoulder. The waist and underarm areas are started by picking up unworked stitches along the bottom of the bodice.

Skirt

Row 1: At Row 3 of the waist, double crochet 2 sts in each stitch of the row below (96 sts).

Rows 2 to 4: Chain 1 st to start one row. Then single crochet, double crochet; and repeat across rest of row. This pattern of alternating single and double crochet is called a granit stitch.

Row 5: Double crochet.

Row 6: Granit stitch.

Row 7: Double crochet.

Rows 8 to 10: Granit stitch.

Rows 11 and 12: Double crochet. End yarn.

Sleeves

Round 1: Slip-stitch 20 sts around armhole.

Round 2: Single crochet to within 3 sts of top of shoulder. In next 6 sts single crochet 2 sts in each st of row below. Continue single crochet to end of round (26 sts).

Rounds 3 to 6: Single crochet.

Rounds 7 and 8: Single crochet 3 sts, miss 1 st, then repeat 3 single crochet, miss 1 st across the row for both rounds until total number of sts is decreased to 16 sts.

Round 9: Double crochet.

Round 10. Single crochet. End yarn.

Repeat Rounds 1 to 10 for opposite sleeve.

Edging

Row 1: Slip-stitch around entire edge.

Row 2 of front edge and neck: 2 slip stitch, 1 single crochet, chain 3, slip-stitch in the same st in which you worked the single crochet. Then repeat the pattern, starting with the 2 slip-stitch, across the row.

Row 2 of hem: slip-stitch 1 to begin the row, then chain 5, miss 2 sts and slip-stitch into the third st, repeat the pattern, starting with chain 5 sts, across the rest of the row.

Finishing the garment. To conceal ends of yarn, thread them on an embroidery needle and pull them through a few stitches of the work, then cut. Some of the yarn ends will be those with which you ended a section. These will already have been secured when you pulled them through the last loop on your hook. But others will be those with which you began a new section, and they will not be secured. Before pulling these loose ends through the work, secure them by taking a few tiny stitches in the same spot, then pull them through the work and cut them off.

If you are making a dress rather than a coat, weave the opening together, leaving only enough for a neck opening. Use the same crochet yarn, and match the rows carefully.

Block the finished garment by washing it with soap and cool water, patting the excess moisture out with a towel, and laying it flat on another towel. Gently push and pull it into shape, pat it down to flatten curled edges, and leave it to dry.

✂ Macramé Purse ✄

Macramé is a craft that requires neither more nor less effort in miniature than in full scale. Whether you make this macramé pocketbook for yourself or for a dollhouse doll, the number of knots you tie and the motions your hands make to tie them are identical.

The only problem you will run into with a tiny piece of macramé is that it is difficult, if not impossible, to see the knot you are tying. For this reason, don't try macramé in miniature until the knotting motions with string come so easily to your hands that you no longer need to check your work by eye.

Complicated as macramé looks, the patterns are made up of only two knots, one of which you use all the time to tie your shoelaces or your bathrobe belt. Designs are formed mainly by shifting from one set of cords to another in different rows and by the changing sequence and right- or left-handedness of the two knots.

Sources

Macramé instruction and design ideas: *Practical Macramé,* Eugene Andes, New York: Van Nostrand Reinhold Company, 1971.

Macramé board: The board used here is a 12 × 18-inch cork-covered bulletin board sold in both hardware stores and lumber yards. Homasote can also be used, wrapped first in brown paper if crumbling edges become a problem. The square panels used as acoustical ceiling tile also may serve the purpose; test by seeing if pins stick in easily and stay put.

Materials

For sampler: 1 ball mason's twine or macramé string
For purse: 1 ball No. 30 DMC Crochet Superba or
  similar crochet cotton, in ecru or off-white

Tools

Scissors
Macramé board
For sampler: Upholsterer's T-pins
For purse: Dressmaker's knit pins, No. 00 embroi-
  dery needle

Knot Handedness

The terminology of right-handed and left-handed knots is of no help to most people. When I was struggling with my own confusion, eyes on the picture, hands on the strings, and brain on the pattern, I found a method that helped keep me straight. The method was to chant each of the motions I was making with the cords. For a twisted bar the words were: Over, over, under, through. Over, over, under, through. For a Solomon bar: Over, over, under, through. Under, under, over, through. And for a single tatted bar: Over, through. Under, through.

Learning Sampler

For those who have not tried macramé before, this 16-cord sampler will give you practice in all patterns used for the purse in the illustration. These patterns are, however, only a fraction of the patterns you could use for your own designs. The books suggested under Sources will give you many other ideas you may want to work into a sampler or a miniature.

Setting up the knotting board. Cut two 6-inch lengths of twine. Knot the ends together as shown. This is the foundation cord. Pin the foundation cord at the top of the cork board, pushing the T-pins right through the knots. The foundation cord should be taut. Stick half a dozen extra T-pins into the board so they will be handy when you need them. To work, seat yourself at a table with the bottom of the board resting in your lap and the top leaning against the table.

Cutting the lengths of cord. Cut 8 lengths of twine each 6 feet long. Fold each length in half to form a loop.

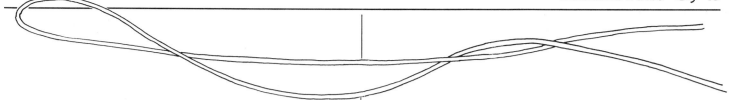

Hitching the cords to the foundation. Hitch each loop to the foundation by: 1. Inserting the loop downward behind the foundation cord. 2. Pulling the 2 cord ends through the loop. 3. Pulling the hitch snug. Each loop forms 2 cords. When you have done this with all 8 loops, you will have 16 cords to knot with. The knotting is done either with a pair of cords tied to one another, or with a pair of cords tied around another pair of cords, called leaders. The number of cords determines the width of the work. Wider pieces are made by hitching more cords to the foundation, always in multiples of 4.

Each loop will form 2 cords. Each cord should be 8 times longer than the piece you intend to make.

Forming a single tatting bar. Two cords are used for a single tatting bar. The bar is made up of half hitches. Like half-knots, half hitches can be left- or right-handed. Repeated identical half hitches will form a spiraled bar; alternating right and left ones form a flat bar like the one illustrated. Tie a left, then a right half hitch. Repeat three times to form the bar shown. Repeat across the row. In the next row put the first cord aside and form the first bar from the second and third cords. At the end of the row, put the last cord aside. Do the third row the same as the first.

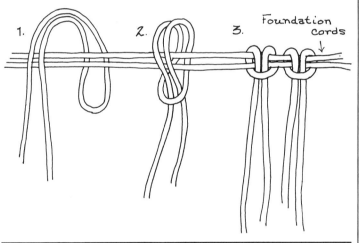

Two loops hitched to the foundation cord form the 4 cords that are the basic multiple for all macramé work.

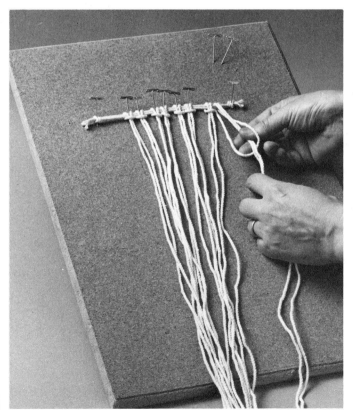

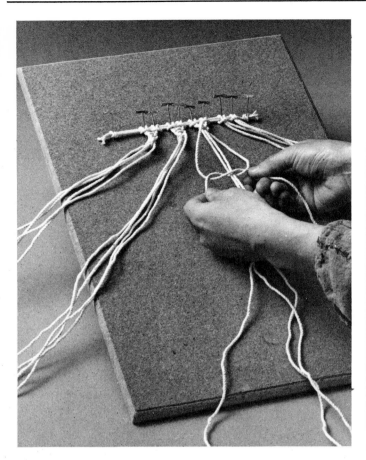

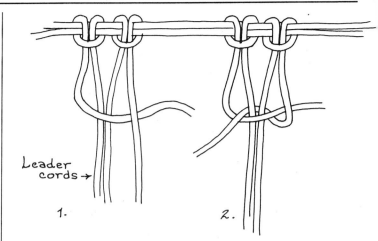

A left-handed half-knot. The 2 outside cords are used to tie the knot. The 2 inside cords are called leader cords.

Forming a twisted bar. The knot shown in this illustration is a half-knot. If this half-knot is tied repeatedly, the knots will spiral down the leader cords, forming a pattern called a *twisted bar.* The direction of the twist will be counterclockwise, using the left-handed half-knot shown here. If you use its opposite, the right-handed half-knot shown in the next illustration, the bar will twist in a clockwise direction. Those who tie knots may recognize the twisted bar as made up of a series of granny knots. Repeat the half-knot 5 times to form the bar shown. Repeat across the row.

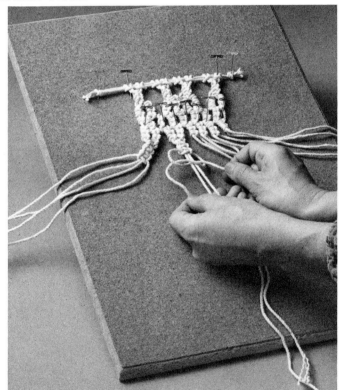

Forming a Solomon bar. The Solomon bar, which lies flat, is made by tying alternating left-handed and right-handed half-knots. First tie the left-handed half-knot, then the right-handed one. Repeat two more times to form the bar shown. Repeat across the row.

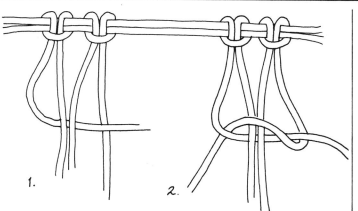

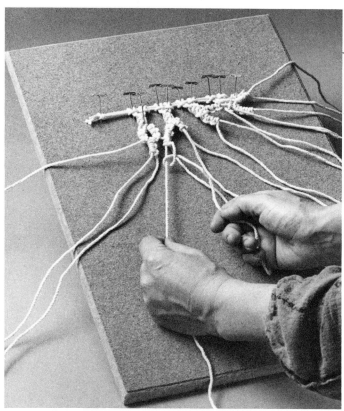

A right-handed half-knot. This half-knot is the opposite of a left-handed half-knot. Where a cord went over the leader cords on the right-handed knot, it now goes under. Where a cord went under, it now goes over.

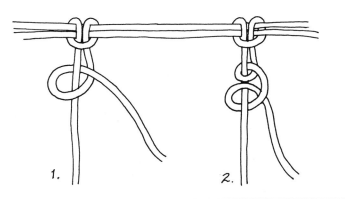

Left- and right-handed half hitches. Only 2 cords are used to make this pattern. The left one becomes the leader cord and is held taut while the other cord is around it. The tying cord goes over the leader to form a left-handed half hitch, under the leader to form a right-handed half hitch. Pins are inserted through the work as needed to keep it taut as you knot.

Forming a single tatting bar. Two cords are used for a single tatting bar. The bar is made up of half hitches. Like half-knots, half hitches can be left- or right-handed. Repeated identical half hitches will form a spiraled bar; alternating right and left ones form a flat bar like the one illustrated. Tie a left, then a right half hitch. Repeat three times to form the bar shown. Repeat across the row. In the next row put the first cord aside and form the first bar from the second and third cords. At the end of the row, put the last cord aside. Do the third row the same as the first.

Alternating square knots. A left-handed half-knot followed by a right-handed half-knot forms the familiar square knot most of us have learned as children. This pretty fishnet pattern is nothing more than rows of square knots tied on alternating pairs of cords. To start, put the first cord aside and tie the first square knot, using the second and third cords. Repeat across all the pairs of cords in the row.

In the second row tie the first knot, using the cord you put aside and the next cord. Repeat across the row. Do the third row the same as the first row to get the diamond pattern.

Fishnet square knotting. Practice may be needed to keep these square knots evenly spaced.

Fringe. To end your sampler, divide the cords into either pairs or foursomes, as you wish, and tie as shown around a pin to form a knotted fringe. Cut the fringe as long or as short as you wish.

Tying knot in fringe around pin. Hold the pin where you wish the knot to fall. Loop the cords around it in an overhand knot, and pull gently, easing the knot up to the pin as you pull. When the knot is in the right spot, tighten it and remove the pin.

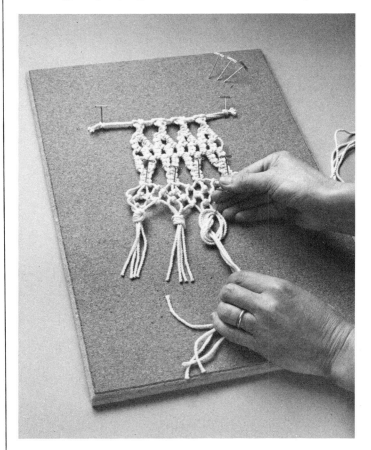

Step by Step

Cutting the cords. Unlike those of the sampler, the foundation cords in this purse have to be quite long because they will be used at the end to form a 3-inch handle. Cut 2 strands, each 48 inches long, for the foundation cords.

The purse itself measures 1½ inches long, including the knotted portion of the fringe. Cut 32 strands, each 24 inches long for the knotting cords.

So that you can do your own figuring for pieces that may differ from this one, here is the arithmetic: for both foundation and knotting cords the arithmetic is based on a cord length 8 times the length of the finished piece, and on a number of cords that is a multiple of 4.

Foundation Cords
Length of handle: 3 inches
Length of cord: 8 × 3 inches = 24 inches
Length of strand to form each pair of cords: 2 × 24 inches = 48 inches
Number of bars in handle: 1
Number of cords needed: 1 × 4 = 4 cords
Number of strands to cut: 4 cords ÷ 2 = 2
Result: cut 2 strands, each 48 inches long.

Knotting cords
Length of purse: 1½ inches
Length of cord: 8 × 1½ inches = 12 inches
Length of strand to form two cords: 2 × 12 inches = 24 inches
Number of bars in purse: 8 per side, or 16 bars
Number of cords needed: 16 × 4 = 64 cords
Number of strands to cut: 64 cords ÷ 2 = 32 strands
Result: cut 32 strands, each 24 inches long.

Hitching the cords. Secure the foundation to the macramé board this time by tying it all the way around, with a bow in the back. Support it with a pin at either side of the work area. Hitch the knotting cords to the foundation cord.

Divide the cords into groups of 4 about ⅛ inch apart, and support the foundation cord between each group with a pin.

Six-knot Solomon bar. The first pattern of the purse is Solomon bars, each made up of 6 alternating right and left half-knots. Begin at the left side of your work, using the first group of 4 cords, and continue across the row.

Alternating 6-knot single tatting bars. The second pattern is made up of 6-knot single tatting bars in 3 alternating rows. Start the first bar using the first 2 cords. Continue across the row. On the second row put the first and last cord aside, then complete the row as before. Pin these 2 cords out of your way to either side and consider them as *out-of-use cords*. At the third row put the first and last cords aside with the other out-of-use cords, continue across the row. Repeat for the third row.

As you continue to work, more and more cords will be put aside with the out-of-use cords. They will all be used in the same patterns later to join the two sides of the purse. The result will be a tubular piece in which no joint is visible.

Ten-knot twisted bar. The third pattern is the twisted bar, made up of 10 identical half-knots. Put the first 2 and last 2 cords aside with the out-of-use cords. Start with the next 4 cords. Work a bar of 10 identical half-knots. Continue across the row.

Alternating 2-cord square knots. The fourth pattern is made up of square knots, each formed by a left-handed and a right-handed half-knot. Put the first and last cords aside with the out-of-use cords. Tie a square knot with the next 2 cords. Continue across the row.

In each succeeding row put the first and the last cord aside. Continue for a total of 5 rows.

Joining the sides. Untie the foundation cord at the back of the board and pull out all pins from your work. Fold the 2 purse edges toward each other until they meet at the center. Pin your work back down in this position. The foundation cords, which will now emerge from the center of the work, can be pinned up out of the way. Part the cords in the middle and pull them out to the sides to get them out of the way. Now pull back into the work area all the untied out-of-use cords. Follow the patterns to tie these cords, starting with the 2 center cords in a 6-knot single tatting bar, and ending with the alternating rows of 2-cord square knots.

Forming the fringe. The fringe is designed to close the bottom of the purse by knotting together cords from both the front and the back of the work.

Unpin your work, and repin it with the two ends of the foundation cord emerging from one side instead of from the center of the work. The surface of the purse facing toward you is now the front of the work, and the side facing away from you is the back. Starting at the left, draw out the 2 pairs of cords that have formed the first square knots at the front and the back of the work. Tie these 4 strands into a 10-knot Solomon bar. Draw out the next group of 4 cords, 2 from the back of the work, 2 from the front. Tie these 4 cords into a fringe, using an overhand knot.

Continue across the row, always drawing out two front and two back cords to form a Solomon bar or a fringe knot. When you have finished the row, the bottom of the purse will be completely closed.

Forming the handle. Unpin your work and repin it upside down. Work the 4 foundation cords into a twisted bar, continuing until it measures about 3 inches.

Unpin your work. Thread each of the cords at the end of the handle in turn into a tapestry needle and run it through the work to secure it at the corner. You can run the cord either horizontally through the top of the purse or vertically down the bars. Snip off the ends of the cords after they are secure.

Mad Money

This purse is exactly the right size to hold a dime. In fact, this one does hold a dime, a real silver dime, with the head of Mercury, dated 1935, the year I was born. Such foolishness, such sentimentality, can be allowed in a dollhouse. And if you are thinking of years hence, when your grandchildren will be puttering about in your dollhouse, discovering this and that, or when—who knows?—a museum curator will piece together clues concerning you, your work, your times, it is certainly a worthy occupation to contrive what mysteries, coincidences, and delights you can.

Besides this revealing dime, we have also taken a first-day-of-issue two-dollar bill and cut it into miniature bills (no doubt thereby destroying its future commercial collector's price —but folly is allowable, too), to fill a small cashbox, which is really my father's silver monogrammed pill box, already an antique.

❧ Leather Shoes ☙

Shoes for dollhouse dolls are among those objects that must be homemade if one is to have them at all. There simply aren't any for sale in sizes to fit dollhouse dolls. Simple shoes such as the ones shown here take only about an hour to make. Since the amount of leather required is minimal, look around for such items as worn-out change purses, wallets, and gloves before spending money on leather from a crafts store. Thin, supple leather is easiest to work with.

Materials
Leather
Sewing thread
Carpet thread for laces
Paper for patterns
Optional: Felt for experimental patterns
Polyester stuffing

Tools
No. 10 "sharp" needle
Embroidery needle for threading laces
Very sharp scissors
Fine-line ball-point pen
Thimble
Tweezers

Step by Step

Making the pattern. The flat pattern shapes that result in three-dimensional shoe shapes are quite mysterious. Before you try to work out variations in style, try those shown here. The exercise may not give you exactly the shoes you want, but it will increase your understanding of how the shapes of the pieces and the resulting curve of the seams form finished shoes. Use the dimensions given to check whether or not these patterns will fit your doll's feet. To make the patterns larger or smaller, see page 27. To save on leather during this experimental stage, use felt instead.

Felt can also be used to make your own original pattern. Cut out the pattern shape to some approximation of what you imagine will work. Hold the pieces together and bend them into shape (or rapidly stitch them up with a few long stitches so you can try the shoe on the doll). Snip off bits of felt where necessary, or cut a new piece to correct a shape that doesn't work. With the temporary stitches removed, the corrected felt pieces can be used instead of paper for the final pattern.

Transferring the pattern to the leather. Lay each pattern piece in turn on the wrong side of the leather and trace around it with a fine-line ball-point pen (pencil doesn't show well enough). Since there is a right and a wrong side to leather, don't forget to reverse the pattern for right and left sides of a pattern piece. In the examples here, only the boot has right and left sides. Transfer onto the leather all the marks shown on the patterns.

Three patterns: boots, moccasins, laced shoe. The marks that indicate how one piece aligns with another are as important as the shape itself. Be sure to transfer these marks onto your pattern and onto the leather. A mark denoted by *a* on one piece should line up with the mark denoted by *a* on another piece when you stitch, and so on for each letter.

Cutting the leather. Very sharp scissors are necessary to cut leather neatly. I use embroidery scissors. When cutting, don't leave any nicks in the edge. Trim them off to leave the edge perfectly smooth.

Stitching the leather. Use a No. 10 "sharp" needle, a single strand of ordinary sewing thread, and a thimble. Hold the pieces to be stitched wrong sides together, being sure points marked with letters line up exactly with one another. Start the thread by pushing the needle out from inside one piece. Secure it by taking several stitches through both pieces at the same spot before continuing. When you get to the end of the stitching, finish the thread in the same manner, with the thread on the inside.

Stitch the seam along the outside of the shoe, using very small overcasting stitches. Take each stitch as close to the edge as possible to keep the seam narrow. Because the pieces tend to get out of alignment as you stitch, be sure to check them frequently.

The boot: This is the easiest of the three examples. Stitch the front and back seams first. Then line up the front and back seams with the marks on the sole, and stitch all the way around. A narrow strip of rabbit fur trim could be added to the top.

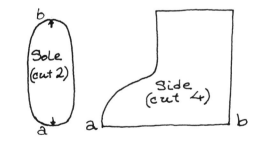

Boot 1⅛ × ⅜ inches

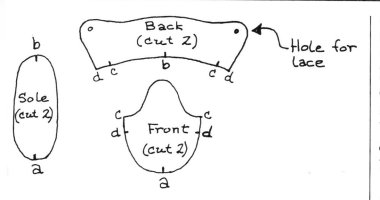

Laced shoe 1⅛ × ⅜ inches

The laced shoe: Start stitching the back piece to the sole at point *b*. Continue to point *c*. Lay the front piece under the back piece with *c* and *d* lined up correctly. Continue stitching through all three layers (sole, front, and back), and then continue on around the front of the shoe until you come to *d* on the opposite side. Lay the unstitched portion of the back piece over the front piece, lining up *d* and *c*. Continue stitching through the three layers, then on around the back to the point at which you began.

The moccasin: The top stitching of the moccasin is done differently from other seams. Each stitch in the sides is twice as long as the stitch in the top piece. The result is an even puckering that shapes the sides of the moccasin. This is easier to accomplish if you do each stitch in two strokes, one through the bottom, one through the top, rather than going through both layers at a single stroke. Be sure to line up the pieces at *a* and *b*. The two seams at the back of the moccasin are stitched in the ordinary way.

Blocking the shoes. After stitching, the shape of the shoes may be rather undefined. Wet the shoes with water. This will make the leather stretchy and malleable. Stuff the wet shoes with polyester stuffing carefully pushed in with the point of your scissors, and push the shoes into shape with your fingers. When the shoes are completely dry, pull the stuffing out with tweezers. The shoes will feel stiffer than before and will keep the shape you gave them.

Making shoelaces. The shoelaces on the tied shoes shown here were made with 20-gauge crochet yarn waxed by pulling it through paraffin. This is not necessary. Carpet thread will do nicely and would have been used here if my ten-year-old had not made off with it. Thread an embroidery needle with the carpet thread and pull the needle through where you wish the lace to go.

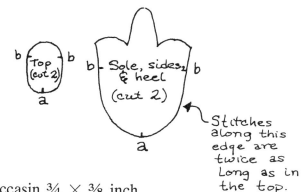

Moccasin ¾ × ⅜ inch

Mattress

attresses don't really look like this any more. These come from my childhood when mattresses had ridges around their edges and buttons through their middles. The thin mattress shown here is padding for a cradle; the thick one is for a bed. The same techniques used for mattresses could be used for thick or thin chair cushions.

Materials
Cardboard or heavy paper
Ticking, twill, or other firm cotton fabric
Thread
Polyester stuffing
White yarn

Tools
Thimble
Scissors
Pencil or tailor's chalk
Needles ("sharps" for sewing; embroidery or other
    long needle for tufting)
Ruler or tape measure

Step by Step

Making a pattern. A mattress is made of three pieces: a top piece, a bottom piece, and a boxing strip that runs all the way around the sides to give the mattress depth. Measure the inside dimensions of your bed and cut a piece of cardboard or heavy paper to your measurements. Check accuracy by placing the cardboard in position where the mattress will go. Trim or recut if necessary.

You may leave the corners of the mattress pattern square, or trim them to a small curve as shown here. It is easier to stitch and turn curved corners than square ones. This is the only pattern piece you will need.

Cutting the pieces. Cut two pieces of cloth from your pattern. Lay the pattern along the lengthwise grain of the fabric. Trace around it with a soft pencil or chalk. Cut the piece out ¼ inch beyond the traced line to allow for a seam. Mark the center line at one end of each piece with pencil or chalk. Keep the pattern piece. You will be using it again later.

To cut the boxing strip, figure out the perimeter of the mattress to get the length of the strip. Decide how thick you want the mattress to be to determine the width of the strip. This mattress, for instance, measures 4 × 6 inches; the perimeter is 20 inches. It is 1 inch thick. With the addition of ¼ inch for each seam, the boxing strip should measure 20½ inches long × 1½ inches wide. To be safe, you may cut the strip longer than necessary and trim it later.

Boxing the mattress. With the right sides together, stitch the boxing strip along the top or bottom of the mattress ¼ inch in from the edge. Start at the center line at one end of the mattress, leaving a ¼-inch margin of the boxing strip free as a seam allowance. Use a small running stitch. Continue all the way around, curving the strip at each corner for a rounded corner, or clipping the seam into the corner if it is to be square. When you are back to your starting point, pin the two ends of the boxing together and stitch up the seam.

Stitch the other mattress piece to the boxing, again starting at the center marking. This time leave a 2-inch opening along one edge so you can turn the mattress right side out.

Right: Stitching the mattress.
1. Start stitching on the boxing at the center line of the mattress, leaving ¼-inch seam allowances.
2. Stitch up the seam that connects the ends of the boxing strip.
3. Sew the other piece of the mattress to the boxing, starting at the center line. Leave a 2-inch space for turning and stuffing.

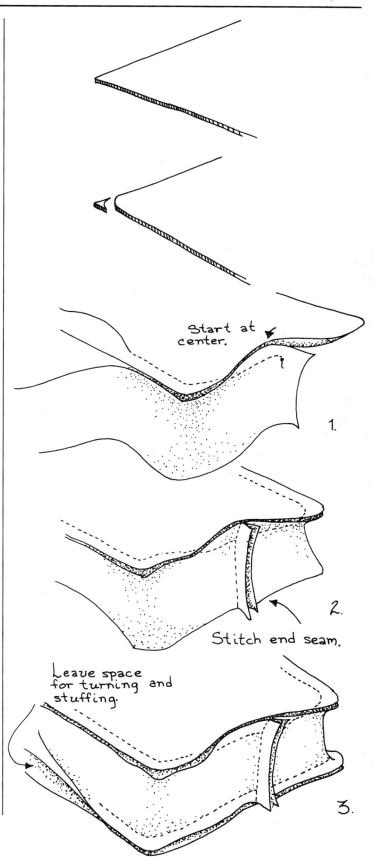

Start at center.

1.

Stitch end seam.

2.

Leave space for turning and stuffing.

3.

Stuffing the mattress. Trim all the seams to ⅛ inch. Turn the mattress right side out. Stuff it firmly. The mattress should not have gaps or feel floppy. If seams or corners look dented in, wet them with a damp sponge, then use a knitting needle to push stuffing into them. Turn in the remaining seam allowance at the gap, pin together, and stitch shut.

Making a tufting pattern. Use the original mattress pattern to work out the tufting pattern. Mark off the pattern into 4 equal divisions along the width and length as shown here. This grid will serve as a guide for positioning the tufts. Make a pencil dot at each point where a tuft will go. Punch a hole through each of these dots with a pencil point.

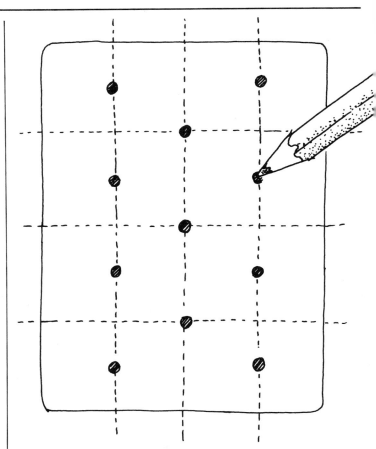

Transferring the tufting pattern to the mattress. Place the punched pattern on top of the mattress. Make a pencil dot through each hole onto the surface of the mattress. Repeat on the opposite side of the mattress.

Tufting the mattress. This mattress is tufted by pulling thread tightly through the mattress to form a dimple at each dot and anchoring the thread around a bit of white yarn to form a tuft in the center of each dimple.

Cut 22 one-inch lengths of white yarn for the tufts. Thread a long needle, double the thread, and knot it at the bottom. Bring the needle into the mattress through a space between stitches along one edge and come up through the nearest dot. Tug lightly at the thread until the knot is pulled in through the space and catches in the stuffing inside.

Push the needle back down through the same dot and out of the dot on the opposite side of the mattress. Before you pull the thread taut, place a length of yarn in the loop of the thread to form a tuft. Repeat on the opposite side so that both top and bottom surfaces are tufted. The tighter you pull the thread, the deeper the dimple will be. When the first dimple is finished, bring your thread under the surface and up through the next dot. Continue tufting until the pattern is complete.

Snip the yarn tufts to ⅛ inch. Rub them with a fingertip to unravel the yarn and form a fuzzy tuft.

Right: Four steps in tufting.
1. Insert the needle into the mattress through a space between stitches and up through the first dot.
2. Down through the same dot, forming a loop to hold the yarn.
3. Out through the dot on the opposite side, with thread pulled tight to form a dimple.
4. Yarn snipped and rubbed to fuzz it to a tuft.

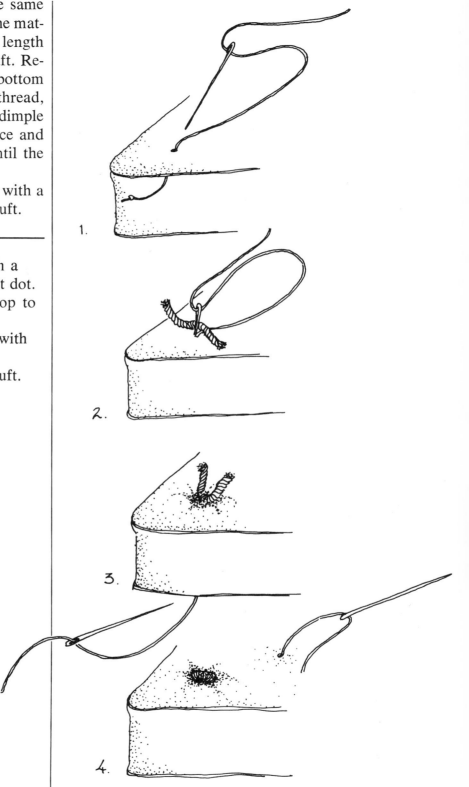

❧ Pillows ❧

Pillows are among the best projects for beginning sewers. Construction is logical, there isn't much sewing to do, and, given pretty fabrics, the results are satisfying. Good fabrics for children to use are felt and ultrasuede because they don't fray. Velveteen is also easy to work with. Besides the simple pillows described here, see also tufting and boxing in the previous chapter. Though both are suggested for mattresses, the same details are often used for pillows.

The "vegetable" pillows shown here are worked in petit point and backed with velveteen. The flowered pillow is worked in crewel embroidery with silk thread on silk fabric. The bed pillow has a separate pillowcase and is stuffed with real down. The half-round boxed pillow is made for the wicker chair on page 143.

Materials
Paper for pattern
Fabric
Thread
Polyester stuffing

Tools
Thimble
Fine-line ball-point pen
Scissors
No. 10 "sharp" needle (or larger embroidery needle for a child)
Large knitting needle or pencil with lead broken off

Step by Step

Making a pattern. Even though the shape is simple, carefully make a paper pattern in square or rectangular shape, using a triangle to get the corners right. If the pattern shape is even a little out of square, the pillow will look even more cockeyed when it is stuffed. Remember that stuffing will make the pillow look smaller. Plan the pattern slightly larger than you want the finished pillow to be.

Transferring the pattern onto fabric. On the wrong side of the fabric, trace around the outside of your pattern piece with a fine-line ball-point pen, then trace another piece, for the two sides of the pillow. Be sure to line up the edges of the pattern with the grain of the fabric, or the finished product will pull into a parallelogram instead of a square or rectangle.

Cutting the fabric. Cut out the two shapes ¼ inch beyond the traced outline to allow for the seams. The outline will be your stitching line.

Stitching the pillow. Use a small running stitch, sewing along the traced outline. Children can begin the thread with a knot and end with several small stitches in the same spot. Adults might prefer both to begin and to end with tiny stitches. Similarly, children do better with their thread doubled, whereas adults sew better with a single thread. Begin the stitching ¼ inch from the end of one side. Continue around the corner, and on around the other three sides. Finish the thread ¼ inch into the side at which you began.

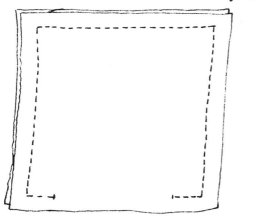

Trimming the seams. Children's stitches may be too large to risk trimming the seams at all (the edges will poke out from between the large stitches when the pillow is turned). If the stitching is small, clip off the corners very close and trim the side seams to ⅛ inch.

Turning the pillow. Turn the pillow right side in. Gently, and with a blunt object, such as a large knitting needle or a pencil with the lead broken off, push out the corners from inside. If this is done with a sharp instrument, you risk poking the narrow seams out between stitches. Press the edges flat between your fingers, or with an iron if necessary. Turn the remaining seam in ¼ inch and press flat.

Stuffing the pillow. Stuff the pillow with polyester stuffing, pushing the stuffing into the corners with the same blunt instrument you used for turning. Stuff rather loosely. The pillow should feel mushy rather than stiff. Knead the pillow with your fingers to distribute the stuffing evenly.

Finishing the pillow. Children may sew up the open seam with an overcasting stitch. Adults should trim the pressed ¼-inch seam to ⅛ inch before stitching, and use a blind stitch instead of overcasting.

Fancy Stitching

Crewel embroidery need not be done on an unusually tiny scale for use on miniatures as it is small and delicate to begin with. These are a few embroidery stitches that are easy to learn and to do. They are the only stitches used to make the flowered design.

Embroidery is done before the pillows are cut out. The cloth is held in place on an embroidery hoop. Cotton embroidery thread is much easier to handle than silk, and it is easier to keep stitches even on a fine fabric than on a coarse one. Use an embroidery needle, which has a longer eye than a "sharp." When you design an embroidered pillow, draw the figure within the actual shape and size of the pillow. Transfer the design onto the right side of the fabric with carbon paper, being sure to line up the edges with the grain of the fabric. The lines will be covered by your stitches.

In each set of drawings the small arrow points to where the needle is brought up through the cloth to start the stitch. The dotted lines represent lines to be outlined or areas to be filled in your design. The thumb is often used to hold a loop of thread in the proper position while completing a stitch. In the French knot both thumb and forefinger are used to hold one thread taut while the knot is made.

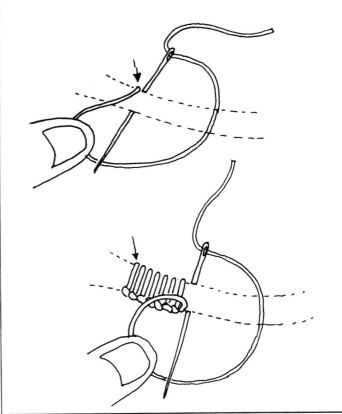

Buttonhole stitch, worked closely to fill in an area.

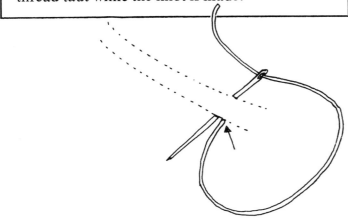

Satin stitch, used to fill in an area.

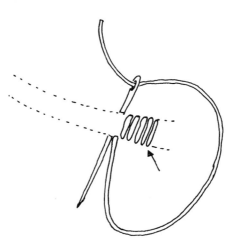

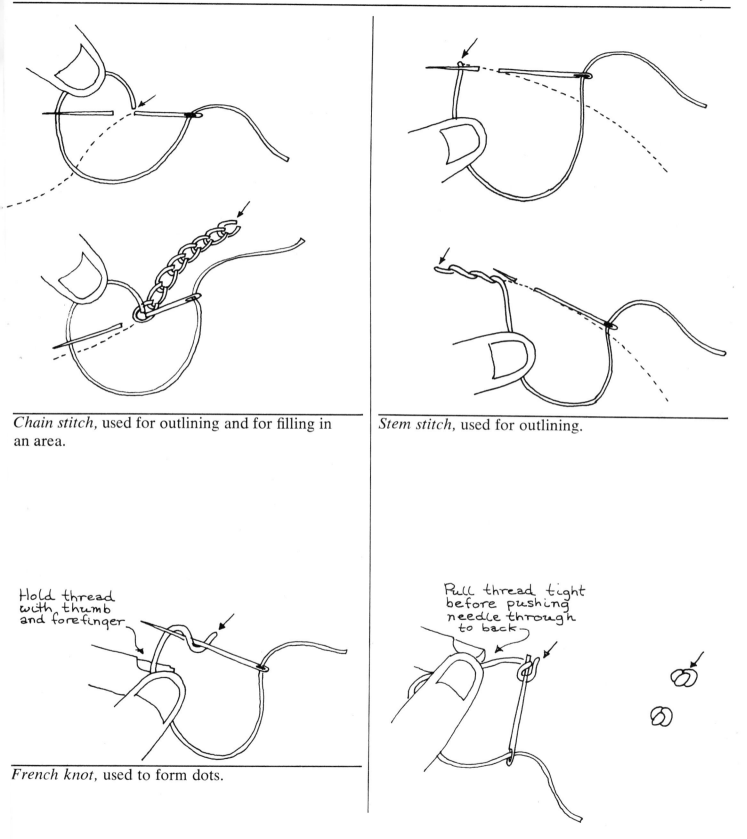

Chain stitch, used for outlining and for filling in an area.

Stem stitch, used for outlining.

Hold thread with thumb and forefinger

French knot, used to form dots.

Pull thread tight before pushing needle through to back

❧ Knitted Blankets ☙

Those who are clever and experienced knitters could probably knit clothing small enough for dollhouse dolls. I have used knitting instead for the easiest of all items, blankets. In fact, blankets are where knitting began —and almost ended—for me. During World War II we were as young girls given two patriotic tasks. One was knitting enormous rough gray squares on thick wooden needles in hot weather. The squares were sewed together for soldiers' blankets. The other task was picking wax beans in a dusty field in the summer sun. The beans were canned for soldiers' dinners. To this day, I am a sweaty, clumsy knitter, and I can't eat canned wax beans at all. The blankets shown here are compliments of my mother-in-law, Rosella Stein, and the pattern samples were done by my son's friend Camilla Lofving.

If you have never knitted before, get basic instructions either from the salesperson in a knitting shop or from a friend. Though there are only a few moves—and none of them are hard—written instructions even when accompanied by the cleverest photographs are very difficult to follow. Once you have been shown, a good book to remind you of the moves and terms is *Mon Tricot Knit and Crochet*, available at yarn shops.

Materials
Yarn—fingering, baby, or similar weight
Scrap of cloth for figuring out blanket size

Tools
Pair of knitting needles, Size 1, 2, or 3. Cable patterns will require a sock needle of the same size in addition to the pair.
Tape measure
Darning needle or yarn needle
Scissors

The Soldier's Blanket

The way we originally made those soldiers' blankets is still as good a way as any for a child to proceed. There is no guesswork about how many stitches to cast on, or any knowledge demanded except how to increase, decrease, and purl (or knit). Cast on one stitch. Purl (or knit) in every row. Increase one stitch at the beginning or end of each row. When one side of the resulting triangle is long enough to fit the doll's bed, begin to decrease one stitch at the beginning or end of each row until you are down to a single stitch again. (Note that increases and decreases can be at the beginning or end of each row, but should be the same throughout.) Bind off the last stitch by pulling the end of the yarn through it. With a needle, weave both ends of the yarn into the blanket to hide them.

Step by Step

Choosing the yarn. Either baby yarn or fingering yarn can be used to make a blanket pattern in a small scale. Baby yarn is limited to white and pastel colors, and though sometimes of wool, it is more usually of synthetics these days. Fingering yarn is wool and comes in more grown-up colors. Besides these two, there are other light yarns of similar weight that you may run into. The only rule to follow is that if the weight is similar to baby yarn, and if the colors appeal to you, by all means use it.

Choosing the needles. Knitting needles are numbered according to size, the lower the number the smaller the needle. The smaller the needle, the tighter the stitches will be and the stiffer the blanket. The larger the needles, the looser the stitches will be and the floppier the blanket. These blankets and samples were knit on No. 1 needles.

Choosing a pattern. If you are not an experienced knitter, try an easy pattern like stockinette stitch (alternating rows of knitting and purling), rice stitch (knit 1, purl 1 in every row), or the hurdle stitch (two rows of knitting, then two of knit 1, purl 1). For fancier stitches, see Fancy Patterns.

Making a stitch gauge. Besides the thickness of yarn, size of needle, and number of stitches, the tension with which a knitter works affects the size of the finished piece. Since everyone is different in this respect, the only way to figure out how many stitches you should start with is to knit a small sample, using the stitch, the yarn, and the needles for the piece you wish to knit. This sample is called a stitch gauge. It tells you the number of stitches per inch.

In whatever pattern you are using, work up a stitch gauge at least 18 stitches across and 1½ inches long. Bind it off and lay it flat on a table. Lay a ruler across it and count the number of stitches that fall within one inch. This number is your stitch gauge. It tells you how many stitches are across 1 inch of your knitting.

Measuring the blanket size. Using any piece of cloth, drape it over the doll's bed you wish to cover. By eye, mark the cloth with a pencil at about where you think it should fall at the sides, the top, and the bottom, being a bit generous in all dimensions. Cut the cloth to size and put it on the bed again. Make any adjustments you still think are necessary. When this piece of cloth is the size you wish your blanket to be, measure it carefully and write down the dimensions. The width and your stitch gauge will be used for figuring out how many stitches to cast on.

Casting on. Multiply the width of the blanket by the number of stitches per inch in your stitch gauge. For instance, if your gauge is 9 stitches and you wish the blanket to measure 6 inches wide, you will need to cast on 54 stitches. For more complicated stitches, check Fancy Patterns for slight adjustments that may be necessary in order to fit in full units of the pattern. Cast on the stitches loosely so your work won't draw at the bottom.

Knitting the blanket. To prevent curling, it is a good idea to purl the first two and last two rows in any pattern, and purl the first and last two stitches in each row. This will give you a narrow, flat garter-stitch border all around. Following whatever pattern you have chosen, knit the blanket until it measures the length you have written down. Bind the last row off loosely.

Finishing the blanket. With a darning needle, weave the ends of yarn remaining into the blanket. If you wish, you can add a crocheted edge, using the same yarn used for the knitting or yarn in a contrasting color. Two edgings will be found on page 40. A fringe at top and bottom will make the blanket look more like an afghan. The simplest fringe is the one used for the rug on page 81, but the extra insurance of glue will not be necessary for soft knitting yarns.

Blocking the blanket. When the blanket is finished, wash it in cool water and mild soap. Pat it dry between towels. Lay it flat on a towel, gently coaxing it into shape and pressing it flat with the palm of your hand. Leave it to dry thoroughly so it will keep its shape.

Fancy patterns

The patterns shown here are only a few examples of the hundreds you can choose from. A particularly good source is *Mon Tricot Knitting Dictionary,* which contains clear photographs and instructions for 333 pattern stitches. Each pattern is based on a multiple of stitches—the number of stitches required to complete one unit of the design. A pattern might say, for instance, "multiple of 7," which means it takes 7 stitches to complete each unit. Or a pattern might say "multiple of 12 + 4," which means that it takes 12 stitches to complete a unit of the pattern, and that there are 4 plain stitches between units to separate them from one another.

To figure out how many stitches you will need to cast on for a fancy dollhouse blanket, make a stitch gauge in the pattern stitch, using a multiple of the number given. For example, the basket weave pattern here is a multiple of 6 stitches, so you could make a stitch gauge of 18 or 24 stitches. Measure your sample to see how many stitches you knit per inch. Multiply the gauge by the total width you wish the blanket to be. If your stitch gauge is 9 stitches per inch and you want the blanket to be 7 inches wide, your answer will be 63 inches. But while this number of stitches would allow you to complete 10 full basket weave units (60 stitches) you would be left with an extra three stitches. Ingenuity is required here. A good solution would be to cast on 64 instead of 63 stitches, and plan for only 9 basket weave units (54 stitches) plus a plain garter stitch border of 5 stitches on each side. So that the border is the same at the top and bottom edges too, you would start the pattern with 5 rows of purling. On the 6th row you would purl the first 5 stitches, follow the pattern for the next 54, and end the row with another 5 purl stitches. This is not the only solution. You could also have figured on 10 pattern units and a garter stitch border only 2 stitches wide. For patterns in which each unit is separated from the next by a plain area, remember there will be one less plain area than there are units. For instance, a cable pattern might be a multiple of 5 + 3 (5 stitches for each cable, three stitches between cables). You would want both to begin and to end with a cable to make the pattern symmetrical. So if you were to figure 8 complete cables (40 stitches) you would figure only 7 spaces between (21 stitches), plus a border of 2 stitches on each side for a total of 65 stitches. All this arithmetic is rather a nuisance, but it does allow you to work the right-size blanket in any one of hundreds of wonderful patterns.

❧ Patchwork Quilts ☙

The secret of miniature patchwork quilts is that they need not be miniatures at all. A standard quilt is made of squares called blocks, which are assembled from small patches and then stitched together to form the large patchwork. The blocks range from about 6 inches square to about 12 inches square. Since a dollhouse bed can be covered nicely by a 7- or 8-inch-square quilt, a single block can serve as a whole quilt. The only trick is to find a block design that, by itself, looks like a whole quilt. There are hundreds of such patterns.

Sources

Patchwork instruction: *Quilting and Patchwork* (A Sunset Book). Menlo Park, California: Lane Books, 1973.

Patchwork design ideas: *American Pieced Quilts.* Jonathan Holstein. New York: The Viking Press, 1973.

Materials

¼-inch graph paper
Fabrics for patchwork
Lining fabric
Thread

Tools

Thimble
No. 7 "sharp" needle
Scissors
No. 1 Pencil

Step by Step

Designing a quilt. Although it is possible to think up patterns that have not been done before, books on patchwork are helpful. Some give instruction on how to lay out the patterns; others simply show finished quilts. Choose a single block of any design that seems to stand on its own as a small quilt. Curved designs and those in which many pieces come together at a point are hardest. The easiest patchwork is a checkerboard of 1-inch squares. Sketch your ideas roughly on graph paper.

Choosing fabrics. Because of the number of seams, heavy fabrics make a clumsy quilt. Silk, fine cotton, and wool challis—or synthetics that imitate these natural fibers—are thin enough and floppy enough for fine work. Although large patterns look awful, you may find one that has highly detailed areas that would make nice patches. Fabrics are sold in minimum quantities of ¼ yard.

Making a pattern. Check the size quilt you need by cutting a piece of cloth to the right size for your bed. For most dollhouse double beds, 7 × 7 inches is right. With a pencil draw the outline of the quilt on the graph paper. Draw the pattern you have chosen. (If you have trouble with the mathematics required for a 7-inch square, allow for a ½-inch border strip all the way around the block pattern. You can then draw the block pattern as a 6-inch square like the first example in the illustration.) The ¼-inch markings on the graph paper will help you check that your design is symmetrical.

   Figure out how many of each shape or size of patch you will need in each of the fabrics you are using. On one of each kind of patch, write the number of pieces required in each fabric that will be cut in that shape. Now with sharp scissors cut out one of each of these different patches to use as pattern pieces. Save the rest of the drawing for reference in case you get mixed up as you begin to assemble the patchwork.

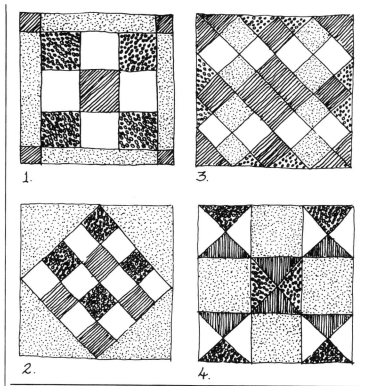

1.

3.

2.

4.

Little sketches like these, colored with colored pencils or scribbled in different textures, will help you decide on a design. This is also the easiest way to figure out the number and kinds of fabrics to use, and the number of patches to cut for each. All these quilts are designed for four fabrics. The fabrics contribute as much to the result as the patchwork pattern. No. 3, for instance, is only a checkerboard laid on the diagonal, but the contrast of lighter and darker fabrics forms a cross. The boldest effects are achieved by solid, contrasting colors. The subtlest effects are achieved by using different prints, all in the same scale and of similar colors and intensities.

Cutting the patches. Lay your fabric wrong side up flat on a table. Place a pattern piece on it, being sure it lies along the straight weave of the fabric. Draw a line around it with a sharp, soft-leaded pencil. This pencil mark will be your stitching line. Cut the piece out ¼ inch from the line—the ¼ inch is your seam allowance. Repeat for all the types of patches in each fabric.

A star is made of 8 identical diamonds. This one was drawn to ¼ the actual size for reproduction here. To draw it to dollhouse scale, make the square that contains the star 5 inches on each side. (Two small squares on this drawing equal 1 inch in yours.) The border is 1 inch wide all around. To sew the star, assemble four diamonds, then the other four diamonds. Stitch the two halves together across the center.

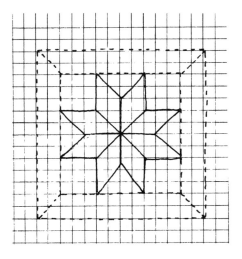

Sewing the patches. Patches are sewed together with a plain running stitch. Use a single thread and a No. 7 "sharp" needle. Several small stitches to secure the thread are preferable to a knot. A thimble is obligatory if your stitches are to be as tiny as they should be. The order in which patches are assembled depends on the pattern. A checkerboard is assembled in strips; then the strips are stitched together. Triangles are usually assembled into squares, which are then stitched to one another. If you get confused, consult one of the "how to" books suggested.

When the patches are all assembled, trim seams to ⅛ inch and press them open. (This is easier to do if you dip your finger in water and spread out the seam with your wet fingertip before pressing.)

Lining the patchwork. Miniature patchwork need not be quilted or tufted. It can simply be a lined coverlet. Use any fine cotton or silk material for the lining. Cut it to the same measurement as the finished patchwork piece. With the right sides together, pin or baste the pieces to one another. Stitch around the outside ¼ inch in from the edge. Leave a 3-inch opening for turning the quilt right side out. Trim the seam to ⅛ inch, clip the corners straight across very close to the stitching line, and turn right side out. Turn the remaining seams in and sew up the opening, using a blind stitch.

For a puffy effect, a piece of patchwork must be either quilted or tufted with knots of string. Either way, an interlining is added between the patchwork and the lining, and the piece is finished at the edges with a bias binding. Polyester stuffing, sold in notions departments, can be used for the interlining.

Basting a quilt. The lining, interlining, and patchwork "sandwich" are basted 1 inch from the edge all around and diagonally from corner to corner.

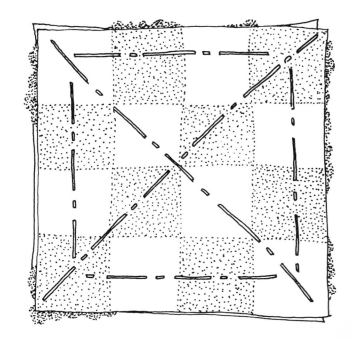

Interlining. Lay the lining on a table wrong side up. Tease out the stuffing evenly until it is the same size as the lining. If it is lumpy, the lumps will show. If it is too thick, the quilt will not fall into place on the bed.

Lay the patchwork right side up on top of the interlining. Baste the "sandwich" together to hold the pieces in place as you work.

Quilting. A quilting stitch is simply a running stitch, worked in small stitches in any pattern that will hold the stuffing in place. The pattern may follow the design, running close along each seam, or it may cut across the design as shown here. Use tailor's chalk to lay out the pattern if necessary on the top of the quilt, and rub it out later. Remove basting stitches when they get in your way.

Partially quilted patchwork. Chalk lines may not be necessary if the quilting pattern bears an obvious relationship to the patchwork pattern. When working out the pattern, remember that you still have an extra ¼-inch seam allowance around the edges that could throw off your symmetry. If you hold a piece of paper ⅛ inch in from the edge of the quilt in this illustration, you will see that some of the quilting lines are not going to come out right when the piece is bound.

Tufting. A tufted quilt is easier than a quilted one. An embroidery needle is threaded with soft cotton string; the threaded needle is pushed down through the center of a patch or at the intersection of seams and pushed back up through all the layers. The two ends are snipped to about three inches, then tied in a square knot and trimmed close to the knot.

A tufted quilt.

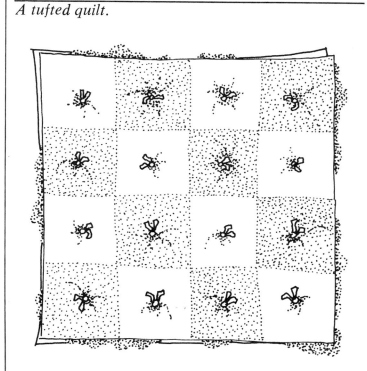

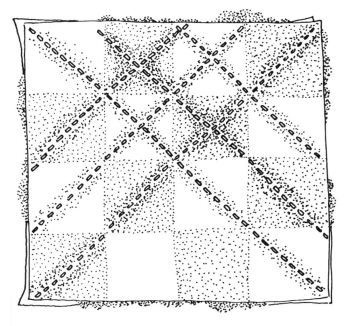

Quilting in a diamond pattern

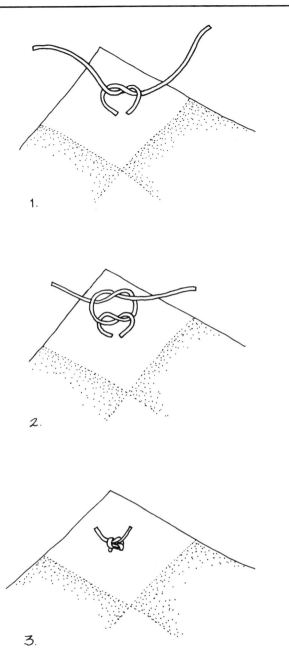

1.

2.

3.

Three steps in tying a tufting knot. Tying a tufting knot in the center of a patch. The knot is a square knot. After a while the soft ends of the clipped string will fray, forming a softer-looking tuft.

Binding. The raw edges of an interlined quilt are covered with bias binding. You can use commercial bias tape or cut your own from one of the fabrics used for patching. Commercial tape comes already turned in at the edges and pressed flat. Choice of color, however, is limited. You may prefer to make your own, following the instructions given here.

Before you begin to bind your quilt, trim the interlining in ¼ inch from the edge so the binding will not be bulky.

Binding a quilt.
1. Diagonal strips, 1 inch wide, are cut from a square of fabric.
2. If a single strip is not long enough, strips can be stitched together, the seam pressed open and trimmed to ⅛ inch.
3. One edge of the bias binding is turned under ¼ inch, basted in place, pressed, and trimmed to ⅛ inch.
4. With right sides together and edges lined up, the bias strip is stitched to the top of the quilt ¼ inch in from the edge. Join the beginning and end of the bias strip with a ⅛-inch seam on the diagonal. Trim all three layers of fabric to ⅛ inch.
5. Two kinds of corners. To make the square corner, snip the extra fabric away and blindstitch the diagonal miter to hold it shut. To make the round corner, trim the patchwork and lining to the desired curve, and gather in the binding as you sew.
6. The binding is folded over to the back, basted in place, pressed flat, and blindstitched.

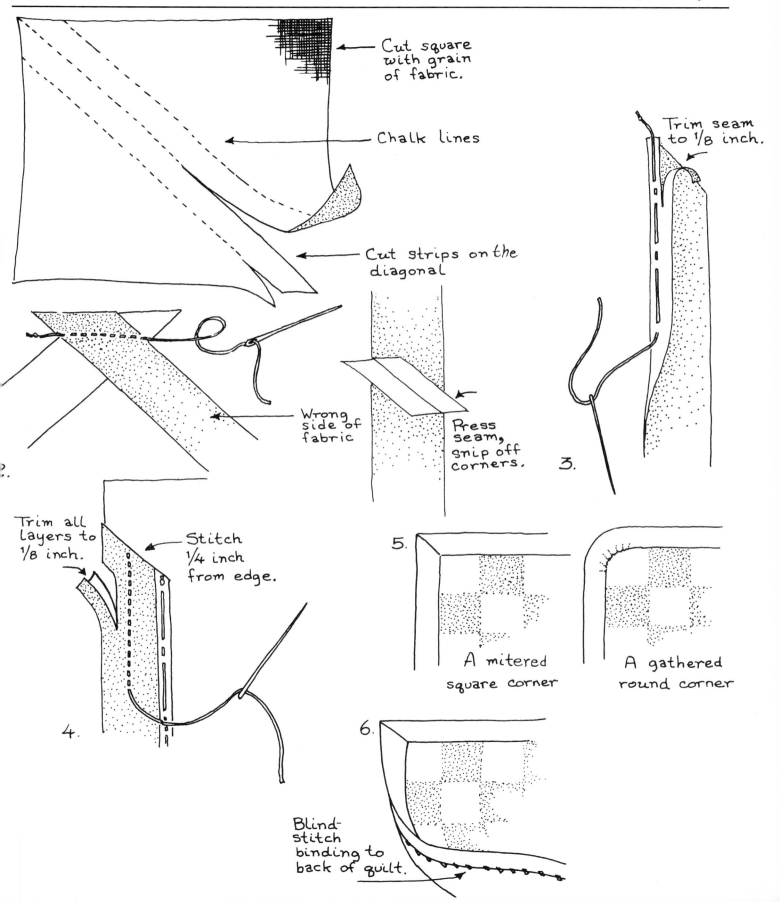

Cut square with grain of fabric.

Chalk lines

Cut strips on the diagonal

Trim seam to 1/8 inch.

Wrong side of fabric

Press seam, snip off corners.

3.

2.

Trim all layers to 1/8 inch.

Stitch 1/4 inch from edge.

5.

A mitered square corner

A gathered round corner

4.

6.

Blind-stitch binding to back of quilt.

ɛ♂ **Woven Towels** ♂ɘ

Tiny fringed towels—or even bolts of cloth —can be woven on an inkle loom. The loom, sometimes called a belt loom, is bought frequently for children or for adults' first experiments in weaving because it is both inexpensive and simple to use. The small size, which sells for under fifteen dollars, can be used for cloth up to 10 inches wide and 68 inches long. Instructions for designing many different patterns come with the loom. These towels were woven from two different kinds of yarn in four colors. The 43 warp yarns (the long ones that become the fringe at the ends of the work) are No. 8 crochet cotton in red, gold, and pink. The weft yarn (the single strand that is woven back and forth through the warp yarns) is No. 20 crochet cotton. The fabric is somewhat too coarse for use as a bolt of cloth. Try using all No. 20 cotton and 91 warp strands for cloth "by the inch."

❧ Braided Rugs ❧

The two braided rugs in the illustration on page 72 were learning pieces. I learned from them how not to design, how not to start, how not to braid, and how not to change colors. After twelve finger-numbing, back-stiffening hours of work on them, I realized that I had a real braided rug in the house that might tell me something I didn't know. Sure enough, it had a simple message: don't change color in more than one strip of cloth at a time. The result of this revelation is the subtly designed and smoothly executed rug shown in the illustration above.

Materials
Fabrics for braiding
Thread

Tools
Thimble
Needle
Shears
Embroidery scissors
Straight pins
Ironing board

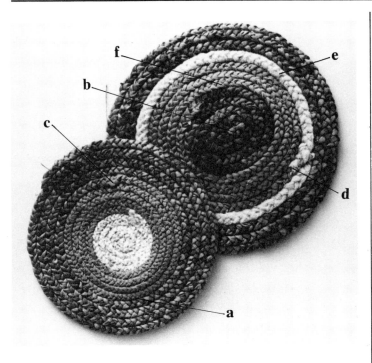

Two "failure" rugs. **a.** This rug is a bad design unless you want an archery target on the floor. **b.** This first turn of braid is too short to form the oval planned. Two bull's-eyes. **c.** A big lump caused by changing color in all three strands at once. **d.** The "disappearing braid" syndrome, caused by trying to sew the end of one braid beneath the rug and sneak another in at the same point. **e.** Too-thick braid, caused by using too-thick cloth. **f.** Lopsidedness. This is caused by ending a color in the wrong place. Each color should end at the same point it began if the number of rows of braid are to be equal all around. In this case, ending at the wrong place was caused by not stitching up the rug as I went along. Unless you keep stitching, there is no way to know where a color change will fall in the rug pattern.

Step by Step

Choosing the fabrics. Thin, soft, but tightly woven fabrics braid well. Combinations of cotton and synthetics seem to fray less than one hundred percent synthetics. Knits do not fray, but they may run easily or be too stretchy to work with. Patterned fabrics can be worked up into interesting textures, but avoid prints that have a definite right and wrong side. Figure on three fabrics to make your design interesting. They should all be the same weight.

Cutting the strips. Cut ¼-inch strips of fabric along the grain of the cloth. You may use the selvage edge, which frays less. Strips shorter than 2 feet won't go far enough; strips longer than 5 feet will tangle too much. Strips 5 feet long braid to about 3 feet, or enough braiding for the border color in the oval rug illustrated. Handle the strips gently to avoid fraying.

Designing the rug. You cannot design a braided rug by drawing it, but you can form a mental image for guidance. From your fabric choices, choose a basic, or ground, color. Make 1 inch of sample braid, using three strands of that color. Make another sample braid, using two strands of ground color and one of another color. Continue to experiment in this fashion, always using at least one strand of ground color. When you have samples that please you, line them up in an order that will allow you, when you braid the rug, to change no more than a single color at a time. In your mind, establish some idea of which combinations will take up larger areas on the rug and which will be accents. Forming a vague image is all you can do until you begin to stitch the braid together and see how the rug looks.

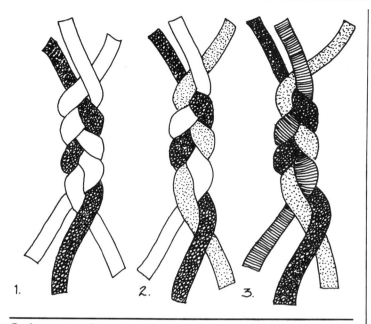

Only one color at a time is changed to get these three different effects.

Braiding the strips. I sit in a chair to braid, leaning forward, forearms resting along my knees. The strips are pinned with a straight pin to an ironing board adjusted to knee height. As the braid gets longer, the ironing board can be shoved back, or the braid can be unpinned and repinned closer to your hands.

Though rug braiding is identical to plaiting a child's hair, it is much more difficult. This is a braid with a right and wrong side. The braids must look smooth on the top surface; the raw edges must be turned toward the bottom. The knack is to pull on the cloth strip as you braid it into place.

The tautness will cause the braid to fold smoothly along the center with the raw edges curled downward. Hold the strip in this folded-up position, edges down as you braid it, tucking edges in with a fingernail when necessary. The resulting braid will have a right and wrong side—smooth on top, rough on the bottom.

As you work, lift the right-hand strip free of the other strips below the braid each time you weave it in. If you don't keep the strips free, you'll get into a terrible tangle. Trim frayed areas on the strips as you notice them. To maintain tautness, move the braid or the ironing board back as you work. When you have completed several inches of braid, start stitching the rug.

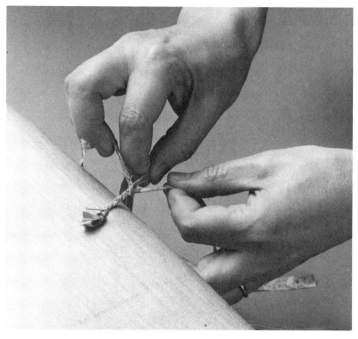

By holding the cloth strip between thumb and forefinger and pulling taut, you can make its edges curl downward; placing raw edges to the back of the braid will result in a smooth surface to the front of the braid.

Stitching the rug. Unpin the braid. Work on the wrong (back) side of the braid. Begin forming the coil in a clockwise direction so you will be able to stitch comfortably from right to left (left-handed people please reverse).

Start a round rug like a clockwise coil, stitching the end of the braid underneath itself right at the beginning. Start an oval as a long loop, stitching

Start stitching at end of loop.

Start stitching at center.

from the loop and toward the beginning of the braid, tacking the braid end in place underneath when you get to it, then proceeding around clockwise. The loop to start the oval rug is 1⅜ inches long.

Secure the beginning of the braid to itself with a few stitches. Then stitch along the sides of the braiding either with long, slanting stitches or with a blind stitch. As you work, keep the rug flat and the outer coil slack. If the outer coil becomes too tight or the work is done on a rounded surface (such as a knee), you could end up with a sombrero instead of a rug.

Stitch the rug up to 2 inches from the end of the braid. Repin the work to the ironing board to continue braiding. Shift from braiding to stitching again when you have a few more inches of braid to work with.

Changing colors. When you feel that your first colored area is large enough, shift to the next color com-

---

To change colors, the old color is snipped to ¾ inch, the new color is placed over it, overlapping about the same amount. Braid both strands in twice to secure the new strip of cloth, then snip off the ends of both the old and new colors where they stick out from the braid.

Sewing up braid. A blind stitch is invisible in the finished rug, both in front and in back. Stitch alternately through the edge of first the inner braid, then the outer braid.

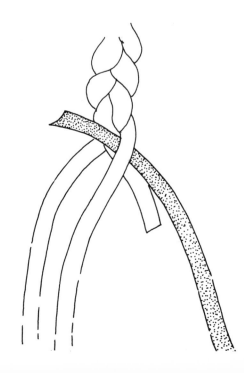

bination. In a circular rug you may shift at any point. In an oval rug, count rows into the center to be sure you are not getting off to a lopsided start.

Snip off the strip of fabric you are discontinuing ¾ inch from the end of the braid. Hold the strip of fabric you are adding on top of the stub of discontinued color, overlapping it ¾ inch. Proceed to braid as before. After the new strip has been braided in twice, snip off any remaining bit of the old color.

From this first color change, make each succeeding change on the same side of the rug and line it up exactly with the first change. The end of the rug should also line up in the same way.

Finishing the rug. The process described so far—braiding, stitching, changing colors—is continued until the rug is of the size and pattern you wish. At that point, all three strips of cloth are cut just at the end of the braid, and the loose end is tucked underneath and held in place with a few stitches. The rug is now finished.

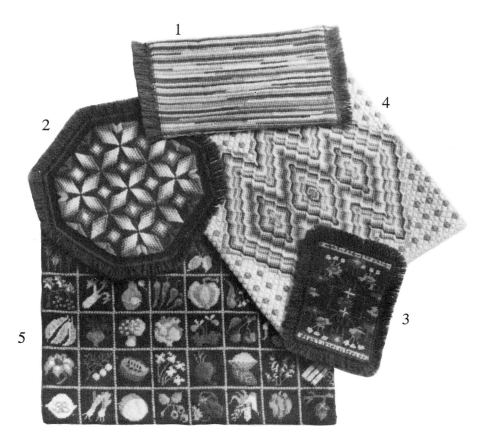

❧ Needlepoint Rugs ❧

Needlepoint is extraordinarily versatile for rugs, since it can ape other techniques convincingly. No. 3 in the photograph resembles an Oriental; No. 1 is a faux-rag rug (the pattern for No. 4 is taken from a hooked rug design). The rest are from out of nowhere, but delicious in their own ways. I work on 18-mesh canvas (18 threads, and therefore 18 stitches, per inch) because I like the thinness of the finished piece and the amount of detail I can work into the pattern. The small stitch is tedious, but the pieces are small, too. Some adults, and probably all children, prefer a larger-mesh canvas. The rug becomes a little thicker, and the design must be kept simpler, but I don't think those details matter that much.

The best yarn for needlepoint is Paternayan, in the range of colors available, the number of shades of each color, the texture, strength, and gloss. Many needlepoint and yarn shops carry it, but not all carry the full color and shade range. Try not to go overboard for brilliant colors. Too-bright color makes a rug leap off the floor of a dollhouse instead of hugging the background. Take it easy; take your time; take home a few samples to work with. Use the samples to make a strip of narrow rectangles of color. Delete from your final choice any colors that jump out at you, unless they are to be for very small details. Soft, subtle, even dull colors make a rug appear to be antique from the moment it is freshly finished.

Opposite: **1.** A rug worked to look like a rag rug, fringed at the ends only. **2.** A combination of tent stitch and pattern stitches, worked in several directions within an octagonal shape. **3.** An Oriental pattern. **4.** A rug worked entirely in pattern stitches. **5.** An example of the detail that can be worked on 18-mesh canvas.

Sources

Design: *The Book of Oriental Carpets and Rugs.* Ian Bennett. London: The Hamlyn Publishing Group, Limited, 1972. *Hooked Rugs.* William C. Ketchum, Jr. New York & London: Harcourt Brace Jovanovich, 1976.

How to: The best book I know of from which to learn both tent and pattern stitches is Carolyn Ambuter's *Complete Book of Needlepoint*, published as a paperback by Thomas Y. Crowell. Needlepoint stores will also help learners, usually free of charge if they are customers.

Materials

Needlepoint canvas, 18-mesh or a larger gauge
Needlepoint yarn
Lining fabric, or white glue for fringing
Woolite or other detergent intended for wool
Tracing paper
White paper

Tools

Tapestry needles, sized for the canvas you are using
Blocking board
Hammer
2-inch nails
Needlepoint marking pen*

Step by Step

Designing a rug. For those who can't draw, books on rugs are the complete answer to design. Photographs in such books are usually about the actual size of a dollhouse rug. Find a design you like, trace it onto tracing paper, and you have your pattern.

---

* Needlepoint marking pens, specially formulated so that the ink does not bleed into the wool during washing or dry cleaning, are available at needlepoint and stationery stores. One brand is Nēpo, made by Sanford's.

The following complications may occur. The photograph may be either too large or too small. Trace it, and take it to a photostat house to be enlarged or reduced to the size you wish. You may like the center motif of one rug but prefer the border of another. Trace both, and use photostats again to adjust the sizes if there is a discrepancy. A design may be what you want but too complicated to execute. Trace the major lines, and add in only those details you can manage.

If you draw well, by all means make up your own designs, as I often do, or use books to help you crystallize a vague idea. Copy and adapt to your own style rather than trace.

Trace first in pencil. Graph tracing paper helps to keep geometric designs symmetrical. When you are satisfied, go over your lines with a black marking pen.

Although full-scale canvases are usually painted, it's annoying to work on a painted canvas in so small a scale. The painted areas are too small to see clearly, the outlines become obscured, and you get all mixed up. A compromise for designs that have a lot of shading is to draw the outline as suggested, then paint in the shading with a single tone of gray or brown. Use oil paint, thinned with turpentine. Work freehand or with the pattern beneath the canvas for reference.

Preparing the canvas. Cut a piece of canvas 4 inches larger both in length and in width than the traced pattern. Lay it on a table. Place a strip of 1-inch freezer tape along one edge, letting it overlap ½ inch. Turn the canvas over and fold the tape down on the back side. Press it to the canvas with your fingers so it sticks well. Snip off the ends. Repeat with the other three edges. This binding will hold the canvas from fraying during even months of work.

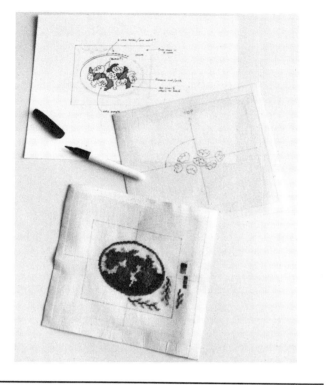

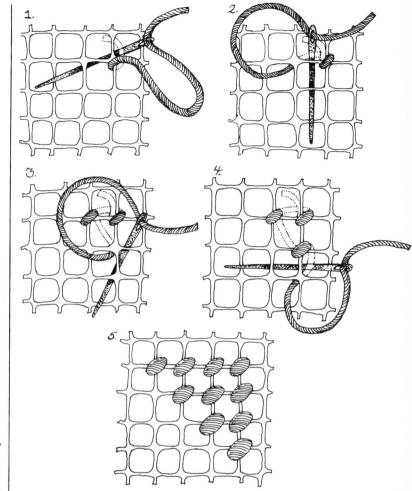

The canvas margin can be used to try out color combinations and pattern stitches, as well as to work out motifs that will be used repeatedly.

Transferring a design onto canvas. Lay a large sheet of paper on a table. Tape the pattern in the center of it. Lay the canvas over the pattern, centering it so that you have two inches of canvas all the way around the edge of the rug design. Tape the canvas in place with freezer tape.

With a needlepoint marking pen, trace the design onto the canvas. For patterns with many lines, you may trace only outlines, work those, then go back to the paper pattern to trace shaded areas or other details onto the canvas. For repeated border motifs or geometric designs, trace only one repeat or figure onto the canvas. Counting stitches when you work the canvas to repeat each design element will be more accurate than stitching over a drawing.

Working the canvas. The basic needlepoint stitch is tent stitch. Beginners work the stitch in horizontal rows because it is least confusing, but this pulls the canvas badly out of shape. Tent stitch worked diagonally is superior if you can manage it. The rug num-

The tent stitch, worked diagonally.

1. A half inch of yarn is left at the back of the canvas as the first stitch is taken. It will be caught and held by the next few stitches.

2. The second stitch, next to the first, begins a diagonal row. Notice that the needle is inserted vertically under two canvas threads to be in position to take the next stitch diagonally below.

3. The diagonal row of two stitches is complete, and the needle is in position to start the next diagonal row. This time each stitch will be diagonally above the previous one.

4. The first stitch in the second diagonal row. Now the needle is inserted under two horizontal threads to be in position to take the next stitch.

5. The second row and a third row (worked downward) are completed. Unless the outline of a shape dictates otherwise, each row is one stitch longer than the preceding one.

bered 2 in the photograph is worked in both tent and other stitches. There are hundreds of these other stitches, and they can form fascinating patterns.

For tent stitch on 18-mesh canvas use a single strand of yarn and a petit-point needle. Larger pattern stitches may require a double strand to cover adequately. Experiment at the edge of your canvas to check. For larger gauge canvases, ask your needlepoint store or look in a needlepoint book for the number of strands and needle size to use. Work outlines and details first. A repeated motif is worked by counting stitches in the design element and threads between elements rather than by following a drawing on the canvas. Fill in solid areas. Work the background in after the figures are completed.

When the design is finished, add two more rows of background color all around. These two rows will either become the seam allowance on a lined rug or be covered by fringe on a fringed rug.

Blocking the rug. A worked piece must be blocked to pull it back to its original shape. Measure the worked piece. Cut a piece of stiff white paper ½ inch larger than the rug in each dimension. With an L-square or 90-degree triangle, check that corners are square. Lay the paper on a board larger than the canvas you have worked. Get out nails and a hammer.

Wash the canvas in Woolite or similar detergent and cool water. Pull off the freezer tape. Rinse well. Pat out excess moisture with a towel.

Lay the canvas over the paper on the board. Pull it or even yank it into shape until you can see a ¼-inch border of the white paper all the way around the worked portion of the canvas. Hammer 2-inch nails at 1-inch intervals through the canvas and partway into the board, starting at diagonally opposite corners and stretching the canvas into place as you go. It should be very taut. If you see that the paper border is uneven at any point, pull the necessary nails and adjust the canvas until it is straight. Let it dry several days before removing the canvas from the board.

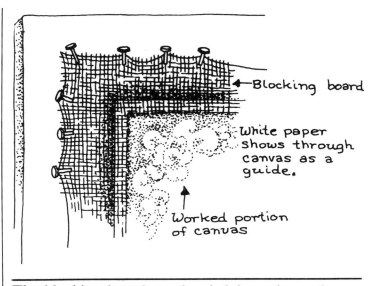

The blocking board can be shelving, plywood, or any composition board that will hold nails.

Finishing the rug. You can finish a rug by lining it, or by fringing it, or both. Use twill or another firm cotton fabric for lining the rug. Use the paper pattern over which you blocked the rug as a lining pattern and cut the lining to that size. Place the lining over the front side of the rug. Turn the rug upside down and pin the rug to the lining. A ¼ inch of lining should show through the canvas all the way around. Baste the pieces together and remove the pins. By hand, using a backstitch, or by machine, sew the lining to the rug on three sides. The stitching line should be exactly 2 rows in from the edge of the rug. Trim the seam to ⅛ inch all around. Turn the rug right side out. Turn in the remaining edge of both canvas and lining, pin, baste, and sew by hand, using a blind stitch.

Press the rug on the lining side with a steam iron over a terry-cloth towel.

To fringe a rug, bravely trim the canvas right to the first row of stitches. Cut several dozen 5-inch pieces of yarn. Divide them into single strands. Cut more yarn as you need it. Fold a strand of yarn in half, thread it through the needle, and pull the loop away from the needle eye.

Work from the top of the rug. Push the needle down through a hole two stitches from the edge of the rug. Bring the needle back up through the loop. Pull the yarn taut, and pull the needle off. Repeat in alternate holes along one edge. When you get to the corner, make fringe in every hole so it looks as thick as along the edges and also so it holds the corners from fraying. Continue along each edge and corner in turn.

Turn the rug upside down and tug at the fringe all the way around to tighten the loops. Run a line of white glue along the base of the fringe, pressing it into the yarn with your fingers and tugging again at the fringe to tighten it. When the glue dries, it will prevent the fringe from loosening and pulling out.

With sharp scissors, trim the fringe to the length you wish.

Fringing a rug.
1. Threading the needle.
2. Forming the fringe.
3. Tightening the loop.

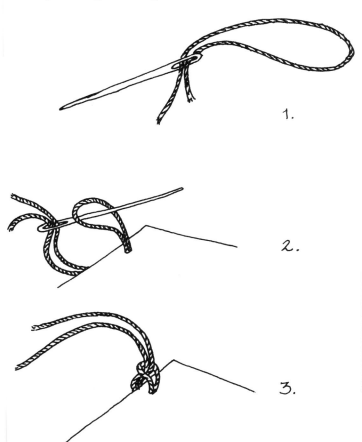

1.

2.

3.

Two Rugs for Beginners

The rag rug in the photograph (page 76) is the first needlepoint I ever did. It is nothing but straight lines, worked horizontally. Choose 10 or fewer colors that look well together. Draw on canvas a rectangle of the size you want and prepare it as in Step by Step. Work in rows, changing colors as the spirit moves you to get a staggered effect in the stripes. When the rectangle is filled in, see Step by Step for blocking and finishing the rug. After lining, fringe can be added to the ends.

A good learning piece for someone who is ready to try working diagonally in tent stitch is a checkerboard. Choose two colors. Work one color diagonally from the upper right-hand corner. When one diagonal row of squares is finished, change to the other color of yarn and work the next series of squares. Be sure to count stitches as you go so all your squares will be equal.

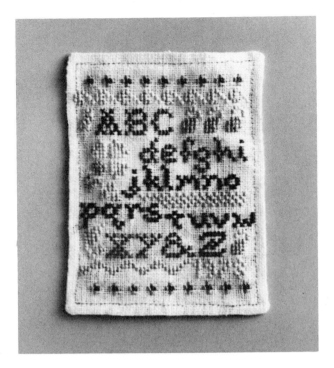

✑ Cross-stitch Sampler ✑

This cross-stitch sampler measures about 3 × 4 inches. In ordinary dollhouse scale, that translates to 3 × 4 feet, or much too large. Without the aid of a magnifying glass, however, it would be hard to make a smaller sampler. Each stitch in cross-stitch is done over 2 threads in the fabric. Since you have to see the threads to count them, there is a limit as to how fine the fabric—and how small the stitches—can be.

Eye fatigue aside, cross-stitch is not difficult, as the many works by six-year-olds in the last century attest. This one is stitched in silk on linen and includes the entire alphabet in a mixture of upper- and lower-case letters. In spite of its size, it looks at home in the nursery.

Sources
Cross-stitch design ideas: *Creating Historic Samplers*. Judith K. Grow and Elizabeth C. McGrain. Princeton, New Jersey: The Pyne Press, 1974.

Materials
Graph paper
Cotton or linen fabric with a thread count of about 34 stitches per inch
Thread to match fabric
Cotton or silk embroidery yarn
Fine lining fabric

Tools
Thimble
Pencil
Embroidery needles
Scissors
Embroidery hoop

Step by Step

Designing the sampler. Samplers, originally used as catalogues of stitches, alphabets, and motifs for household reference, are usually worked as blocks of lettering interspersed with broad or narrow borders. But since the lettering on this sampler is so large in comparison with the total area, rows will not line up neatly. Some letters take up much more width than others; some rows fall far shorter or longer than they should. One solution is to stagger the rows of letters, as in the example in the illustration, then fill in the gaps with motifs that fit. Graph paper can be used to lay out an idea and check the fit. Metric graph paper, which is much smaller than the usual graph paper used here, will give a better idea of how the over-all sampler will look. You can either fill in the squares with tiny crosses to represent the actual look of the stitches or fill the squares in solidly.

Choosing the materials. The fabric on which you work must have countable threads of even thickness. The gauge, or number of threads per inch, will determine the scale of your design. The fabric used here is a rather loosely woven linen with 34 threads per inch. Since a stitch is taken over 2 threads, there are 17 cross-stitches per inch. The capital letter B is 6 stitches across, or about ⅓ inch on this gauge fabric. A fabric with fewer stitches per inch will force a larger scale; a fabric with more stitches per inch will allow you to work in a smaller scale. Fabric stores may be able to measure the gauge with a clever device of their own to save you the difficulty of trying to count threads.

The yarn you use can be either cotton or silk. Cotton is widely available; silk is harder to find and quite costly. Both silk and cotton come multistranded. The silk used here, for instance, was 6-stranded, but only 3 strands were used for the stitching as 6 would have been too bulky. How many strands you use depends on the fabric you choose. Experiment until the cross-stitch looks neither too skimpy nor too bulky.

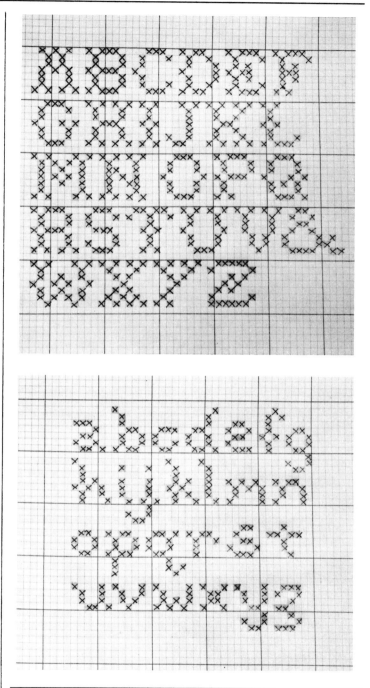

There are many possible alphabets, but these two are about the smallest I could find for both upper and lower case.

Stitching the sampler. Cut a 10-inch square of the fabric. Mount it in an embroidery hoop and stretch it taut. Thread an embroidery needle with the first color you want to use. Right-handed people will find it easier to work the design from right to left if they have a graphed pattern to follow. If you are working without a graphed design, it would be confusing to work the letters backwards, so work toward the right.

To start the thread, bring your needle up through the fabric, leaving only ½ inch of thread dangling at the back. Hold this end in place with your finger as you take the first few stitches. Catch the thread end into the stitches as you go. To end a thread, bring it to the back of the work and pull it through three or four stitches, then snip it off close.

The diagrams here show how to do cross-stitch. It is confusing at first, since you are making a horizontal movement with your needle in order to form a diagonal stitch. The stitching will become logical with experience. Count threads between stitches as carefully as you count threads for each stitch. Move the embroidery frame to a different area of the design as necessary.

Finishing the sampler. Remove the embroidery frame and trim the excess fabric from around your sampler. Leave an extra ¼-inch margin all around. Line the sampler with a thin cotton fabric in the same way as described for a patchwork coverlet (page 66). Add a single row of running stitches, worked in ordinary sewing cotton, ⅛ inch in from the edge all the way around to frame the work neatly.

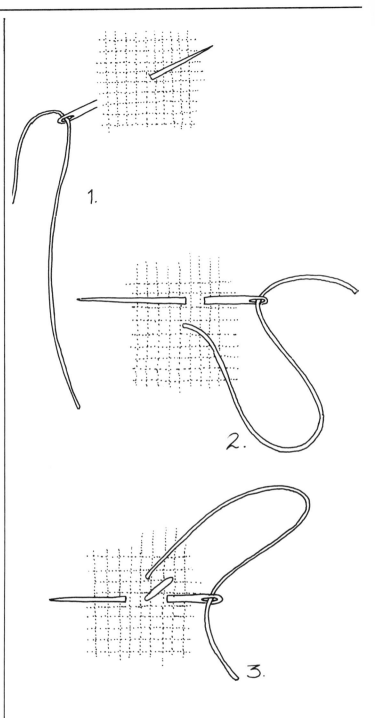

1. Needle enters at lower left corner of first stitch.
2. Making the first arm of the cross.
3. Finishing the first stitch and coming up to start another next to it.
4. First arm of the second cross.
5. Finishing the second stitch and coming up to start another below it.
6. First arm of the third cross.
7. Finishing the third stitch.
8. Three completed cross-stitches.

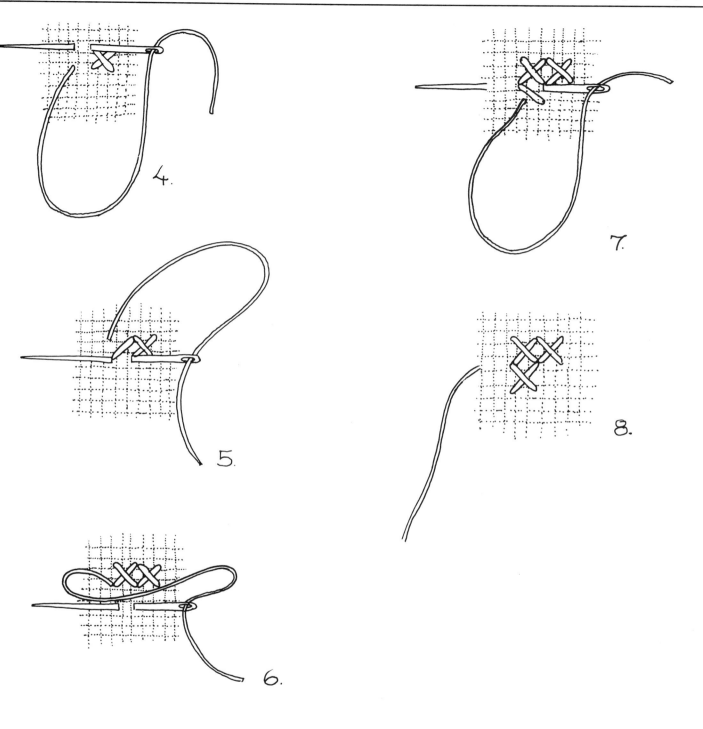

4.

5.

6.

7.

8.

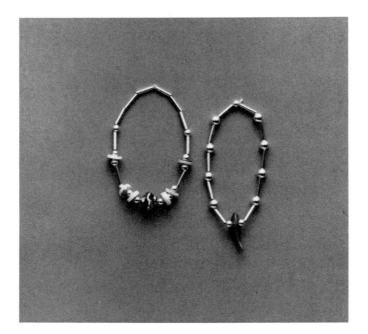

᎒᎒ **Bead Jewelry** ᎒᎒

Craft stores and jewelry supply houses sell lovely varieties of beads, many of which are small enough to make jewelry for dollhouse dolls. These two necklaces are made with real silver beads, turquoise, and small flat beads cut from pink seashells. They were strung with a bead needle on a fine thread specially made for beadwork. Both are available wherever beads are sold. A needle threader is needed to thread the bead needle. The necklaces were made large enough to go over the doll's head. The two ends of the thread were secured by tying them in a square knot.

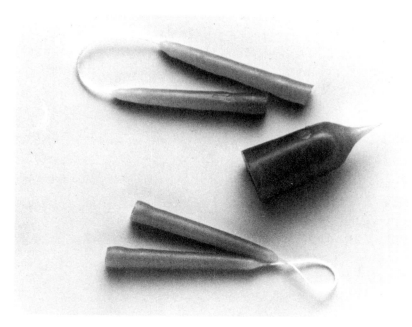

❧ Candle Dipping ❧

irthday cake candles, the usual answer to the need for tapers in a dollhouse, have a way of always looking like birthday cake candles. Their shape is wrong: flat at the top instead of tapered. Except for white, those birthday party colors are wrong too. Dipping your own tapers is not only a good solution but easy and satisfying. The technique is to build up layers of wax to the desired thickness by repeatedly dipping a wick into melted wax. The work is simple enough for quite young children, but they have to be supervised: the melted wax is quite hot and is also flammable. Candle wax is sold at craft stores, but you can easily melt down your own candle stubs and remove the wicks.

Materials

Candle wax (To get one cup of melted wax, you will need somewhat more than that bulk in solid wax.)

Cotton crochet yarn for wicks*

Tools

Small saucepan

1-cup Pyrex measuring pitcher

Pocket comb

---

* Knitting stores usually sell J. & P. Coats Knit-Cro-Sheen which you can use as wicks. The candles here were made with DMC crochet yarn, which is harder to find.

Step by Step

Preparing the wick. Cut a 4-inch length of cotton yarn for each wick. A 4-inch wick will make a pair of candles about 1½ inches long. Loop a wick around the teeth of a comb as shown. The two ends of the wick should hang about ½ inch apart. Count the number of teeth over which you have looped this first wick so that you can make the other pairs of candles exactly the same.

Melting the wax. Place the solid wax into a 1-cup Pyrex measuring pitcher, breaking up the pieces into smaller chunks, with a knife if necessary. Place the pitcher into a small saucepan filled with an inch of water. Put the saucepan and pitcher on the stove and heat slowly. Don't let the water boil, as violent bubbling might upset the pitcher. Add more chunks of wax as needed to keep the level of melted wax at the 1-cup mark. When all the wax is melted, remove the pot from the stove.

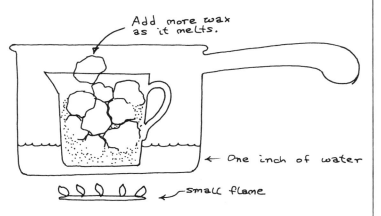

Dipping the candles. Lower the comb with its looped wick down into the melted wax until the comb touches the rim of the pitcher. The comb acts as a stop, automatically controlling the depth of each dip. Lift the wick out again, and allow this first coat of wax to harden. When it is quite stiff, straighten out the wick ends with your fingers.

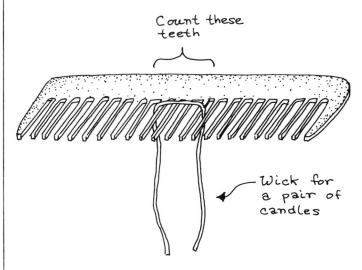

To add each new layer, dip the wick into and out of the melted wax very quickly. If you dip too slowly, the previous layer will melt off and the candle will fail to grow thicker or else it will become lumpy. Between dips let the two candles cool down for at least 30 seconds. The cooling will help prevent that layer from remelting. As you dip, your candles will grow in length as well as in thickness, and the bottom may become misshapen. Don't worry about it, as this dripped area below the wick will be trimmed off. Continue dipping until the candle is as thick as you wish.

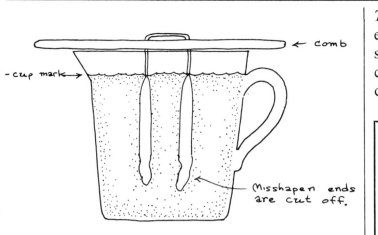

Controlling the temperature of the wax. If your candle does not take shape evenly and quickly, the wax is probably too hot or too cold. If it is too cold, you will see an opaque film of wax hardening around the rim of the pitcher. Reheat the wax until it is clear again. More often the wax is too hot and is remelting previous layers at each dip. Remove the pitcher from the water bath with a potholder and try again.

Trimming the candles. When the candles have hardened, lay them flat on a table, and with a sharp knife slice off the bottom, below the wicks. This operation can be saved until all the candles are finished so you can line them up and cut them all to the same size.

Bayberry Wax

Bayberry candles are made from the waxy coating that surrounds the berries. Large quantities of berries are picked late in the summer and boiled in water in a large kettle. The wax melts and rises to the surface, where it is skimmed off. When hard and dry, the wax is remelted for dipping candles. If you live in bayberry country, this might be fun to try, as the amount of wax needed for dollhouse candles is not overwhelming.

❧ Soap Carving ❧

These three bars of sandalwood soap were carved by my children from a nearly used-up cake of bath soap. They rough-shaped them with a paring knife but finished smoothing the shape with their fingernails. The box is cut with scissors from the thin cardboard of index cards, glued together with white glue, and covered with bits of English soap labels.

ᏹ Flower Drying ᏹ

Nature has already seen to it that flowers come in miniature. Many tiny flowers are actually better candidates for drying than larger ones. Once dried, they can be used in flower arrangements and wreaths. You can also prepare potpourri for small containers in your dollhouse, or hang herbs to dry in its kitchen or storeroom. Pressed flowers, which you might also like to try, are on page 105.

There are several varieties of flowers that can simply be hung upside down in small bunches to be dried like herbs. These include sea lavender (pinkish in color), tansy (yellow), strawflower, and baby's breath, which is all white. Everlasting comes in yellow or white. Try this same method for local grasses, many of which have decorative seed heads that look well in small flower arrangements.

The best small flower to dry by the silicone gel method is statice, which comes in vivid blue, pink, white, or yellow and is shaped something like a tiny gladiolus. Try the spiky blooms of heather, too. Some of these varieties are wild, but many others are among the ordinary garden flowers that you can plant from seed packets. The packets usually mention that the bloom is recommended for drying.

Above: The large flowers in this arrangement are globe amarinth. The very delicate ones are gypsophila (baby's breath). The medium-size blooms are everlastings, statice, and the more delicate star flower.

Materials
Freshly cut flowers
Silicone gel

Tools
Shoebox, cracker tin, or similar container with lid
Kitchen spoon
Sable paintbrush
Embroidery scissors
Tweezers
Fingernail clippers

Step by Step

Preparing the drying box. Fill the box or tin with 2 inches of silicone gel. Set out a kitchen spoon so it is handy for adding more gel after you have prepared the flowers.

Picking the flowers. Pick early in the morning before the sun has wilted the blooms, and choose blossoms that have just opened rather than those that have matured. Besides the small flowers already suggested, try larger, compound flowers, such as goldenrod or hydrangea. They can be dissected into smaller blooms before drying. Using scissors, cut a few flowers at a time so you can start the drying process before they have wilted. If this is difficult, store the blossoms in tightly sealed plastic bags in the refrigerator until you are ready to dry them.

Preparing the flowers. Cut each stem to 3 inches or less. Remove the leaves from most specimens. Very neat leaves, like those of heather, can be left in place. Sharp, pointed embroidery scissors will be helpful in doing a neat job.

Drying the flowers. One at a time, stick each bloom into the gel, stem end down, flower head up. Leave an inch of space all the way around each flower. When the flowers are all in place, gently sprinkle more gel from the spoon until the blossom heads are completely covered and the box is filled. Cover the box with its lid and set it aside in a warm, dry place. The top of the refrigerator and a wall cabinet near the stove are both good choices. Let the flowers dry without disturbing them for 10 days, or according to instructions on the package of gel.

Removing the dried flowers. After the prescribed number of days, remove the lid, tip the box, and gradually spill the gel back into some other container (it is too expensive to discard, and it may be used over and over again until you can see the tops of the flowers. With tweezers, lift each flower out and place it on the table. With a sable artist's brush, brush off the grains of gel that adhere to the flowers.

Flowers are stuck into layer of gel, then covered with more gel to the top of the container.

Container

2 inches of silicone gel

Arranging the flowers. These flowers are so small that their stems will support them without the usual addition of florist's wire. Use any suitable container, from a basket to a pitcher, tub, or pail. If the top opening is small, you will not need to support the arrangement. If the opening is large, like that in the basket in the illustration, you will either have to insert branchy flowers like baby's breath first to pro- vide a supportive framework for single-stemmed blooms or use a small block of the crumbly Styro- foam that florists use for arrangements. Use it dry, not wet. In general, insert the tallest flowers in the center of your arrangement first, then add shorter blossoms all around the outside. If stems are too long, use fingernail clippers; they work better than scissors on tough or wiry stems.

Dried Herbs and Potpourri

Rosemary, thyme, lavender, tarragon, and dwarf sage are small of leaf and easy to dry. Cut sprigs 2 inches or less, tie in bunches of no more than 3 sprigs each, and hang to dry in a shaded, airy place indoors. Beige carpet thread looks rustic and is easy to work with. To hang bunches of dried herbs in your dollhouse, buy the smallest eye hooks you can find. The ones I have are ½ inch long, and the eye measures less than ¼ inch. With wire cutters, snip the eye, as shown, to form a hook. Screw these hooks into wall or ceiling with needle-nose pliers.

Any fragrant combination of dried herbs, spices, and flowers is called a potpourri. Here is a reduced potpourri recipe for miniature containers in a dollhouse:

6 petals from a fragrant rose
1 sprig of lavender blossom
1 pinch ground cloves
¼ teaspoon grated orange rind
6 rosemary leaves
1 sage leaf

Dry the fresh ingredients by spreading them on paper towels indoors. Let them dry for a week. Mix the dried ingredients together gently and distribute among small boxes, bottles, or jars.

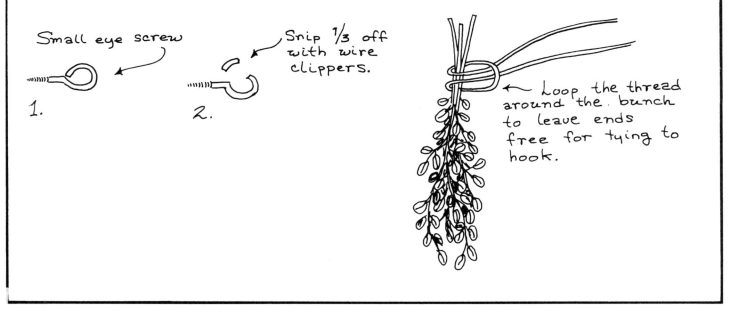

Small eye screw

1.

2.

Snip ⅓ off with wire clippers.

← Loop the thread around the bunch to leave ends free for tying to hook.

❧ Decoupage Boxes ❧

These boxes were made from the actual patterns given here. They are constructed of 2-ply Bristol board, a thin but very stiff cardboard available in art stores. They could be left plain, but these were decorated by the method called decoupage—covering an object with pieces of paper. Magazine pictures are perfect for this, especially photographs of art. Several of these boxes were covered in Pompeian frescoes, compliments of *Smithsonian* magazine.

Materials

2-ply Bristol board, or shirt cardboard
White glue
Pictures from magazines, or other decorative paper
Tracing paper
Acrylic polymer medium

Tools

Utility knife
Steel rule
Pencil
Embroidery scissors
Artist's brush

Step by Step

Making the patterns. The easiest way to use the patterns here is to copy them on a copier, cut them out, and then trace around them onto cardboard. If a copier is not available to you, trace the patterns instead onto tracing paper, then use carbon paper to transfer them onto cardboard. Be sure to pay attention to which lines are solid, which broken. The solid lines are cutting lines; the broken lines are fold lines.

Cutting out the box. Cut along the solid lines with a utility knife and steel rule (see p. 100). Still using the knife and rule, score along the broken lines. Scoring means slicing only partway through the cardboard so it will fold cleanly along the cut.

Before you go on to the next step, fold the sides of the box up and check that they are even with one another and come together, straight and neat, at the corners. Bend the sides of the oval or round box around the base to see whether or not the strip is the right size. Try on the tops for size. Both tracing and cutting can easily go awry, and different thicknesses of cardboard will throw the patterns off, too. The tops especially are likely not to fit if the cardboard you use is thicker or thinner than the pattern is designed for.

Recut or trim portions that don't fit well.

Gluing the box together. The sides of the oval and round boxes are bent around smoothly and glued on top of the base. For all the other boxes, the sides are bent upward and glued to one another along the edges. Tops are glued in the same way. Use white glue sparingly. Hold the pieces in place for a few minutes until the glue sets.

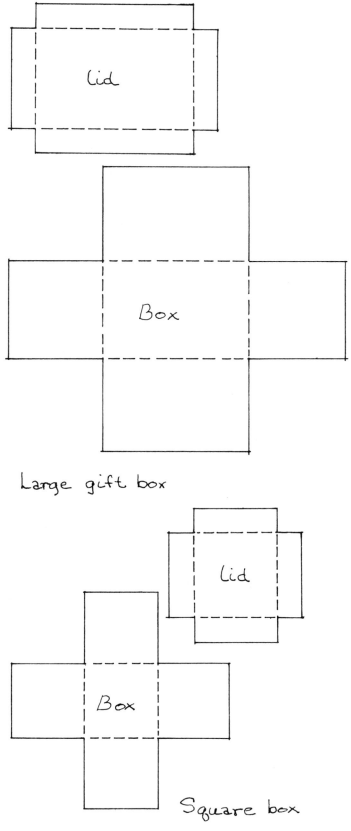

Large gift box

Square box

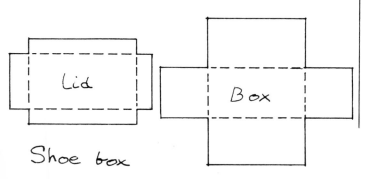

Shoe box

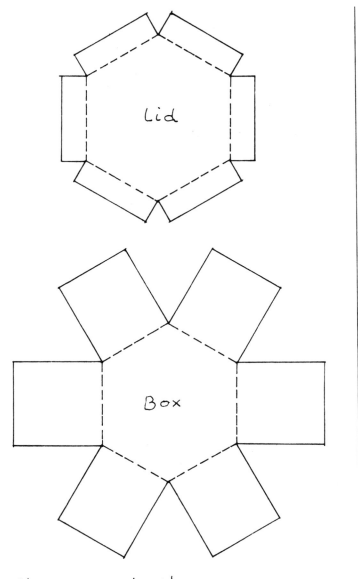

Lid

Box

Hexagonal hatbox

Round cereal box

Lid

Cut the side strips
of oval and round
boxes a bit
longer than
pattern.

Trim later.

Box

Oval box

Lid

Box

Cutting the side strip. The easiest way to cover the sides of the box or lid is to wrap a strip of paper all the way around it. The strip should be about ¼ inch wider than the height of the box so there will be a ⅛-inch margin to fold down into the inside of the box or lid and over onto the bottom or top. Be sure the strip is long enough to go completely around the box, with ⅛ inch to spare for an overlap.

If you are working with a picture that you want to position in a certain way on the sides of the box, cut it out roughly first, then wrap it around the box in the position you want. Press the paper against the top and bottom edges to form a crease. This crease will be visible enough to guide you when you cut the strip out.

Gluing the side strip in place. Thin white glue with water so it spreads easily. Brush it onto a small portion of the side of the box or lid with an artist's brush. Lay the glued portion of the box down onto the wrong side of the paper strip, placing it exactly in the middle so the strip overlaps equally at both edges. Continue gluing the strip in place a bit at a time until you come back to where you started. Trim the strip if necessary to leave a ⅛-inch overlap, and glue the overlap down.

Covering the top and bottom. To cover the top of the lid and the bottom of the box, trace each outline on the picture you wish to use. If you are using a picture you want to position in a certain way on the top, cut it out roughly, position it on the lid, and press against the edges to make a crease in the paper. Use either this crease or a traced line for a cutting guide. Cut to the inside of the line. The piece will probably still be too large, but try it and snip away more if you have to.

Brush the whole top of the lid or bottom of the box with glue, and press the paper in place.

Finishing the box. When the paper covering is finished and dry, the whole box can be protected with two coats of acrylic polymer medium (a clear plastic coating). Varnish is another possibility, but I found that it was a solvent for the printing ink and lifted some of the color off the surface. If you like, you can also paint the inside of the box or lid with tempera paints before varnishing.

1. Gluing strip of paper to side of finished box.
2. Gluing the flaps down inside the box.
3. Gluing the flaps down over the bottom.

1.

Box is centered on strip →

This end of strip can be trimmed if too long.

2.

← Slit corners

3. Notch corners

Gluing the flaps in place. To fold the edges of the strip down into the inside of the box or lid, clip the strip at each corner (or for the oval or round box, clip at ¼-inch intervals) to form flaps. Glue each flap down into the inside.

To fold the edge of the strip over the bottom of the box or over the top of the lid, notch instead of clipping. Notch each corner (or for the oval or round box notch at ¼-inch intervals). Glue each flap over onto the top or bottom.

❧ Photo Album ❧

This photograph album harks back to those we pored through as children, trying to believe that those strange creatures were really our parents as children. Because I'm certain the idea that parents were once children will remain incredible to each generation, I have filled this album with pictures of my own children, so that my grandchildren will find it strange.

Similar albums can be used as scrapbooks, ledgers, and journals, for stamp collections (one or two stamps per page), or even to harbor small pressed flowers. The end sheets of the albums can be made from miniprint wallpaper samples, end sheets, or colored illustrations from discarded books, origami papers, or construction paper.

Materials

Cardboard: 3-ply Bristol board, shirt cardboard, or cardboard from pads
Black cotton broadcloth
Black cotton embroidery yarn
Colored or figured paper for end sheets
Black charcoal paper for pages (from art store)
White glue

Tools

Cutting board
Thumbtacks or pushpins
Scissors
Embroidery needle
90-degree triangle
Pencil
Utility knife and fresh blades
Steel rule
1/16-inch drill bit and drill (jeweler's hand drill, or hobbyist's drill from hardware store)
C-clamp, large enough to go over your table edge and cutting board.

Step by Step

Cutting the boards. This album measures 2 × 3 inches, but you may adjust that size to your own needs. Lay two pieces of cardboard on top of one another on the cutting board, and tack them in place on the board with thumbtacks or pushpins. With a sharp pencil and triangle draw the rectangle that will be your cover size. You can do this with the help of a ruler or just by eye.

Cut through both layers of cardboard by holding a steel rule along each line and running the blade of a utility knife along the edge. If you do this carefully, both boards should be exactly the same size.

To open and close properly, both back and front album covers are actually two pieces, which act as a hinge when covered with cloth. Using steel rule and utility knife, cut through each piece of cardboard ½ inch from the spine edge.

Cutting the lining paper. Using the larger of the cover pieces as a guide, cut two pieces of lining paper ⅛ inch smaller in each dimension. Set the pieces aside, as they will not be used until the boards are covered with cloth.

Covering the boards. Place both pieces of one cover on top of the cotton broadcloth, slightly separating the pieces as shown. Be sure they are lined up straight with the grain of the fabric. With a pencil, mark the cloth around three sides ¼ inch out from the edge of the board. On the spine side, mark the cloth ¾ inch out from the edge of the board. Cut around your mark with scissors. Repeat for the other cover.

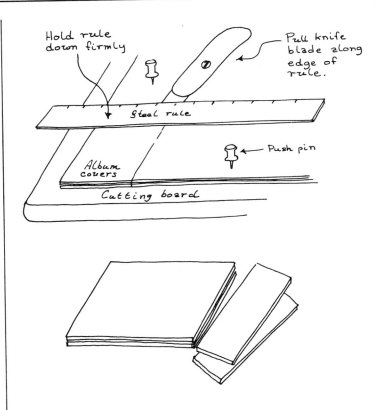

Cutting with straight edge and utility knife. Hold the steel rule down tightly with one hand, cut with the other. If you are cutting through many layers or through thick material, be sure to hold the knife straight so your cut does not come out beveled. Don't try to cut all the way through heavy material in one stroke. Rather, make the first cutting stroke lightly, then repeat it as many times as necessary until you have cut through the full thickness.

Spread white glue thinly and evenly over both pieces of one cover. Lay the pieces glue side down on one piece of cloth, leaving the correct margins and space. Press the boards flat with your fingers so the cloth sticks at all points. Repeat for the second cover.

Clip the corners of the cloth as shown, and notch it at the spine edge.

Spread white glue over the spine piece and in a ¼-inch strip next to it. Fold the ¾-inch cloth margin over the glued area and press flat with your fingers.

Spread glue in a ¼-inch strip around the remaining three edges, and fold the ¼-inch cloth margins over the glued areas, pressing them flat with your fingers. Repeat with the cloth margins on the second cover.

Lining the boards. Spread white glue evenly on one piece of lining paper and position it over the inside

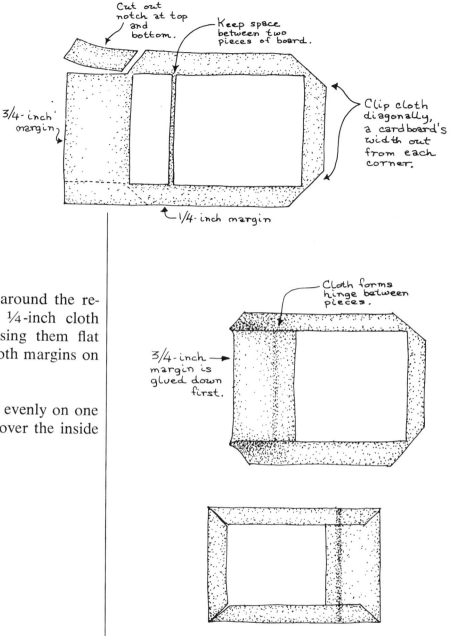

of the larger piece of the cover, leaving a ⅛-inch margin as shown. It should not go over the hinged space between the pieces. Press the lining flat with your fingers. Repeat for the second cover.

Cutting the pages. Fold a piece of charcoal paper in half, then in quarters, then in eighths. This folding will give you 8 leaves, or 16 pages in your album. You can fold it once more for 32 pages, but the extra thickness will make cutting more difficult.

On the surface of the folded paper, use a triangle to draw a rectangle ⅛ inch less in each dimension than the completed album cover. The rectangle should not include any of the folded edges. Hold the folded paper down on a cutting board with thumbtacks or pushpins. Cut along your lines with steel rule and utility knife. The paper will tend to stay more accurately stacked if you cut off the major fold last. If after you have finished the cutting you discover the page edges are not even, trim them with steel rule and utility knife, not with scissors.

Making the cord. The cord with which this album is tied is made with cotton embroidery yarn formed into a single chain. The illustration shows how single chaining is done. Secure one end of the thread to a drawer knob or chair back. Reach through the loop with thumb and forefinger to pull the next loop through. Tighten the loop above before pulling through the next one. End the chain by pulling the string completely through the last loop. You will need about 6½ inches of chained cord, which requires about triple that length of embroidery yarn.

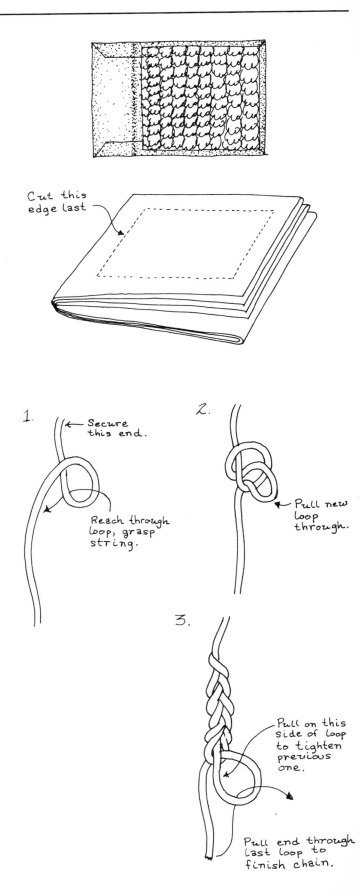

Assembling the album. Lay the cutting board on a table and get out the C-clamp and drill. Straighten the album pages so they line up perfectly and place them between the two covers, being sure you have even margins all the way around. Hold the album together tightly. Look sideways at all the edges again to check that the pages are in the right position. Correct if necessary. Without letting go of the album, hold it down on the cutting board and place the clamp over album, board, and table. Tighten the clamp carefully. Once the album is secured in the clamp, you can let go of the album. Drill two $\frac{1}{16}$-inch holes with either a jeweler's hand drill or an electric hobbyist's drill (p. 155). The holes in this album are centered vertically in the ½ inch spine piece and are ¼ inch in from the top and bottom edges. Leave the album clamped until you are ready to thread the cord through it.

Thread the end of the chained cord onto an embroidery needle. Loosen the clamp and carefully lift the album so the holes are still lined up. Push the needle down through the top cover and up through the bottom cover. Take the needle out, tie the ends of the cord with overhand knots, and tie the cords together in a bow.

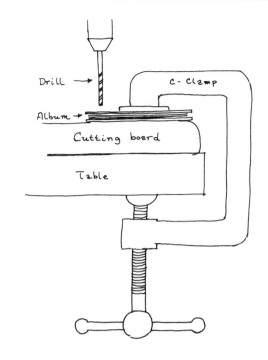

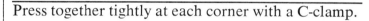

Press together tightly at each corner with a C-clamp.

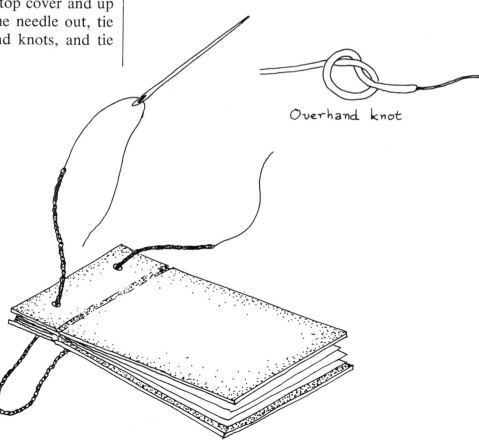

Overhand knot

Filling the Album

Dry mounting. The best way to mount paper on paper is a method called dry mounting, which uses rubber cement instead of a water-soluble glue. The adhesion is excellent, and there is no chance of the paper buckling or blistering from moisture. First mark with a pencil on the page the position of the entry you will be gluing down. Spread the page with rubber cement applied thinly with the cap brush. Spread rubber cement on the back of each photo, stamp, or whatever entry you wish to place on that page. Wait for the glue on both surfaces to dry completely. When both are dry, press the entry to the page, using your pencil marks as a guide. When all entries are in place, rub off excess rubber cement with the end of your finger and erase your pencil marks.

But where do you get miniature photographs? Aha! By one of four clever methods. The first method, called cropping, requires only that you pore through the snapshots you already have and snip out bits that can stand on their own as tiny photos (a face, house, or piece of landscape).

The second and third methods both require negatives and someone who has the equipment to print black-and-white photographs—not hard to find, as the group includes twelve-year-olds in the junior high photography club, and many amateur photographers.

One of these methods is to print negatives directly onto what is called contact paper, which makes prints exactly the same size as the negative. The quality of contact prints is not as good as other printing, but also does not require an enlarger, which is necessary in the next method. Anybody who has an enlarger can furnish you with prints that are just a hair larger than the negative you provide—still very small, but of good quality. It is polite when using either of these latter two methods to pay for the printing paper.

The fourth method requires no negatives of old snapshots but does require a decent 35 mm camera. It is a tedious method, but is the only one that will give you the white edge around each photo that has become the earmark of a genuine old-fashioned snapshot. First, select the snapshots you want to reduce. Next, dry-mount them to a flat surface (wall, plywood, or heavy cardboard). Now, with good, even lighting step back and photograph the photographs. The result, when developed by others, will be a single print of the tiny snapshots you want in your album. Cut them out with steel rule and utility knife.

An Album of Frogs

This tiny book, an album of frogs, so to speak, was made by Rafael Stein when he was in the second grade. It depicts the ubiquitous frogs of his imagination in the roles of rock star, garbage frog, football player, surgeon, astronaut, architect, and mad scientist. More intriguing still, it moves from a spatial view (bird's view of a football field, ant's view of a rocket) to a close-up of the hero.

As to how it was put together, the pages are stuck one to another with a strip of tape between. The covers, thin cardboard covered with illustrated paper, are stuck to one another the same way. And again, the cover is stuck to the first pages in front and the last page behind in the same way too. Not complicated, not hard, and not very time-consuming.

Pressed Flowers

Choose tiny flowers, such as star grass or baby's breath, or dissect larger flowers that are actually made up of mini-flowers, such as Queen Anne's lace or goldenrod. The faster the flowers dry while being pressed, the better they will hold their color. A relatively slow method is the traditional one of pressing the flowers in a large book between paper towels, with a heavy stack of books on top to increase the pressure. A better method involves two pieces of shelving board, each from 6 to 8 inches square, paper towels, and four C-clamps. Lay three or four layers of towels on one of the pieces of board, arrange the flowers so they do not touch one another, lay more layers of towels on top, and cover with the second piece of board. Clamp this "sandwich" together tightly with a C-clamp at each corner. The flowers should be ready for mounting in 10 days or less.

Mount pressed flowers in the album with tiny droplets of white glue.

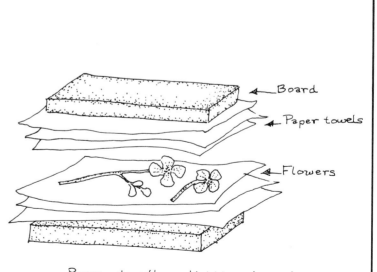

Press together tightly at each corner with a C-clamp.

❧ Bookbinding ❧

The technique used to make this book is only slightly modified from the method a real bookbinder would use. Like any fine hand-bound book, it is made up of signatures (sheets of paper folded into fourths, eighths, or sixteenths), which are stitched through their spines around tapes that hold them in a stack. The endpapers are sewed in, too. The spine is reinforced, and the book is covered in leather. The result is a book that opens easily to any page.

The big difference is that these pages are blank. They haven't a word to say to us. I intend to remedy that. After this book is finished, and the garden is planted, and the garage is cleaned, and the dollhouse, fabrics, wood scraps, metal filings, paints, glue, string, and paper are all at last picked up and stored out of everyone's way, I will start a journal. In hand-printed lettering this little hand-bound diary will someday tell what was for dinner, how the weather was, who broke the ashtray, and how many puppies the dog had way back in 1979. There are only 192 pages to fill.

Sources

Paper: For the pages, airmail sheets from a stationery store, preferably the soft type rather than the crisp, crinkly variety. For the endpapers, brown wrapping paper from a stationery store or cut from paper bags, or use printed gift paper in a small pattern.

Leather: Worn-out wallets and purses.

Materials

White glue
Scrap of fine cloth or seam binding
Soft, thin cotton string
Thin white paper
Contrasting paper for endpapers
Leather
White thread

Tools

Scissors
Hobbyist's knife with straight pointed blade
Steel rule
Triangle
Medium tapestry needle
No. 7 "sharp" needle
Thimble
Vise
Cardboard or two scraps of thin wood

Step by Step

Cutting the sheets. The signatures in this book were made by folding sheets of paper into sixteenths, but I think that was a mistake. The pages would have come out more even and the book would have lain flatter if the signatures had been made with one less fold.

Using whatever sheet size your paper happens to be, fold it in half, then quarters, then eighths. Keep the edges perfectly even and run your thumbnail along each crease to make it crisp. (This number of folds gives you eight leaves, or a sixteen-page signature.) Judge the size and shape of your folded sheet. It may be of unlikable proportions or too large for the size book you have in mind. With scissors, trim the free edges at the bottom to correspond to the height you want the book to be. Don't cut off the folded top margin. Refold the last crease to make the signature the width you want the book to be. Cut off the excess, again along the free edges, not the folded ones.

When the signature is trimmed, open out the sheet of paper again. Your trimming was probably not exactly squared, so check the sheet with a triangle and trim it again until it is true at the corners and straight along the edges. This sheet is now the correctly sized sample for all the sheets you will be folding into signatures.

Figure out how many signatures you want. For instance, 8 sheets will give you 8 signatures of 16 pages each for a total of 128 pages. The more signatures, of course, the fatter the book will be.

Cut out as many sheets as you need, all to the same size as your sample. Discard the sample.

---

1. Draw lines to indicate the size you want the book to be.
2. Trim along the bottom line; refold along the vertical line; trim off excess.

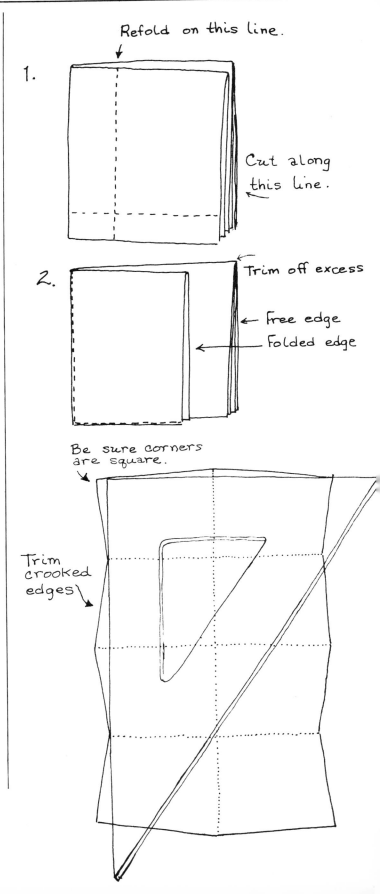

Refold on this line.

1.

Cut along this line.

2.

Trim off excess

Free edge

Folded edge

Be sure corners are square.

Trim crooked edges

Folding the signatures. Fold each of the sheets as you did the sample, being as careful as you can to keep the edges lined up and the folds crisp.

Pressing the folded signatures. Stack the signatures with their spines lined up and the folded top edges together. Sandwich the stack between two small pieces of cardboard or wood. Insert the sandwiched stack into the vise and tighten as far as you can. Leave the signatures in the vise for several hours to press them flat before removing them.

Making the endpapers. The endpapers in this book are stitched to the first and the last signatures so they become an integral part of the binding process. Choose a colored or printed paper that is not too thick. Cut two strips of the paper exactly as high as your book page, but 2½ times wider. Using a signature as a guide, fold each endpaper as shown. This folding method will allow you to sew the endpaper along with a signature.

Stitching the signatures. Place one endpaper over the first signature of the book and another over the last signature so that the stack begins and ends with an endpaper. Take the whole stack of signatures and line them up exactly by tapping the spine and then

Folding the endpaper.
1. Fold endpaper in half.
2. Fold free edges of endpaper over spine edge of signature.
3. Trim top flap to half its width.
4. Fold bottom flap over top one, then again behind endpaper.
5. Insert signature into fold, ready for stitching.

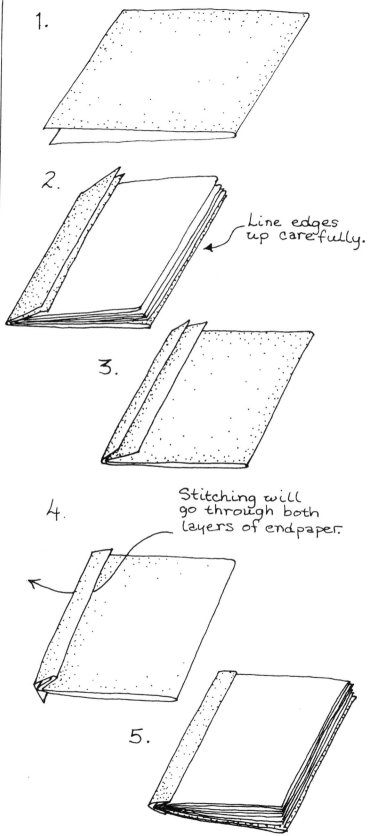

1.

2. Line edges up carefully.

3.

Stitching will go through both layers of endpaper.

4.

5.

the top edges against a flat surface. Hold them lined up exactly, and mark three lines straight across the spine with a pencil. One line should be in the middle of the spine, and the other two about ¼ inch in from top and bottom. Be sure the pencil has left a mark on each of the signatures.

Now open out each signature in turn, and pierce it with a needle through the spine in the pattern shown. The three middle pairs of holes are each to one side of each pencil mark on the spine. The pencil mark indicates where the string that holds one signature to another will lie. The holes to each side is where the thread will form a stitch through which the string will be pulled to hold it in place.

Thread your needle with a single strand of white thread. For each signature, insert the needle into the first hole from the outside of the spine.

Leave several inches of thread dangling, and bring the needle back out through hole No. 2. Bring the needle around the dangling end and through the loop formed to secure it. Pull this knot taut. Insert the needle into the inside again through hole No. 2 and bring it to the outside through hole No. 3. Continue down through hole No. 4, back out through hole No. 5, down through hole No. 6, out through hole No. 7, down through hole No. 8, back out hole No. 9, and down again at hole No. 10. Bring the

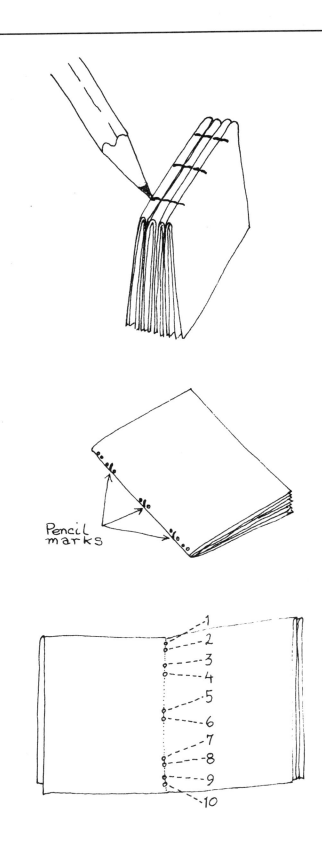

Pencil marks

needle out at hole No. 9 again. Push the needle through your last stitch, and through the loop of thread as shown, and pull the knot taut. Cut the thread.

Repeat this process for each of the signatures.

Attaching the signatures together. Cut three 8-inch pieces of thin, soft cotton string. Thread the first on a tapestry needle. Stack the sewed signature, spines together and folded edges at the top. Push the needle under the stitches that straddle the first mark on the spine, being sure to catch all the signatures, and pull the string partway through so you can remove the needle. Thread the next string onto the needle and repeat at the center mark. Repeat with the third string at the third mark. The signatures are now loosely held together by the three strings.

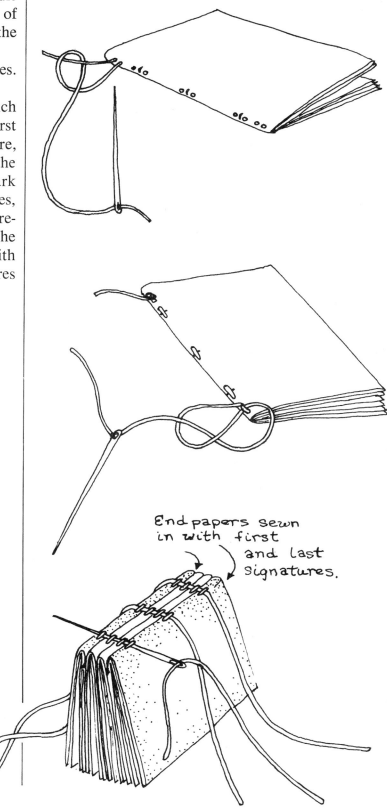

End papers sewn in with first and last signatures.

Gluing the strings down. Lay the book down, press the stack flat, and gently tug at each of the strings on one side to tighten them around the spine. Cut the ends to about ¼ inch. With the tapestry needle, tease out the ends to fray them so they will lie flat when glued. With white glue, glue each string end to the endpaper, pressing it flat with a finger. Turn the book over and repeat it on the other side. The string ends will not show in the finished book, because the endpaper will be glued to the cover.

Reinforcing the spine. Cut a scrap of fine cloth or seam-binding tape to the same dimensions as the book's spine. Spread white glue thinly on the strip of cloth and press it down over the spine. Hold the book firmly and with your finger probe at the strip to be sure it is in contact with each individual signature before the glue sets.

Slitting the pages. With the pointed blade of a hobbyist's knife, slit the folded edges of the endpapers and signatures.

Pressing the book. The book should be pressed at this point preparatory to covering it. This time, though, sandwich the book so the cardboard or pieces of wood leave the spine itself free. Insert it into the vise with the spine just above the vise. If you can manipulate it well enough, the spine should be slightly bowed outward in the middle. Press the book for another few hours before removing it from the vise.

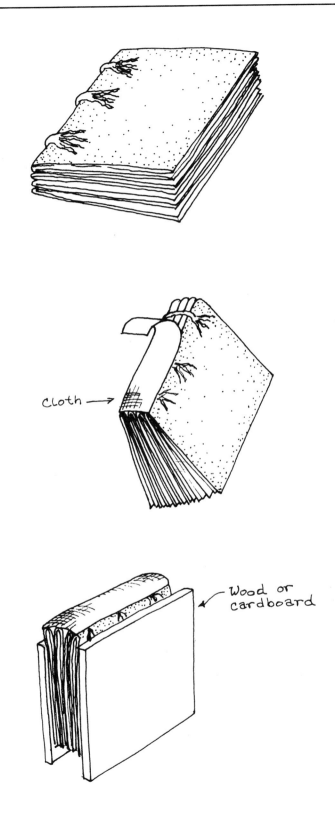

Covering the book. Using knife and steel rule, cut a strip of leather 3/16 inch higher than the signatures. Wrap it around the book to gauge how long the strip should be. The cover should project equally beyond the endpapers at top, bottom, and side of the book. There should be a little slack around the spine, too, so it will bow out at that point. Mark the length with a pencil, but cut beyond your mark. You can always trim the sides of the cover if they project too far beyond the endpapers.

Spread glue evenly over one endpaper. Lay the book down at one end of the leather strip, keeping a small, even margin of leather showing around the endpaper at top, bottom, and along the side. Let the glue set thoroughly.

Spread glue on the other endpaper. Let the leather bow over the spine, then press it to the endpaper, again being sure there is an even margin of leather showing around the perimeter of the endpaper. If there is a little too much leather showing along the side, trim it with the knife and a steel rule after the glue has set.

Shaping the cover. A nicely bound book is grooved along the spine to emphasize the bow. To do this, moisten the leather on the front and back covers of the book along the spine with a fingertip dipped in water. Try not to get the paper wet. Sandwich the book between cardboard again to protect the surface, leaving the spine itself free. Place it in the vise with the spine just above the vise. Press the book overnight. When you remove it from the vise, the bowed spine will stand out better from the covers. If you wish to emphasize this even more, dampen the area again and draw a knitting needle along each cover to form a groove alongside the spine.

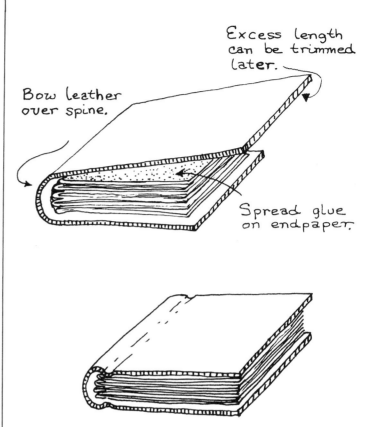

❧ Oil Painting ❧

I have never painted a full-size canvas, and I'm afraid to try—my mistakes would be so large. Given enough fiddling time, it's hard to imagine a tiny canvas that would not be pleasing. The two paintings here are copies, as is the primitive shown on page 117. As an encouragement, let me assure you that while I can't draw people at all, I can paint them. There's a lot you can fudge with oil paint. You can refer to books to find paintings to copy. The simple lines and lack of realistic shading make primitive landscapes, portraits, and still lifes a good starting point. Other sources might be your own photographs of landscapes or houses, old children's book illustrations, and still lifes you set up for yourself.

The Basics—Oil Painting

Oil paints are finely ground pigments mixed with oil and packaged in tubes. For small-and-seldom painting, buy the smallest tubes. Turpentine is the solvent to use both for thinning the paint and for cleaning brushes. Buy artist's round sable brushes, Nos. 0, 1, and 2. Squeeze out the colors you wish to use in small blobs on a palette or a plate. Keep the tubes tightly shut after use. Pour a little turpentine into a small container. A ¼ cup measuring cup or custard cup is fine. Keep a rag or paper towels close by for wiping the brush clean between colors.

To thin paint, dip the brush in turpentine, then dab it lightly at the edge of a blob. Repeat until you have a smear of paint that is as thin as you like it. Usually you would use thinned paint to fill in areas roughly at the start of a painting and use thicker paint as you refine the painting.

To mix colors, dab at a bit of this, a bit of that, and mix them together in a free space on the palette. You do not have to clean the brush at each dab. When you want to change to a completely different color, however, dip your brush in turpentine and wipe it clean on the rag.

To keep paints from drying out when you wish to continue another day, cover the palette with plastic wrap. Always clean your brush thoroughly when you're done for the day. The rag should come out completely clean on the last wipe. To clean a palette, scrape off the blobs and wipe it with a rag and turpentine.

Materials

Oil painting canvas*
1/16-inch-thick cardboard
White glue
Oil paints
Turpentine
Damar varnish
Rag or paper towels
Framing
No. 00 brass wire
⅜-inch No. 20 brass escutcheon nails**

Tools

Artist's round sable brushes, Nos. 0, 1, and 2; flat
  artist's brush
Small container for turpentine
Palette or plate for mixing paints
Triangle
Scissors
Utility knife
Breadboard or other cutting surface
Miter box and straight-backed saw
Needle-nosed pliers

---

* Many art stores sell miniature canvases already prepared for the miniature painter. But however small they look in the store, they may be startlingly oversize in a dollhouse. The portraits shown here are only 1½ inches square before framing. Small as your needs are, art stores will not sell a few square inches of canvas. Canvas comes in 36-inch-wide rolls and, like fabric, is sold by the yard.

**From a tools-only hardware store or a miniaturist's supply house (see page 181).

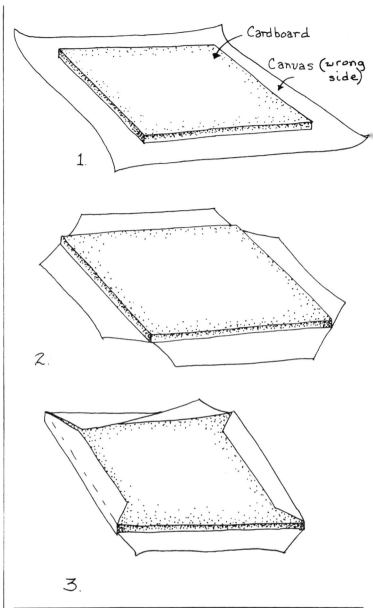

Steps in preparing the canvas.
1. The canvas is cut ½ inch wider and ½ inch longer than the cardboard.
2. When the canvas is glued in place, the corners are notched so the canvas will not overlap when the flaps are folded over.
3. The flaps are folded over and glued in place.

Step by Step

Preparing a canvas. Decide on the shape of your painting. If necessary, use the method on page 166 for scaling an actual painting down to dollhouse size. Cut a piece of paper to the right proportion and hold it against the wall in your dollhouse to see if it's the right size. Remember that the frame will add about ¾ inch to the size. Adjust as necessary.

Using an L-square or 90-degree triangle, lay the shape out on heavy cardboard. I use the $\frac{1}{16}$-inch cardboard backs of artist's sketching pads. With a steel straightedge and utility knife, cut the cardboard out.

Cut a piece of canvas ½ inch wider and ½ inch longer than the piece of cardboard. Canvas has a right and a wrong side. The right side, which feels smoothest, is the side you paint on. The wrong side, which feels somewhat rougher and fuzzy, will be glued to the cardboard.

Spread white glue evenly over the cardboard and place it glue side down on the wrong side of the canvas. Position the cardboard so that ¼ inch of canvas shows evenly on all sides.

Let the glue dry for ten minutes, then snip the corners as shown. Spread glue on the four flaps, fold them over the cardboard, and press them in place. You can begin to paint as soon as the glue is dry— about an hour.

Starting the painting. Some people sketch in major portions of their composition before starting to paint. Others don't. Use a pencil if you prefer some guidelines. Don't bother with details; they will soon be obliterated with paint. The lines you draw will serve only to delineate basic areas of color.

Work at a table. Get your paints, brushes, turpentine in a dish, palette, or plate, and rag or paper towels ready. Mix the color you want to start with and fill in that area, using thinned paint. Move from one area to another until the canvas is covered with paint and the rough shape of your painting is visible. For a portrait, this would mean that areas like face, hair, arms, clothing, and background are now all filled with solid blocks of color.

Refining a painting. For the amateur painter, the process of refining is hit or miss. I may put in two dots for eyes to see if they are in the right place. They can always be covered by more paint if they're not. I may work up some rosiness here, a line of detail there, a lightening or a darkening of background. When a try fails, I shift to another area where I feel more certain. Little by little, the painting "becomes." It is only toward the very end that I add such touches as eyebrows, colored flowers in the grass, a white highlight on the edge of a cloud.

If you are really stuck, try looking at real paintings very close up. Shadow, light, and color are achieved by methods you can see from a foot away, even when the over-all result looks unachievable from a distance.

Varnishing a painting. Oil paintings are protected when dry with a coat of Damar varnish. Drying, however, may take a month. Apply the varnish with a flat artist's brush so it goes on evenly. Let it dry several days before framing.

Framing a painting. Set the miter box at 45 degrees to cut the corners of the frame pieces. Cut one top piece and one side piece first. Cut both of them 3 inches longer than the canvas. Tape them together at the mitered corner with freezer tape. With the framing pieces upside down, place the canvas in position as shown. Mark both frame pieces at their corners to show you where to make the next cut.

Remove the tape and miter the other end of each piece at your mark. Check again for fit, and recut if necessary. Cut the other two frame pieces exactly like the first two. When all four pieces are cut, lay them together and check again that the miters meet nicely and the canvas slips into place. If all is well, glue the frame together with white glue, holding it tight with your hands for a few minutes until the glue sets.

When the frame has dried for several hours, glue the canvas into place. Squeeze a thin line of glue around the inside perimeter of the frame where the canvas will rest, wipe any excess glue off with your finger, and set the canvas in place. Check if any glue has oozed out onto the painting. If it has, remove it now with a damp sponge. Press the canvas against the frame for a few minutes until the glue sets.

---

1. One top and one side piece are cut first, both 3 inches longer than necessary. One end of each is mitered.

2. The two pieces are temporarily held together with freezer tape, and a mark is made on each to indicate the next mitered cut.

3. The other side and the bottom piece are cut exactly the same as the top and first side. After gluing, the back of the frame is strung with wire between two small nails for hanging. Hold the nails in place with needle-nosed pliers if necessary while you hammer.

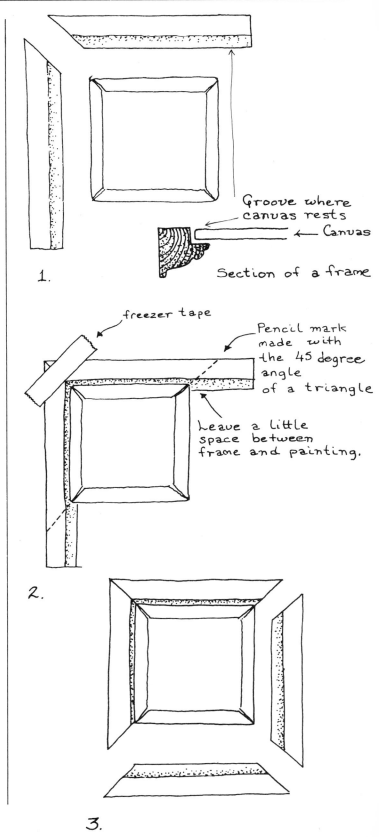

Groove where canvas rests

← Canvas

Section of a frame

1.

freezer tape

Pencil mark made with the 45 degree angle of a triangle

Leave a little space between frame and painting.

2.

3.

To hang the picture on the wall, you will have to wire it like a real painting. Set the framed picture face side down on a soft cloth. Hammer a nail into each side, about ½ inch from the top of the picture. Wind soft wire around one nail head, then the other. The wire should be slightly slack, but not so much so that it will show above the painting when it is hung.

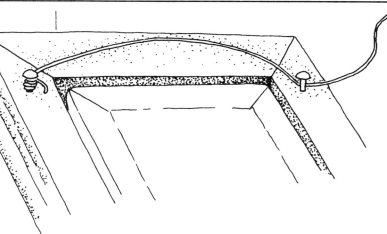

Frames

Take your painting with you when you search for a frame. What looks small and delicate to you in isolation may look amazingly gross in context. Fancier frames can trick the eye into seeming to be those ornate, carved frames often used on full-size oils. Plain frames, no matter how narrow, look bulky because of their thickness.

Whether or not it is worth it to you to do your own framing depends on how difficult it is to find a molding that works at dollhouse scale. If you have gone to half a dozen places and finally found the right molding, my advice is to try to buy at least three feet of it and make your own frames. The reason is that frame design seems to change rapidly—what you found this time may be unavailable the next. If a frame shop will not sell its moldings, of course you will have to have them do the framing and take your chances on the availability of that particular design in the future.

❧ Dough Breads ❧

asiest of all foods, and certainly the most convincing, are loaves made from inedible dough baked to a uniform hardness. They are not as imperishable as clay, falling victim in summertime to sogginess and mold, and in the winter to the nibblings of mice. These disadvantages can often be avoided, however, with a thick coating of varnish.

This craft is definitely not for grown-ups only. Kids are just as good at it.

Above: The French bread was slashed diagonally across the top. The oval rye loaf was decorated with caraway seeds and left to brown in the oven longer than the other loaves. The round white loaf was slashed in a crisscross pattern and sprinkled with cornmeal. The poppyseed and sesame seed rolls were sprinkled with their respective seeds. The braided loaves were braided in the usual manner, and the croissants were made from flat triangular pieces of dough rolled up.

Materials
Flour
Salt
Water
Decorations: poppy, sesame, caraway seeds; corn-
meal; coarse salt
White glue
Varnish
Glossy finish: 1 egg yolk mixed with 1 tablespoon
water

Tools
Cookie sheet
Mixing bowl
Paring knife
Small paintbrush
Pastry brush
Plant mister
Waxed paper

Step by Step

Making the dough. In a bowl mix together with your hands 2 cups flour, ½ cup salt, and 1 cup water. If the dough is too sticky to shape, add flour. If it cracks when you shape it, add water. Set the oven now to preheat at 300 degrees.

Shaping the loaves. Shape the loaves as you would real bread, referring to a cookbook for the fanciest shapes. The shapes shown here are all quite easy. The cuts are made, before baking, with a sharp paring knife or a razor blade. Don't add any seeds yet. Bake within 20 minutes to avoid cracking.

Baking the bread. Place the loaves on a cookie sheet. To prevent cracking, dampen the loaves very lightly with a plant mister just before putting them in the oven. After one hour brush the egg yolk and water mixture over the loaves with a pastry brush to glaze them, and leave them in the oven another 15 minutes or until golden brown and hard. These times may not be accurate for the size loaf you are making. To check that your loaves are hard all the way through,

turn the largest ones over and probe the bottom with a skewer. If the dough inside is at all soft, the loaves will soon deteriorate. To prevent further browning, turn the oven down to 200 degrees and continue baking until the loaves are hard.

Decorating the bread. To sprinkle the loaves with any of the suggested seeds, cornmeal, or salt, spread white glue thinly over the surface with a small paintbrush. While the glue is still wet, sprinkle the seeds, cornmeal, or salt over the surface. In about 20 minutes, when the glue is dry, shake off any excess material.

Preserving the bread. In order for these loaves to last for a long time, they must be made completely moisture-proof with several layers of varnish. Use a glossy varnish. Working on waxed paper to avoid sticking, either paint or spray the varnish, being sure to cover every bit of surface on each loaf. Repeat for three coats, allowing the varnish to dry throughly between coats.

❧ Clay Food ❧

The meats, fish, breads, fruits, and vegetables shown opposite were surprisingly easy to make. Even a very young child can roll self-hardening clay between his hands to form oranges or hot dogs. Round loaves of bread, chicken drumsticks, and bunches of grapes are not much harder. How convincing the finished product is depends more on the painting than on the sculpting. Luckily, oil paints can be fiddled with endlessly until, by accident or design, they give that touch of reality that makes these foods a cut above commercial ones.

Materials
Self-hardening clay
Oil paints
Turpentine
Damar varnish
Carpet thread for stringing foods
Waxed paper

Tools
Round toothpicks
Razor blade for cutting foods
Round sable artist's brush No. 0
Palette or plate
Long needle for stringing foods
Bread board

Step by Step

Rough-shaping the clay. No matter what shape of food you want to end up with, start by rolling a ball of about the right size. The rolling assures that the clay is free of cracks or air spaces, and rolling is also a way of telling whether or not the consistency is right. If the clay has cracks that don't go away easily, wet your fingers and mush the clay around. If it is too sticky to roll well, leave it to dry for 15 minutes and try again.

Place the piece on a flat surface if it is to have a flat bottom—for instance a loaf of bread. Work the piece up in the air if it is to have a round shape, such as an apple or a carrot. Squeeze the ball gently here and there with your fingers to coax from it the shape you wish. It needn't be a perfect shape for now.

Fine-shaping the clay. Allow the pieces to dry from half an hour to an hour, depending on size. When you can pick the piece up without denting it by mistake, it is ready for final shaping. With a round toothpick, gently scrape away at any bulges or unevennesses. Where you want dents, say for the bottom and top of an apple, dig out the clay with the same tool. To smooth the whole piece, rub the side of the toothpick along it.

If you want to add pieces together, as with a bunch of grapes, wet both surfaces with your finger and press them lightly together. If they come apart later, you can always put them back together with white glue. To make sliced bread and sliced cheese, finish the whole piece first. Then use a razor blade to do the slicing.

When you are finished, put the pieces aside to dry for at least a week before painting.

Painting the food. With oil paints, brush on the basic color over the whole surface. For bread, this would be a shade of brown, for an apple either red or green. Work on waxed paper, using a fingernail to hold the piece in place, tipping it this way and that so your brush can reach all surfaces. Some paint will come off on the paper and on your finger, but this will not ruin your work.

While the paint is still wet, work in other colors, again holding the piece in place with a fingernail. A green apple might call for a pinkish glow on one cheek, a loaf of bread for a darker crust on top. Again, don't worry that the paint will be ruined where it touches the paper. Even the sausages, illustrated here, which were mottled in white all the way around, were simply nudged along with the tip of the brush to get to the bottom surface, and the paint did not smear in the process.

Let painted pieces dry from several weeks to a month before you varnish them.

Varnishing the food. Use Damar varnish and a round sable artist's brush. Work on waxed paper, holding the piece with a fingernail and tipping or rolling to get at all surfaces. Use the varnish sparingly so pieces do not end up sitting in puddles. The varnished pieces will not be stuck to the waxed paper when they are dry. Drying may take from several days to a week.

Hints on Highlights

Page 115 will give you some basic information on oil paints. But a hint about blending in lighter or darker colors on these tiny foods may be helpful. Work on still-wet paint. Using a No. 0 round sable artist's brush, dab tiny spots of the color you wish to blend in in the area you are highlighting or shading. Wipe your brush dry on a rag or paper towel. Now lightly jab at the dots with the point of the brush. The jabbing action will slightly mix in the background color. To blend further, dry your brush again and dab some more. This method will give you a livelier surface and better blending than if you tried to premix each shade and brush it into place.

Of Sausages and Fish

Any food that must be strung on thread for hanging (unless it is an open shape like a bagel) must be strung or pierced for stringing before the clay is dry. Sausages are strung like beads with needle and carpet thread while they are still quite wet. If they get out of shape during stringing, they can be coaxed back into shape afterward. These sausages were bent to a curved shape after stringing so they would hang convincingly in a loop. Leave several inches of thread at each end for later tying and hanging. The sausages are rather a nuisance to paint, all strung together, but it can be done.

To prepare fish for later stringing, pierce the still-wet clay in the gill area with a needle, moving it about to enlarge the hole somewhat to allow for shrinkage in drying. After the fish have been painted and varnished, string them up with a needle and carpet thread.

The provolone cheeses here are wrapped for hanging after the clay has dried, but the grooves are pressed into the clay while it is wet with the side of a round toothpick. The strings can be tied on after the cheese has been painted and varnished. Use beige carpet thread. Start with the vertical string, wrapping the cheese exactly as you would wrap a ribbon around a package. Before tying, check that the strings are in the grooves. Tie the ends of the string into a square knot at the top instead of a bow, then make a second knot about an inch up the strings to form a loop.

To tie the horizontal strings, thread a needle with the same carpet thread. Insert the needle under one of the vertical strings, and leave several inches dangling. Bring the needle to the next vertical string, insert it once, and then again to form a loop that will hold it in place. Lightly tug at the thread to tighten the loop. Proceed around the next two verticals, looping each time. When you get back to where you started, insert the needle under the vertical

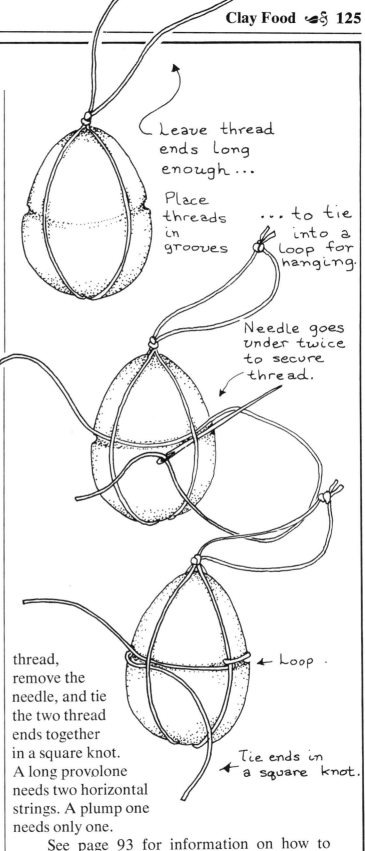

Leave thread ends long enough...

Place threads in grooves

...to tie into a loop for hanging.

Needle goes under twice to secure thread.

← Loop.

Tie ends in a square knot.

thread, remove the needle, and tie the two thread ends together in a square knot. A long provolone needs two horizontal strings. A plump one needs only one.

See page 93 for information on how to make small hooks for hanging these foods in your dollhouse.

❧ Pottery Dishes ❧

There are two time-honored methods by which pottery is made. One is to form the shape of bowl or plate by coiling long rolled strips of clay. The other is to place the clay on a horizontal wheel and shape it with the hands while the wheel is spinning. The beautiful thin-walled crocks on the dollhouse mantelpiece (on page 185) were "thrown" in this way by an expert potter who claims it is as easy to form a 1-inch bowl as a 10-inch one. Since I can't for the life of me manage even a 10-inch piece, and since a potter's wheel is not to be found in the average home, and since coiling in miniature is just too hard, I have come up with another method for making crockery. It is not time-honored and not perfect, but it is enjoyable and appealing. The method actually is modeling, as one would model a statue rather than a set of dishes. If you are already a potter, of course, you will want to use the skills you have. Although the pieces in the illustration were fired in a kiln, the same instructions can be used for either self-hardening clay or the sort that is fired at a much lower temperature in the home oven.

Sources

For all sculpture materials and tools, Sculpture House, Inc., 38 East 30th Street, New York, N.Y. 10016. Send for their mail-order catalogue, or look under "Sculptors' Equipment and Supplies" in the Yellow Pages.

Kilns

Unless you are a serious ceramist or potter, you are not likely to have or want to buy so expensive an item as a kiln. There are probably kilns in your community, however, and arrangements can usually be made to use one. Before I had my own small kiln, the art teacher at my children's elementary school would allow me to include a few pieces along with the children's work she was firing. This cost the school no extra money, and because the pieces were small, they did not take up needed space. A nearby community crafts center also has a kiln which is used in cooperative firings several times a week. Other possibilities to look into are neighbors whose hobby is pottery or who teach the craft. If any kiln is going to be used exclusively to fire your pieces, offer to pay for the electricity used and for the time it may take another person to oversee the operation. Don't try to run a kiln on your own unless you have been adequately instructed in its use. Each kiln is somewhat different and comes with its own instructions for firing. Used improperly, a kiln is very dangerous.

Materials
Firing clay

Tools
Sculpture tools similar to those illustrated
Kiln
Firing cones (see page 130)

Step by Step

Choosing the clay. Most art stores do not sell firing clay. It is sold by sculpture supply houses, one of which is suggested under Sources. Each type of firing clay has a different texture or color and may fire at a different temperature. Before you buy, check whether the clay will fire to a red, pink, or white color, whether the texture is smooth or gritty, and at what temperature the clay should be fired. The temperature may be given as a "cone" number. Page 130 explains what a cone is. Unless the package also tells you the number of cone to use in firing, write it down for future reference. Firing clay is sold by the pound in one-pound packages. The clay is already moist and is wrapped in plastic inside the box.

Preparing the clay. Take from the plastic bag the amount of clay you intend to use now, then reseal the bag to prevent the rest of the clay from drying. Roll the clay into a ball and throw it down onto the table. Repeat this several times to remove any air bubbles that might be in it. Trapped air bubbles expand during firing and may cause the piece to explode. In the rare event that the clay feels too hard to work, dip your hands into water and work the water into the clay until it becomes softer.

Designing the piece. Design pottery in your head rather than on paper. The task of trying to draw a three-dimensional picture is greater than the task of interpreting from a mental image directly into the clay. Think out ahead of time such features as rims or handles, as well as over-all shape. Let the clay and your own hands change your mind as you really get into the shaping process.

Rough-shaping the piece. For convenience's sake, a bathtub rather than a dish is used in the illustration to demonstrate the rough and finished shaping of a piece. The principle is the same for any piece you wish to make. With the clay soft and moist, shape the crude outlines of the piece with your hands. It should be larger in all dimensions than you intend it ultimately to be. If you are making several identical shapes, work on all of them simultaneously. The reason for this is that clay shrinks as it dries. If you make one piece in a set now, then try to copy it after it dries; you won't know how large to form its copy in wet clay to allow for shrinkage. Be sure to include in this rough shaping any protrusions, such as feet, handles, rims, and bases. Don't scoop out any clay from inside the shape. You are shaping only the outside at this point. Any bowls, cups, or pitchers should be solid. Even a plate should be left flat across the surface rather than scooped to a concave shape. Handles should not have holes through them yet, either.

Before you try to refine the shape by using sculpture tools, the clay has to dry somewhat. If it is a large piece like the bathtub, you may have to set it aside in its rough state for most of a day. If it is as small as the dishes illustrated here, you can probably proceed with the next step within half an hour.

Refining the shape. When a piece is ready for refining, the clay should have hardened to the extent that it no longer yields to poking with your fingers. When you pick the piece up, it should not deform under the pressure of your hand. Your fingers should not leave depressions. If the over-all shape still deforms or if the pressure of your fingers still dents it readily, leave it to dry some more. Refining is done with the sculpture tools illustrated, or with substitutes such as butter knives, toothpicks, and demitasse spoons. Real tools make a real difference. Using first the bladelike tool No. 10, begin to remove excess clay. A scraping rather than a cutting motion gives you more control. Incise shallow lines to remind you of where a rim protrudes or what the final shape of a handle should be. Remove only small scrapings of clay at a time. Tempting as it is, don't start yet to scoop out any hollow areas or holes.

These three sculpture tools are all you need for shaping small objects. Each is shown in full and side view. Catalog numbers, stamped into the handles, identify each tool.

As the clay begins to feel harder and more leathery, switch to the hook-shaped end of tool No. 22, which can be used more delicately. As you work, turn the piece a little at a time to keep your shaping symmetrical. It may help to revolve the piece slowly in front of a bright window to see the outline in silhouette. Go on to the next step only when the outside shape is virtually finished.

Scooping out the shape. When a piece is ready to be scooped out, the clay is dry enough so that even a good deal of pressure from your fingers will not deform it, and almost no work remains on the outside of the piece. The reason so much caution is raised on this point is twofold: First, the scooping action requires a good deal of pressure, and if the walls of the piece aren't leather-hard, they will push outward or crack open. Second, after scooping, there isn't enough clay left to make changes in the outside shape of your piece. Pieces other than concave ones like bowls and cups must be scooped out too. No portion of your work may be greater than ¾ of an inch thick if you are going to fire it. Even though it is not part of the design, the pedestal of the sink on page 24 was scooped out from the bottom.

Use the wide end of tool No. 22 for scooping broad areas, and either end of tool No. 42 for scooping into narrower areas. The motion to use when starting is similar to scooping ice cream out of a container, except that caution must be used not to apply too much pressure for fear of scooping right through the wall. As the walls become thinner, switch to tool No. 10 and go back to the scraping rather than the scooping motion. Continue scraping until the inside shape is as well defined as the outside.

Smoothing the surface. When a piece is ready for smoothing, the surface has begun to look lighter in color and have a chalky feel to it. Use the hooked end of tool No. 22 to work lightly over the entire surface to get rid of scrape marks made earlier. The motion to use at this point is more a rubbing than a scraping one. Tiny bits of sandpaper can be used to smooth the inside of a shape. A flat jeweler's file may be helpful to even out a rim or base. Even a toothpick makes a good tool for rubbing back and forth along the entire surface to erase scrape marks. When you are satisfied with the smoothness of a piece, set it aside to dry completely.

Firing the piece. A piece is ready to fire after it has dried at least a week, for a small piece, at least two weeks for one as large as this bathtub. The kiln in which you fire it will have its own instructions for use and may require that you heat it in stages, first low, then medium, then to a high temperature. In general, the piece to be fired is placed in the cold kiln on prism-shaped pieces of clay or commercially bought "stilts" so that air can circulate evenly around it and it won't stick to the kiln floor. A cone of ceramic material is placed in the kiln along with it, positioned so that it can be seen through a peephole in the kiln designed for the purpose. Each type of clay achieves optimal hardness at a particular temperature, and different types of cone (differentiated by number) begin to melt at particular temperatures; for instance, cone 06 melts at a little over 1860 degrees. To know when the temperature inside the kiln has risen to the optimal temperature for the clay you are using, a cone that begins to melt at that same temperature is used. When a peep through the peephole reveals that the cone is beginning to bend and sag, the kiln is turned off.

It is left unopened for at least 12 hours to cool before it is safe for you to open it to see how your piece has turned out.

If you have to stop . . . The demands of everyday life do not often allow one to finish without interruption a project as demanding, say, as a whole set of dishes. More likely, you will have to interrupt your work, possibly when the clay is just right for the phase you are in. When this happens, simply wrap the work in plastic wrap, leaving as little air around each piece as possible. If you have to stay away for longer than overnight, dampen a rag (just slightly, or the clay will become wetter rather than stay the same) and lay it loosely over your work before covering it with plastic.

❧ Glazed Dishes ☙

Few projects in this book are as exciting, as miraculous as glazing pottery. First you have a slightly bumpy, lopsided plate. You paint onto it a chalky, nondescript colored glaze. Then you pop it into the kiln, contain your curiosity until it has baked for an hour or more and cooled for another twelve hours, and then you open the lid. There is your plate, its bumps smoothed over and its lopsidedness no longer obvious beneath a glistening, gorgeously colored glaze. It is like a plate coming true.

Above: The eggs in these bowls were used to test the glaze colors before deciding which ones to use on the dishes. Instead of a wasted firing, this ploy results in a pretty collection of Easter eggs. If the glaze sticks to the stilts in the kiln, break them off and file down the bumps with a jeweler's file. The small defects will hardly show.

Opposite: These jugs were shaped and glazed by a child.

Not that this was so at my first attempt. The glazes I originally tried were intended for school use and therefore contained no lead. The glaze came out thin and translucent, showing up every original defect. The colors were muddy or garish. Most of the earthy glazes I like—at least those that will melt at cone 06 (about 1860 degrees)—contain lead and are not intended for use on objects anyone will eat off of. The drawback, of course, is that young children can't be permitted to use such lead products for fear of poisoning.

The glazes used on these dishes are made by Duncan, Fresno, California 93727. Write to them to find a dealer in your area or a mail-order art-supply house that will fill a small order, or look under "Ceramics—Equipment and Supplies" in the Yellow Pages for a dealer in this or other brands.

The cups here were glazed in Duncan's AR 620 Rusty Amber, a mottled mixture of the two colors that resembles some Early American kitchen ware. The bowls are 20024 Cocoa Marble, a tan and brown glaze that also looks like that period. The plates are 20054 Blue Fantasy, a steely blue background with areas of dull gold streaked into it. The sink and bathtub on page 24 are an ivory undercoat with a clear crackling glaze applied over it to produce the "crazed" look of an old piece.

Instructions for applying each glaze are clearly set forth on each bottle. In general, three coats of the glaze are simply painted on with a round artist's brush. Some glazes have crystals on the bottom of the bottle (these are the second color) which are distributed over the surface on the last coat. After painting, the ware is simply placed in the kiln on stilts and left to fire to the correct cone temperature. The glaze on these dishes was applied after the clay was fired once, but glaze can also be applied on the unfired clay to save yourself the second firing.

❦ Twig Furniture ❧

Very few pieces of this Victorian craft have survived. Perhaps that is because the small twigs from which such furniture was made become fragile with age, but more likely it is because it was then merely a childhood pastime, too quickly, cheaply, and easily accomplished to be valued. What has survived is, of course, quite valuable now. Easiness alone would not warrant the inclusion here of twig furniture if the results were not both useful and charming. This bench is at home in a rustic store, as shown on page 21, or on a porch or in a garden. Twig furniture makes an excellent post-Christmas project, as the branch ends from any of the usual species of Christmas tree can be used. If children's fingers begin to hurt from pushing the pins in, let them work on a breadboard so that as soon as a pin has been started in the right spot, they can turn the piece of furniture over and press the pin in by pushing its head against the board.

Materials
Fresh ends of branches from fir, spruce, or pine trees (Christmas trees can be used)
"Ball-point" dressmaker's pins

Tools
Small pruning shears, wire clippers, or pocketknife for cutting twigs

Step by Step

Cutting the twigs. Look over the surface of the tree for twigs that are straight and long and about 3/16 inch thick. At least a few of these twigs should have buds at their tips to use as decoration. Cut off more twigs than you need so you will have plenty to choose from as you build the piece of furniture. Strip the needles from all the twigs and discard the needles. Lay the stripped twigs on a table along with clippers and pins.

Building the frame. The principle behind construct-any piece of furniture from fresh evergreen twigs is that the pin that holds two pieces together must always go through the side of one twig and into the end of another. The pin will be easy to stick through the side of the first twig because the side is still green and soft. It will be almost as easy to stick into the center of the second twig because these fresh branchlets have soft, pithy centers. When this method of construction is used, you never have to worry about pins sticking out from the furniture; the only portion of the pin that is visible is the head.

Before you start to cut actual lengths of twig for your furniture, look at the drawings to enable you to understand the basic frame structures. Figure out where you want to use the decorative buds. Then start to cut and assemble the frame. The order in which twigs are pinned is not crucial, but it is helpful to cut those twigs that are the same size together so they are accurate. As a guide, the bench in the photograph is 4 inches long. The back is 3½ inches high from the floor to the top of the buds, and 3 inches high to the top of the back railing. Seat height is 1¼ inches. The arms are 2½ inches from the floor. The bench measures 2 inches from back to front.

Filling in the design. After the basic structure of the piece of furniture has been pinned and can stand up on its own, decide how you wish to fill in the spaces in the back, sides, head and foot boards, or seat. Parallel slats or crisscross arrangements are both easy.

Finishing. There is really no pressing need to do anything more to your piece of twig furniture once all the pieces are pinned in place. If you wish, you may shellac or varnish it when the wood has thoroughly dried (a month). If you want to disguise the multicolored modernity of the pins, apply brown oil paint to the heads with an artist's brush.

Insert each pin through the side of one twig, into the end of another.

Only the basic structure of this bench, chair, and bed has been finished. Cross bracing has been added at the bottom of the chair because it is shaky without it. Diagonal bracing has been started on the bed. It will be completed at each of the remaining three corners.

To these basic structures will be added other twigs to form slats for the bed and its decorative headboard, the chair and bench backs and seats, and a crisscross pattern in the bench arms, which will serve both as bracing and decoration.

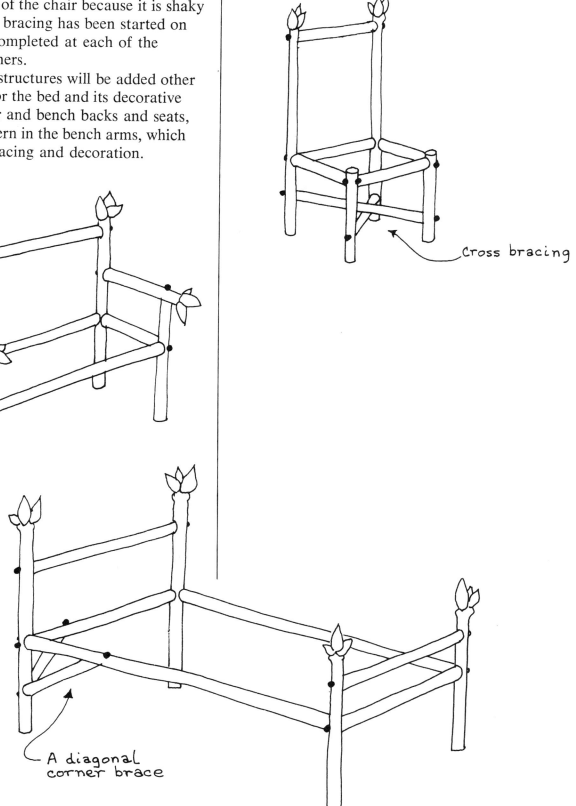

Cross bracing

A diagonal corner brace

❧ Basketry ❧

This basket gave me three days of trouble and ten sore fingers. I can save you trouble, but only calloused experience can save you sore fingers. The trouble was caused by trying to work in miniature with normal-size cane. The smallest sizes are not stocked by many sources, so I have suggested a mail-order source that was prompt and reliable.

Cane, sometimes called reed, is actually neither. It is the core of an extremely long, woody vine called the rattan palm. The smooth, lustrous outer portions just under the bark are split off to be used as chair caning. The central core is run through cutting machines of various diameters to produce the round cane often used in baskets and wicker furniture. Like many of the materials needed for miniatures, it comes in quantities that seem grotesque compared to the size of the object you wish to make. The only way around the problem is to find a basketmaker from whom you can beg a few strands of the right diameter.

Sources

Basketry instructions: *The Techniques of Basketry.* Virginia I. Harvey. New York: Van Nostrand Reinhold Company, 1974.

Cane: Peerless Rattan, 45 Indian Lane, P.O. Box 8, Towaco, N.J. 07082. Send for mail-order catalogue.

Materials

Size 0 cane for weaving
Size 1 cane for the ribs*

Tools

Awl
Wire snippers
Large bowl for soaking
Needle-nosed pliers

---

* It is easier to shape a basket if the ribs are somewhat less pliable than the weaving strands, but if you wish, use only Size 0 for the whole basket.

Hobbyist's knife with pointed blade
Breadboard as cutting surface, or work table

Step by Step

Soaking the cane. Select 2 strands of Size 0, which will be used for the weaving, and 1 strand of Size 1, which will be used for the ribs of the basket. The second strand of Size 0 is for insurance, as a single long strand should be enough to complete this basket.

In a large bowl filled with warm water, soak the coiled strands for 10 minutes. Keep the water available for resoaking the basket-in-progress whenever it becomes less pliable. Well-soaked cane is so flexible that it can be tied in a knot without breaking.

Starting the base. Cut 8 pieces of Size 1 cane, each 12 inches long, with wire nippers. Using a hobbyist's knife with a pointed blade, split down the center of 4 of these pieces for about an inch. The easiest way to do this is to stick the point of the blade through the center of the cane and into your working surface at the beginning of the cut; then gently pull the cane against the blade rather than try to pull the knife along. The cane tends to split straight.

Poke the other 4 pieces through the split centers of the first four to form a cross as shown.

Weaving the base. The type of weaving suggested here involves twisting 2 strands together between each rib as you weave in rounds around the basket. The 2 strands are formed by looping 1 long strand. Loop the longest strand of Size 0 cane in half. Place the loop over one arm of the cross. Twist the 2 strands once around each other, turning clockwise. (You can also turn counterclockwise if it feels more natural to you, but once you have chosen a direction in which to turn you must stick with it.)

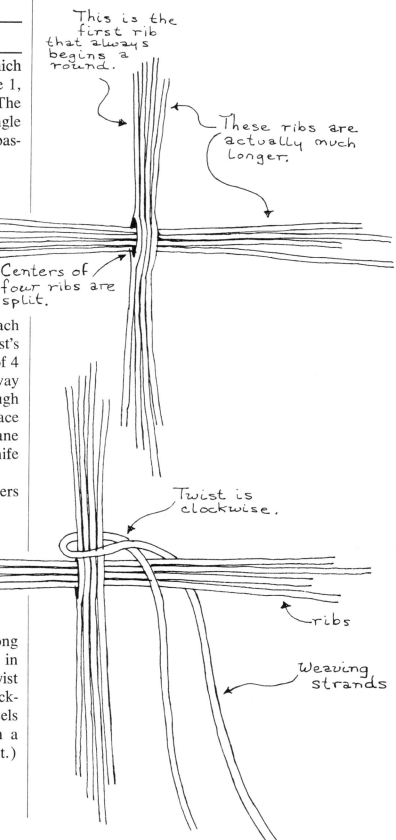

This is the first rib that always begins a round.

These ribs are actually much longer.

Centers of four ribs are split.

Twist is clockwise.

ribs

Weaving strands

Catch the next arm of the cross between the 2 strands, and twist again. Repeat this weaving motion for 2 rounds around each of the 4 arms of the cross.

For the next rounds you will be dividing the ribs into 8 groups of 2 ribs each. Bend them apart evenly as shown, and continue to twist between each group of 2 for the next 2 rounds. As you weave, keep the work flat between your fingers to achieve a flat, non-tippy base for the basket.

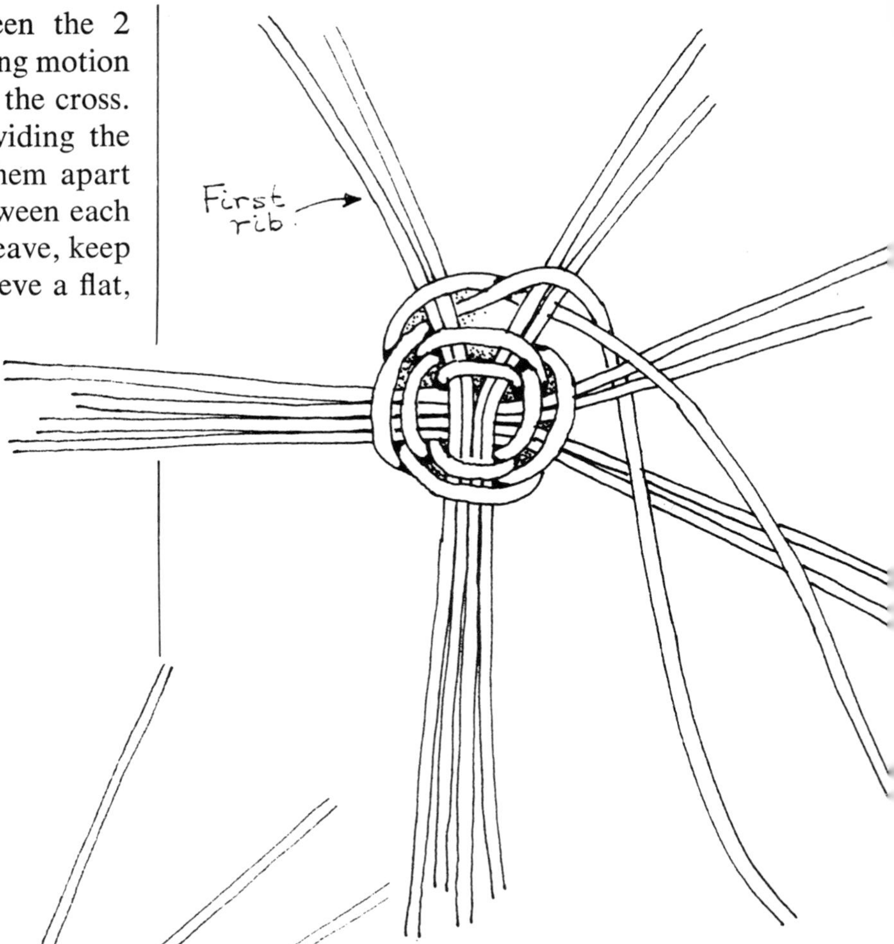

The last round of the base is done by dividing the groups of ribs again, this time 16 single ribs. Do this round carefully so that the ribs are evenly spaced all around. The base is now finished.

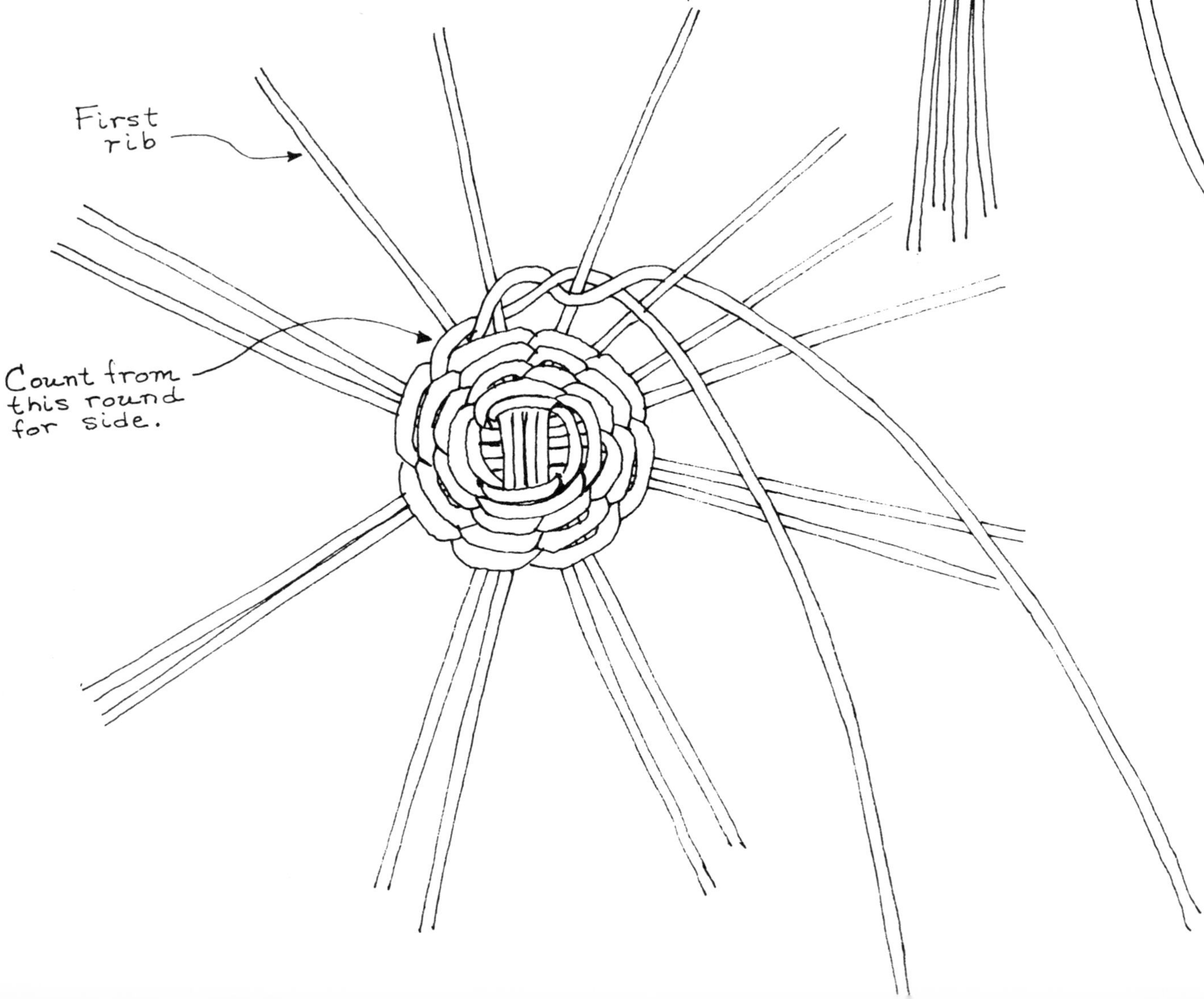

First rib

First rib

Count from this round for side.

Forming the sides. From now on, work in your lap (or rather in the air above it, using your lap for support as needed). Keep the weaving canes to the outside of the basket. Use your left hand to bend the ribs upward to shape the sides as you twist and tighten the weaving canes with your right hand.

Since your left thumb will be inside the basket as you work, you will find that you can use it to bend the rib around which you are twisting temporarily outward while you get the weaving canes around it, then push inward with your other fingers while you pull that twist tight. Considerable pressure is needed both to push the sides inward and to pull the twist tight, accounting for the sore fingers mentioned earlier.

Resoak both the basket and the trailing weaving strands as soon as they become less flexible. Also, you will find that the trailing strands get twisted around each other, impeding your work. Untwist them as needed.

Continue to shape the rounded sides of the basket for a total of 10 rounds (counted from the first round on single ribs, which was the last round of the base). In this example, in the last 2 rounds the sides of the basket were pushed even farther inward and the weaving strands pulled even tighter to narrow the basket slightly at the top.

To count rounds, locate a rib and count the number of strands that lie over it. If you look carefully at your basket sideways, you will see where a round begins: the edge suddenly looks higher at that point, becoming even only when you have woven up to the rib just before it. If this location of the beginning of a round is hard for you to judge, there is another way to keep track: make a pencil mark on the first rib around which you placed the loop when you began the base. This rib will always be the first one in each round.

Stop weaving at the end of round 10, but don't cut off the strands yet.

Adding a new strand if you run out. There is a chance you will run out of one or both weaving strands. If you see that both are coming to an end soon, cut one of them shorter so that they are of uneven lengths. This at least will prevent having to add 2 strands at the same spot. When you get to the end of the shorter one, simply place a new strand next to it, leave 2 inches of the old strand and 2 inches of the new one projecting so you can cut them later, and continue weaving, using the new strand in place of the old one.

Weaving the edge. The edge of a basket is woven from the ribs only. The weaving strands are simply cut after the basket is dry. To help in the edge-weaving, use an awl to pry open a hole large enough to stick the rib through, and needle-nosed pliers to pull the rib tight.

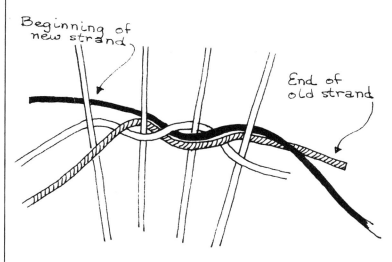

Cut all the ribs to 2 or 3 inches above the rim of the basket. Resoak for 10 minutes in warm water. 1. Working clockwise, bend each rib (rib No. 1) in turn around the outside of its neighbor (rib No. 2) and downward into the basket. Continue until all the ribs loop behind a neighbor and down into the interior of the basket. 2. Take each rib in turn and poke it back out of the basket underneath the loop formed by the next rib (rib No. 3). Continue around the rim until all the ribs are sticking outward. 3. Now poke each rib in turn back into the loop formed by the next rib (rib No. 4). Continue around until all the ribs are sticking inward again. These ends are cut off when the basket is dry.

These instructions will be easier to follow when you are actually working on a basket. When you have it in your hands, you will see that the action is only weaving in and out around one rib after another.

Making a handle. Cut two 6-inch lengths of well-soaked Size 0 cane. Using an awl to pry a space alongside a rib, poke both pieces down through the side of the basket as far as you can get them. When they are secure, twist the two strands together. Bend them to form a handle, and, allowing for how far you are going to push them into the opposite side of the basket, snip them off to the length you want with the wire nippers. The handle in the example shown here is taller than a normal basket. Pry a space on the opposite side of the basket and push the ends (untwisted) down as far as you can. A twisted handle tends to go awry, so straighten it with your fingers before it dries. Leave the basket to dry now.

Finishing the basket. When the basket is thoroughly dry, snip off the projecting ends of the ribs and weaving strands with wire snippers.

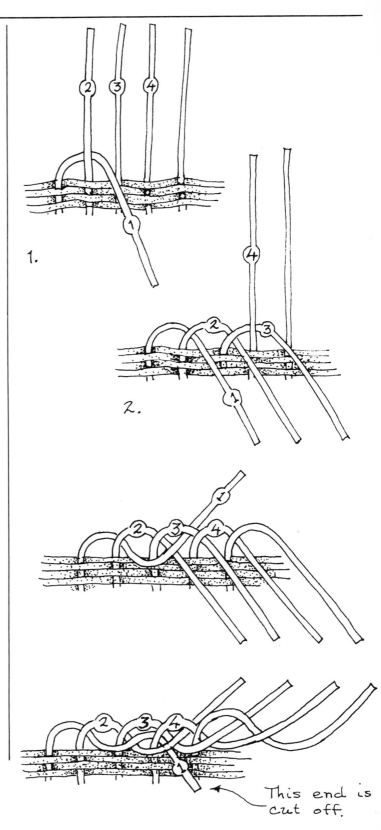

1.

2.

This end is cut off.

❧ Wicker Chairs ❧

Making wicker furniture is harder than making baskets only in that there's twice as much weaving to do. Otherwise the skills are the same, so if you can make one, you should be able to make the other. The decorative braid—actually a Turk's head knot made with a single strand of cord—is tedious, but it is optional, as the chairs look just fine without it.

There are many ways to construct wicker furniture. The method given here seemed to me the most straightforward, and it can be used for a love seat as well. The seat is a piece of wood cut to shape and drilled with holes evenly spaced all around the edge. The ribs are stuck through the holes and then woven around with a looped strand of cane, as in the weaving of a basket. By the way, as you will see when you have half completed weaving the base, the same seat shape, in the same size, makes a darling wicker dog bed. Those who get discouraged easily can always stop right there.

These chairs measure 2½ inches wide at the base and are 3 to 3½ inches high at the back. Seat height is 1 inch (1½ inches with the pillow).

Sources

Design: Home-furnishing magazines; *All About Wicker*. Patricia Corbin. New York: E. P. Dutton, 1978.

Dremel Moto-Tool: Hardware and hobby stores

Cane: Peerless Rattan, 45 Indian Lane, P.O. Box 8, Towaco, N.J. 07082

Plywood: Lumberyard, but only in 4 × 8-foot sheets. See Cigar Box Furniture, pages 167–168, for other wood you might use.

Materials

No. 1 and No. 0 cane
⅛-inch plywood
Heavy paper for pattern
Rubber cement

Tools

Pencil
Needle
Fine-line ball-point pen
File
Bowl to hold water for soaking
Small wire snippers
Needle-nosed pliers
Awl
Dremel Moto-Tool, stand, and 1/16-inch drill bit (or hand drill)
Hair dryer

Step by Step

Designing the chair. Except for the seat shape and the over-all look of the chair, it is difficult to decide in advance exactly what the chair will look like unless you are experienced with shaping wicker. Looking through books on wicker and home-furnishing magazines can give you plenty of ideas to aim for, however.

Making a pattern for the seat. Trace the pattern here or draw your own. The pattern should be on quite

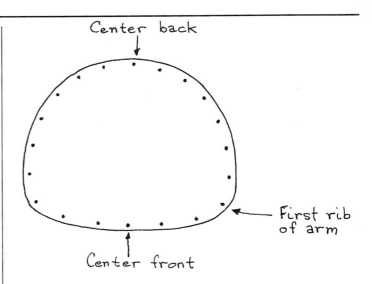

heavy paper as you will be temporarily gluing it to the seat to use as a drilling template. The holes should be no more than ¼ inch apart so the ribs will be close enough together for neat weaving, and as close to the edge as you can drill so the seat will not stick out beyond the weaving. You will need an even number of holes. It is helpful but not absolutely necessary to place the first hole at the center back so you can keep better track of symmetry. Also be sure that a hole falls at each side exactly where you want the arms to end. Draw the holes on only one half of your pattern.

Fold the pattern along the center line to cut it out evenly. While it is still folded, prick through the hole marks with a needle so they can be marked symmetrically on both halves of the pattern. Pencil dots over the prick marks.

Cutting the seat. Trace around your pattern onto ⅛-inch plywood with a fine-line ball-point pen. Even out the edges with a file until the seat is exactly the same as the pattern.

Drilling the seat. Brush rubber cement onto the seat and before it dries press the pattern onto it so it fits exactly. With a 1/16-inch drill bit and the drill mounted on its stand, drill through both pattern and wood at each of the hole markings all the way around the seat. Pull the pattern off the seat when the holes are finished.

Inserting the ribs. Cut No. 1 dry cane with wire snippers into 8-inch pieces. Cut as many pieces as there are holes in the seat. There are 20 holes in this pattern. Insert a piece of cane into each hole, letting 4 inches protrude from the bottom, and 5 inches from the top of the seat. The canes are left dry for insertion because they swell when they are soaked and become too thick to stick through the holes. The ribs at the front of the seat will be cut off, but not until the base is woven.

Soaking the cane. Soak No. 0 cane in warm water in a bowl for 10 minutes. Hold the bottom ribs of the chair in the water too, but try throughout the weaving of the chair to keep the wood seat from getting soaked. A little moisture won't hurt it, but soaking could make the plywood warp and delaminate. Re-soak the chair and the weaving strands, as they become less pliable during work, by hand-holding the chair in the water. Soak more strips of cane as you need them.

Weaving the base. Starting at a side rib, weave a looped piece of cane around and around the base as explained in the chapter on Basketry (page 139). Continue for 6 rounds, flaring the back of the chair base only in the last two rounds. Finish off the base as described in the chapter on Basketry (page 140).

With wire snippers, clip off the ribs that project up through the front of the seat. They can safely be clipped off flush with the seat (but be sure you don't clip off ribs that are needed for weaving the arms—all the ribs except 5 across the front of the seat in these chairs are needed for arms and back).

Weaving the arms and back. Unlike the base, the arms and back of the chair are woven back and forth in rows instead of rounds, with the cane being brought around the rib at the end of each row to reverse direction. Begin the loop of cane at one of the arms. With the chair facing you, you will find that when you work from left to right, you will be working from inside the chair as you did with the basket and the chair base. But when you work from right to left, you will be working from the outside of the chair. The only difference is that (and this happens automatically) you will be using your index finger instead of your thumb to push out a rib while you twist around it. There is one disconcerting aspect of weaving in rows instead of rounds. Because the twist is always clockwise, both arms will be strongly pulled to the left and the shape of the chair will be very distorted. This is taken care of in the final soaking and shaping.

For the low-backed chair, weave 7 rows to achieve the right height for the arms. For the high-backed chair, weave 5 rows to achieve the right height for the arms. Don't flare the ribs out at all yet; the arms will be pulled into a slight flare as you continue shaping the back.

When you have completed the right number of rows to get to the desired arm height, you will begin to shape the curve of the back by decreasing the number of ribs used for weaving each row. Decreasing is done by simply stopping short at the end of a row, leaving one or more ribs unworked, and turning at that point. The following row is then stopped short an equal number of ribs on the opposite side of the chair to keep the shape symmetrical. Flare the back out slightly, but keep the sides vertical. See page 141 for information on how to add new weaving strands if you run out.

In both these chairs, you are starting with 15 ribs around arms and back.

For the low-backed chair:

Rows 8 and 9: Decrease 3 ribs at the end of each row (9 ribs).

Rows 10 and 11: Decrease 1 rib at the end of each row (7 ribs).

Rows 12 and 13: Decrease 1 rib at the end of each row (5 ribs).

Rows 14 and 15: Decrease 1 rib at the end of each row (3 ribs).

When row 15 is completed, snip off the cane ends several inches from the chair.

For the high-backed chair:

Rows 6 and 7: Decrease 1 rib at the end of each row (13 ribs).

Rows 8 and 9: Weave all 13 ribs.

Rows 10 and 11: Decrease 1 rib at the end of each row (11 ribs).

Rows 12 and 13: Weave all 11 ribs.

Rows 14 and 15: Decrease 1 rib at the end of each row (9 ribs).

Rows 16 and 17: Weave all 9 ribs.

Rows 18 and 19: Decrease 1 rib at the end of each row (7 ribs).

Rows 20 and 21: Decrease 1 rib at the end of each row (5 ribs).

Rows 22 and 23: Decrease 1 rib at the end of each row (3 ribs).

When row 23 is completed, snip off the cane ends several inches from the chair.

Weaving the edge. At this point, the arms and back of your chair go upward stepwise instead of in a nice curve. Although those steps will always be there, they are disguised by weaving two more rows from the first rib of one arm all the way around the back and down to the first rib of the other arm.

Start a new loop of cane around one arm and weave two rows, pushing the twists as tight as you can against the previous weaving to achieve a neat curve. When the two rows are completed, clip the ends of the strands off several inches away from the chair.

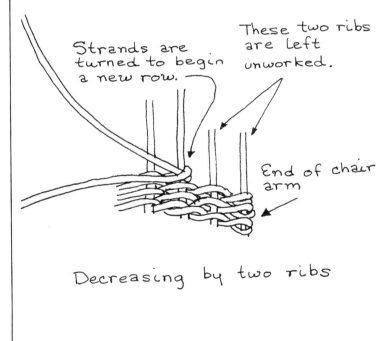

Strands are turned to begin a new row.

These two ribs are left unworked.

End of chair arm

Decreasing by two ribs

Weaving the ribs. Because the ribs of the chair arms and back don't form a round, as with a basket, you can't use the same method of weaving the ribs as you did for the base. Instead, a much easier method is used.

Soak the rib ends well. Starting at the first rib of one arm, bend it over in a loop and stick its end down beside the next rib through three rows of weaving. If you can't stick it down because the space is too tight, insert an awl alongside the rib and push it down through the weaving to make a big enough space. When the rib is inserted through three rows, push the end out toward the back of the chair and pull it taut with the pliers.

Repeat this, working from the arm toward the back with each rib inserted down into the weaving beside its neighbor. Stop when you have gotten to the center rib, and repeat the process, starting at the other arm and working up to the center rib. Now all the ribs are taken care of except that center one. It will be simply snipped off when the chair is dry.

Shaping the chair. At this point your chair will be alarmingly lopsided.

Prepare for the final shaping of the chair by weaving in any strands that have not been taken care of yet. This will include the ends of the strands with which you wove the last two rows—turn them back toward the chair around the first rib and tuck them in. You may also want to bring to the back any ends that now protrude into the inside of the chair. Cut these and all other strand ends 1 inch from the chair so they don't get in your way during shaping.

Soak the entire back of the chair well by holding it in the bowl of warm water. Get out the hair dryer and either set it in a stand if it has one, prop it on a pillow, or enlist the aid of someone who can hold it for you for the next few minutes.

With both your hands, force the arms and back of the chair into the shape you wish and hold them firmly in that position. Direct the hot air from the hair dryer onto the chair, and keep holding the shape while it dries. This takes only a few minutes. Stop holding only when the chair is completely dry. It will keep the shape you gave it without any trouble now. Snip off all the ends of cane close to the work.

Unless you want to try the decorative Turk's head braid around the edge of the seat, the chair is now finished except for a pillow. Several simple pillows will be found on p. 56. Instructions for boxing are on p. 53, and for tufting on p. 54.

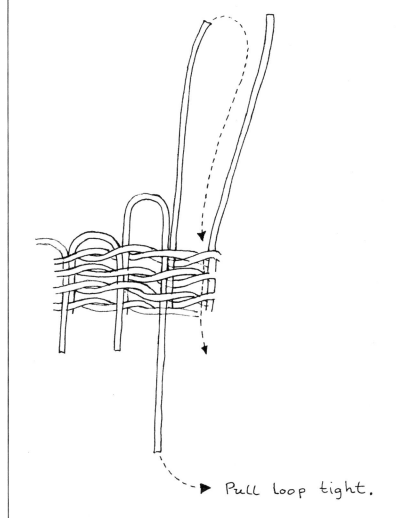

Pull loop tight.

A Turk's Head Braid

If you remember the various woven string bracelets and rings that garnished many schoolchildren several years ago, you are already familiar with the look of a Turk's head knot. Of the many variations, this is the simplest. It is woven over the hand from a single strand. The braid is first made large enough to slip over the base of the chair, and is then tightened in place around the seat edge.

Choose the most supple piece of No. 0 cane you can find. Soak it well. Hold one end of it under your thumb as shown, and wind it so there are three strands over your palm. The braid is formed by pulling one loop over another and weaving the free strand over and under the loops.

Follow the drawings step by step until you get the hang of it. When you have completed 13 weaves, stop. (You can count weaves by following any single strand and counting one weave for each time it crosses another strand.) When you are finished, the 2 ends should be beside each other.

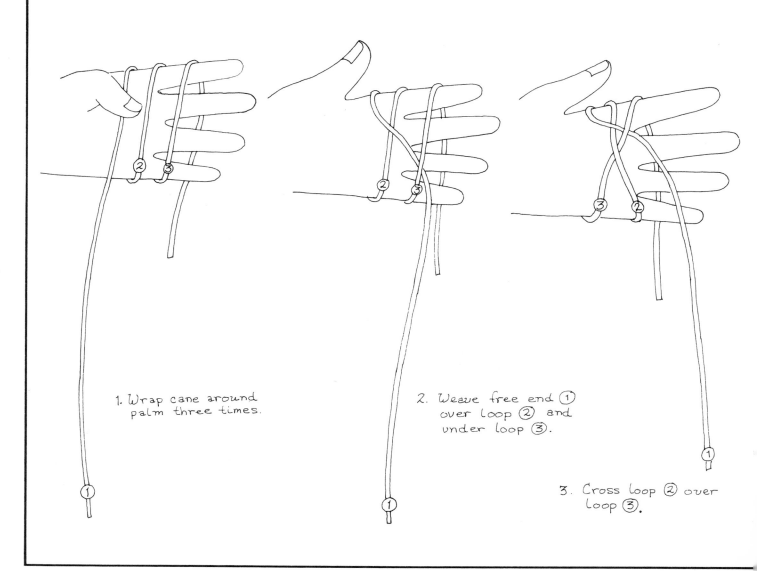

1. Wrap cane around palm three times.

2. Weave free end ① over loop ② and under loop ③.

3. Cross loop ② over loop ③.

Soak the Turk's head well and slip it over the chair into position. The knot is tightened around the seat by pulling out a loop at any point along any strand with an awl, then following that strand around the braid, pulling out a larger loop each time with the awl until you get to one of the 2 ends. The end is then pulled taut, and the process begins again by pulling out another loop anywhere along the braid. The work is slow, but the knot does get tighter each time. Because you have to tug at the loop quite vigorously to make headway, be sure to keep the braid wet by dipping your finger in water and running it along the braid frequently.

When the knot is getting close to finished size, pull it around the seat so the two ends are in the back. When it is tight enough to stay in place along the seat edge, clip the ends to 2 inches, insert them into the weaving of the chair, and snip them off close.

Five steps in making Turk's head.
1. Wrap cane around palm three times.
2. Weave free end 1 over loop 2 and under loop 3.
3. Cross loop 2 over loop 3.
4. Weave 1 over loop 2 and under loop 3 again.
5. Cross loop 3 over loop 2. Continue the braid by repeating steps 2–5.

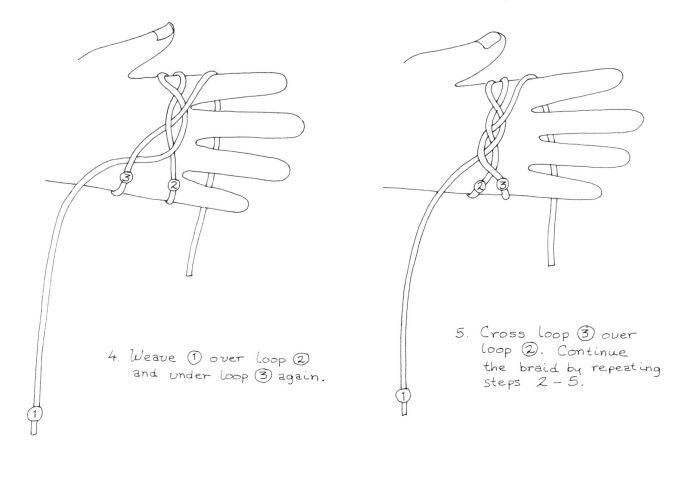

4. Weave ① over loop ② and under loop ③ again.

5. Cross loop ③ over loop ②. Continue the braid by repeating steps 2 – 5.

❧ Mops, Brooms, and Carpet Beaters ❧

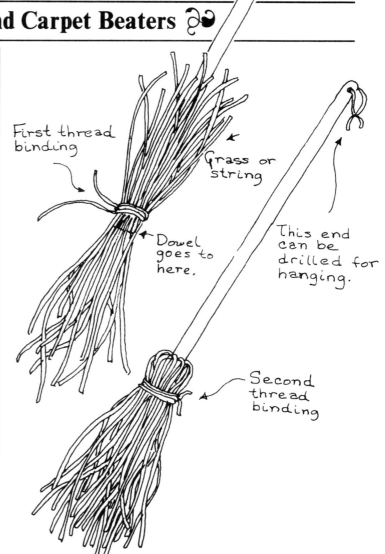

First thread binding

Grass or string

Dowel goes to here.

This end can be drilled for hanging.

Second thread binding

Handles for mops and brooms can be cut from ⅛-inch dowel, available at lumber-yards and sometimes at hobby shops. Five inches is a good length. For the head of a mop, use white crochet cotton from a yarn shop or thin, soft cotton string from a hardware store. For the head of a broom, use grass. There are so many dozens of grasses that you will have to experiment with your own local varieties to see which remain strong and somewhat pliant when fully dried. The broom opposite is made of what we call poverty grass. Pick it green, but not tender (that is, wait until July). Spread the grass on paper towels to dry until it is withered but not brittle.

To make either mop or broom, hold the strands in a bundle around the handle and bind them with thread around their middles ¼ inch from the bottom of the dowel. White glue is spread below the binding to insure that the strands won't pull out. When the glue is dry, bend the top portions of the strands down over the binding, and bind around the outside of the bundle as shown. Trim the bottoms even.

The wicker carpet beater here is made from a single strand of No. 0 cane. Soak the cane, then form the knot as shown, first in its single form, then doubling it by weaving one end of the cane in and out of the knot alongside the first loops.

Bind with thread below the knot, rub white glue over the binding to secure it, then clip off the free ends of the cane. Bind again at the end of the handle to form a loop for hanging.

Variations of this knot, from *The Ashley Book of Knots,* can be used to form wonderful doormats from string. An example can be seen in the photo on page 21.

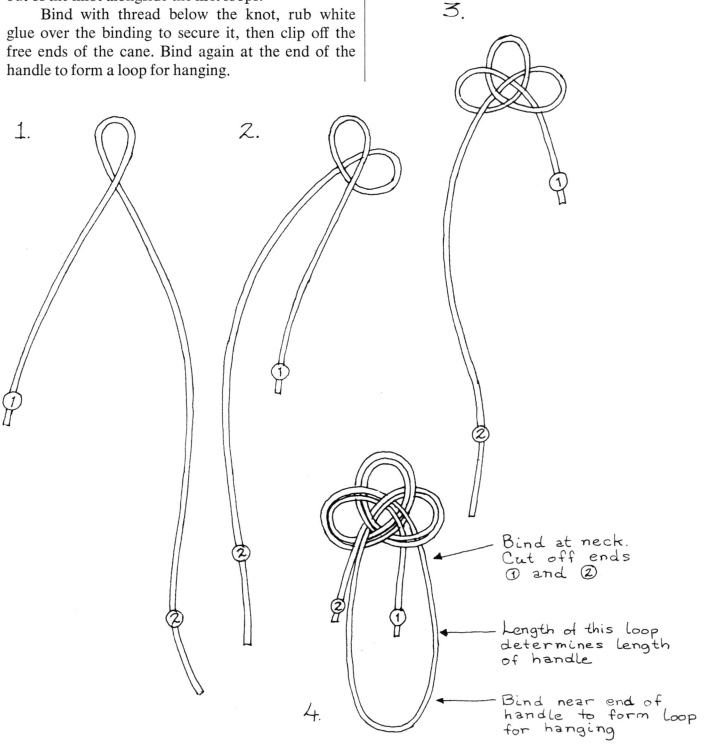

3.

1.

2.

4.

Bind at neck.
Cut off ends
① and ②

Length of this loop
determines length
of handle

Bind near end of
handle to form loop
for hanging

❦ Hangers ❧

These wood and wire hangers were used to hang all the doll's clothes in the photograph on page 26. Use the pattern here to mark and cut pieces of ¼-inch wood to the right shape. Smooth and correct the curves with fine sandpaper. Cut a 2-inch length of 16-gauge brass wire (available at hardware stores). Bend the question-mark-shaped hook with needle-nosed pliers at one end. Put the wood hanger in a vise and drill through the center portion from top to bottom with a 1/16-inch bit. Push the straight end of the wire down through the hole. Snip the wire off flush with the bottom of the hanger at the length you wish. Then push the wire through farther, lay the straight end of it on the edge of the vise, and pound it flat with a small hammer. Now pull on the hook end until the flattened end of the wire is firmly embedded inside the hanger. Paint or stain to finish (pages 186–189).

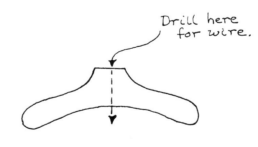

Drill here for wire.

❧ Clothespin Dolls ❧

Clothespin dolls are hard to make by whittling but easy to make with an electric rotary shaping tool. I use the Dremel Moto-Tool. The doll on the right was made by my ten-year-old son, Aram. Judging from the hairline, it is a self-portrait. He used both the Moto-Tool and a utility knife without injury but after careful instruction and demonstration. Once he saw how to use the vise and the tools and had watched the whole sequence by which a doll is made, he made his own doll without any help at all. He did discard a few malformed arms and swore somewhat during the painting. He deviated from my sample by sculpting a neat little behind for his "bad boy" figure. Feel free to deviate too. Bodies can be curvaceous, legs can have knees. And pieces can be added: the topknot on the tallest doll here was shaped from the top of another clothespin and glued in place.

Materials

One-piece hardwood clothespins
White glue
Fine sandpaper
Tempera or acrylic paints
Low-luster varnish (for tempera paints only)
⅜-inch brads (for movable limbs only)

Tools

Wire snippers
Vise
Coping saw
Electric rotary shaping tool or whittling knife
Shaping tool accessories: teardrop-shaped steel cutter, fine sanding disk, 1/32-inch drill bit (for movable limbs only)
Utility knife
Small files: flat and half round
Artist's sable brushes, Nos. 1 or 2, and No. 0
Hammer (for movable limbs only)

The Dremel Moto-Tool

Owning this tool and a selection of accessories will free you to make all sorts of objects that would be tedious or perhaps impossible with manual tools. The machine is basically a high-speed drill (30,000 rotations per minute). Drill bits, down to 1/32 inch in diameter, are available, as is a drill stand that allows you to make perfectly vertical holes. Sanding disks replace most hand-sanding and filing. Steel cutters replace whittling to shape even hard woods, or to incise details such as eyes and mouths. The Dremel Moto-Tool is carried by many hardware and hobby stores. The accessories shown here are the ones used to make these clothespin dolls.

CAUTION: Always hold the piece you are working on in a vise when using electric cutting tools. One slip while hand-holding could mean a chunk out of your own flesh. Use a very light touch, brushing against the surface of the wood rather than digging into it.

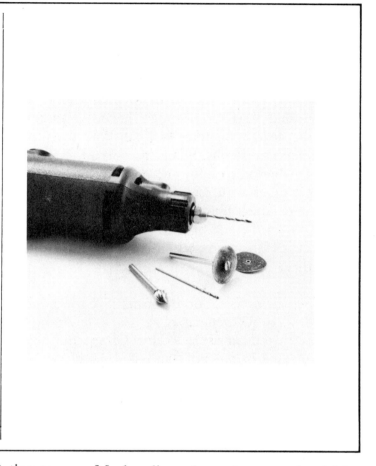

Step by Step

Choosing the clothespin. Choose a clothespin that has no splits, splintery areas, or holes. Paint will cover light-colored better than dark-colored wood. Some clothespins may be too flat-headed to shape well. Snip the wire band off with wire snippers.

Marking and cutting arms and legs. Mark the height of your doll with a pencil line where you wish the feet to end. Holding the clothespin horizontally in a vise, cut off the pieces along your marks with a coping saw. The extra pieces will be the arms. Hold these pieces along the body; move them up and down until the thinner "hand" ends look in the right position to you. Mark a line where the arms should be cut off at the shoulder. Don't cut them yet, though, as they would become too small to work with easily.

Rough-shaping the pieces. To shape with a Moto-Tool, hold the body horizontally in a vise. Cushion the doll in a scrap of cloth to keep the vise from denting it. Attach the steel cutter No. 121 to your tool. Shape the front of the legs and feet as shown in the photo. Then turn the body and shape the backs of the legs. Hold each arm vertically in the vise, hand end up. Shape as shown in the photo, cutting below your shoulder mark so it will be easier to saw the excess off later. When both arms are shaped, put them into the vise horizontally together, flat sides touching and hands even with each other. Cut across the shoulder mark with a coping saw. The shoulders will be squarish and too thick. Whittle them to a thinner, rounded contour with a pocketknife or a utility knife.

All rough-shaping could also be done by whittling. It is slow work, though, because clothespins are made of hard birch.

Smoothing the pieces. Insert the sanding disk accessory on your Moto-Tool. Round and smooth the contours that have been rough-shaped; round the top of the head a bit too. You can hold the pieces in your hand to do this. Stand the doll up. If it falls, flatten the bottoms of the feet or make them even with each other with the sanding disk. A hand file will smooth areas that are hard to get at with the Moto-Tool, or it could be used for the whole smoothing process. Finish smoothing by hand, using fine sandpaper.

Attaching the arms. Glue the arms in position with white glue. Hold them in place for a few minutes before setting them aside to dry. Or see the boxed section on making movable limbs if you prefer.

Painting the doll. Use a hard (No. 3) pencil to draw face and clothing. The hard lead leaves a light line that the paint will cover easily. Use the best-quality sable artist's brush for the painting. Size No. 1 or 2 is good for solid areas, size No. 0 for details and lines.

Paint either with acrylic paints, which are waterproof when dry, or tempera paints, which must be coated with varnish to waterproof. Acrylic paints are more garish in color, less opaque, and more difficult to paint fine lines with than tempera paints. The best tempera paint for this work is called gouache, a velvety high-quality tempera that comes in tubes. Paint all solid areas first, then paint details. When gouache is dry, brush on two coats of low-luster varnish, allowing it to dry between coats. The varnish will slightly darken and brighten the colors.

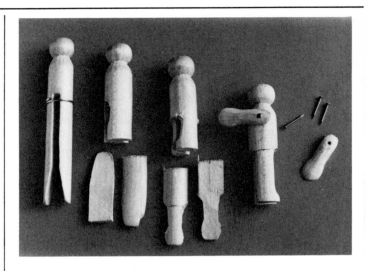

Forming the doll. A clothespin without splits or rough spots is chosen. The wire is snipped off, the length of the legs is marked, and the pieces are cut; the legs and arms are roughly shaped. Then the arms are cut to the right length, and all pieces are smoothed by whittling, filing, and sanding. Here the arms have been drilled to make them movable; one arm has been nailed in place.

Movable Limbs

To make movable limbs, shape the doll as shown here. The arms are the same as the glued version, but the trunk of the doll is shaped to receive separate legs. Both arms and legs can still be gotten out of the clothespin bottom.

The limbs are held in place with small nails called brads. Drill through the tops of the arms and legs, using a 1/32-inch bit. The hole will be slightly larger than the brad, so the limbs will swing freely. Hold each limb in place on the body and mark its position by pressing a brad through the hole to make a dent in the body. Pencil a dot in the dent so you can see it better.

Drill into the body ⅛ inch at each pencil dot to make just enough of a hole to start the nail into it. Push ⅜-inch brads through the holes in the limbs, into the holes in the body. Then hammer them the rest of the way in. If you can't obtain ⅜-inch brads, cut longer ones down with wire snippers.

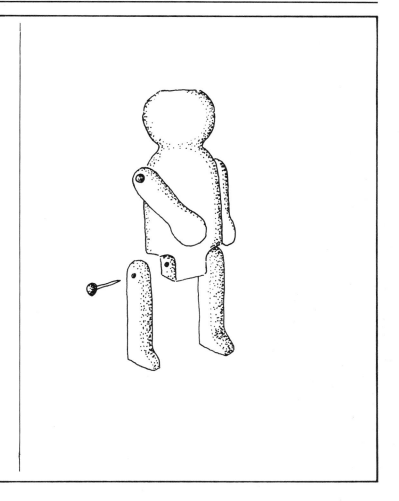

❧ Whittled Rocking Horse ❧

C hips flying . . ." begins the description of the genuine whittler at work. "Chunks splintering . . ." begins my description of me. Whittling is not as easy as it looks. And this example is not even proper whittling. Each craft has its own integrity. The genuine whittler starts with a solid block of wood, using only his blade to shape the figure. Neither saw, file, nor sandpaper ever touches his work. I cheated on this horse from beginning to end. The over-all shape was sawed. File and sandpaper smoothed the chunked and splintered places. Only on flanks and shoulders, where the whittling came out semiprofessional, are the original cuts exposed to view.

Sources

Whittling instruction: *Let's Whittle*. Ben. W. Hunt. Milwaukee, Wis.: Bruce Publishing Company, 1962.

Whittling design ideas: *Wood Carvings: North American Folk Sculptures*. Marian and Charles Klamkin. New York: Hawthorn Books, 1974.

Opposite: A bit doggy in face, and more plow-than-pleasure-horse, this figure still has charm.

Materials

White pine or other wood
Lohite or carpenter's glue for combining two blocks
    of wood if you need extra thickness
Finish: varnish, stain, or oil paints; solvent
Fine sandpaper
Crochet cotton

Tools

Whittling knife and hone or hobbyist's slim blade
    knife handle and blades
Hand or electric drill
Coping saw, hobbyist's saw, or electric scroll saw
File
Paintbrushes: any small brush for varnish, artist's
    round sable brushes Nos. 2 and 0 for oil paints
C-clamps for gluing two blocks of wood together

Step by Step

Designing the piece. Often the designs of people who "can't draw" are livelier and more charming than the expert's work. But if you won't give freehand drawing a try, look in the suggested books for figures that appeal to you. Draw the piece in profile, to actual size, on stiff paper. If you are tracing a profile from a book, and it is not the right size, see page 78 for photostating to reduce or enlarge your tracing. Or follow the instructions here.

With scissors cut your design out to use as a pattern. To draw the rockers on this rocking horse, set a compass to a radius of 2¾ inches, or trace the bottom line of the rocker around a bowl or plate that is about 5½ inches in diameter.

Choosing the wood. Clear white pine, sold as shelving, is a good soft wood for whittling. Mahogany is excellent, too, but must be obtained from a sculpture supply house rather than a lumberyard. Shelving is ¾ inch thick, or sometimes 1 inch (called five/quarter stock at lumberyards). If your piece is to be thicker than the available lumber, glue two pieces together with white glue or carpenter's glue. Clamp

with C-clamps at each corner for several hours or overnight before proceeding. The glue bond will not be visible in the finished piece and will not interfere with cutting.

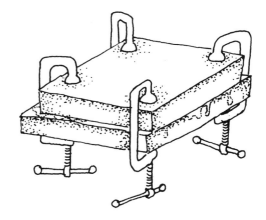

Tracing the pattern onto the wood. Place the cutout pattern on the wood in the position you think it should go. Now check the direction of the grain of the wood. If the grain cuts across narrow areas of your design, those parts can break off easily. Turn your pattern and see if you can find a position that will give the most strength in the most vulnerable spots. No matter which way you choose, there will be some fragile area of your figure. This horse's ears could easily break.

Sawing the shape. Cut around the outline with a saw. You can use a hand coping saw, holding the wood in a vise, but it is difficult to keep the cut from slanting inward or outward on so thick a piece of wood. An electric scroll saw or a hobbyist's saw, either of which automatically cuts a true vertical, makes the job easy.

To cut interior spaces, drill a hole larger than the saw blade. Insert the saw blade into the hole, re-attach it to the saw, and cut around the perimeter of the inside space. In the rocking horse there was not only the space between the belly and the rockers that had to be cut out, but also the space that separated the right- and left-hand legs and rockers from one another. This sort of cut cannot be made at this point. It would weaken the wood of both legs

A right and wrong way to lay out horse in relation to the grain of wood.

1. Wrong way to lay out this horse. The rockers, among the thinnest portions of the design, would break off too easily.

2. Right way to lay out this horse. There are still vulnerable parts, such as the ears, but it is a better solution.

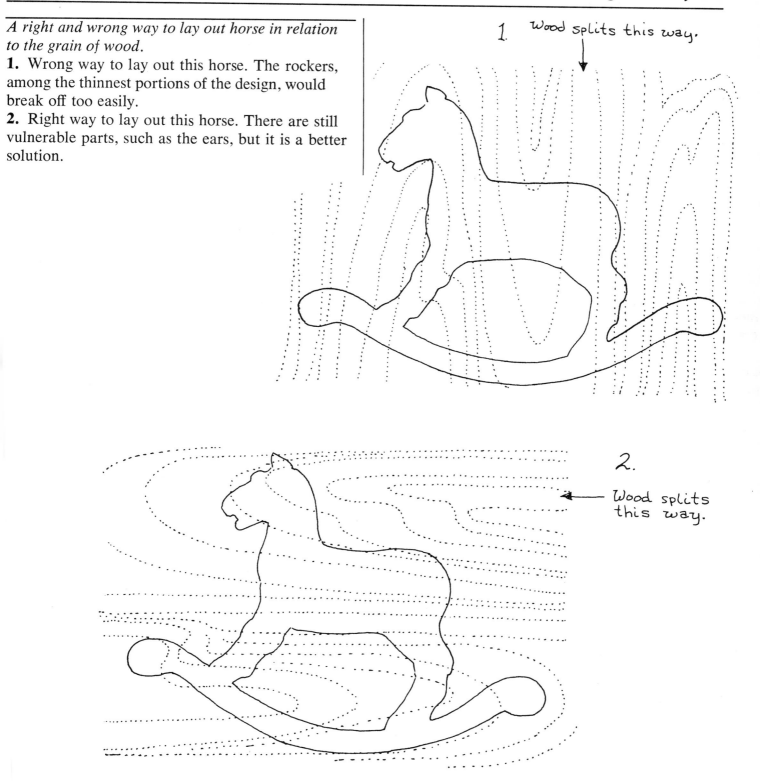

1. Wood splits this way.

2. Wood splits this way.

and rockers. The cut was made after all the whittling on the rest of the horse was nearly finished. The cut was done by holding the horse upside down in a vise and cutting by hand with a coping saw. Awkward cuts like this are dangerous, if not impossible, to do with an electric saw.

Whittling. Whittling is the art of understanding the grain of wood. Books on the subject go into detail about the ways in which the piece is held, the angle of the knife, and the types of cut. Experience teaches as well, and most mistakes will be made while the piece is still large enough so that they are not disasters. The biggest lesson is that the easiest cut— flaking along the direction of the grain—is the one cut *not* to make. The wood just keeps splitting away like a piece of kindling, coming away in large chunks where you don't intend it to. All cuts should be against or diagonal to the grain.

The first cuts, when there is still plenty of wood to remove, can be large. The closer the piece is to finished the smaller the cuts should become. At the end, each cut removes only a tiny flake of wood. Typically, a cut should result in a short curved, almost scooped-out chip.

As you get used to the work you will find that sometimes you make cuts toward your thumb, as in peeling an apple, and sometimes away from your body, as in scraping a carrot. Whenever the cuts fail to come away cleanly, change your blade or sharpen it. A dull blade chips the wood instead of slicing it. A half hour or less of whittling will dull a blade.

As you whittle off your pattern lines, replace them with new pencil marks so you don't lose the shape of your piece. As necessary, pencil on details such as ears, eyes, or other protrusions so you don't whittle away needed wood.

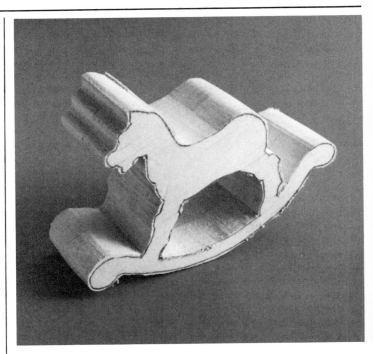

The rocking horse sawed along the outline and in the interior space between belly and rockers. It is now ready for whittling.

Finishing the figure. Use a small, flat file to get rid of traces of bad whittling. Sand with fine sandpaper areas you wish to be really smooth. Your piece has to be treated with some surface covering so it will not become soiled. Choices are paint, varnish, or oil stain followed by varnish, shellac, or wax. Follow directions on the container for all the usual wood finishes. I preferred oil paints for finishing the rocking horse because white pine is not a particularly handsome wood. Page 124 has tips on painting three-dimensional figures in artist's oils.

The horse's tail. The tail of this rocking horse is made of crochet cotton.

Cut a dozen or so 3-inch strands and hold them in a bunch to get an idea of whether or not the tail will be the right thickness. Add or subtract strands from the bunch until it looks right to you.

Working over waxed paper, dip the end of the bunch of strands in white glue and bind them with thread around and around very tightly while still wet for a distance of ¼ inch; allow to dry. Trim the strands at the rump end of the tail. Measure the thickness where the thread is bound. With the horse in a vise, drill a hole in the rump slightly wider than the tail thickness and ¼ inch deep. Pay attention to the angle: the angle of the hole determines the angle at which the tail will stick out from the rump. Squeeze a drop of glue into the hole and insert the tail. When the glue is dry, trim the tail to the desired length.

The mane is made in a similar manner from smaller bunches glued into a row of holes ⅛ inch apart from the forehead to the base of the neck.

Making the horse's tail.
1. Dip the end of a bunch of crochet cotton strands into white glue.
2. While they are still wet, bind the strands tightly around with thread for a distance of ¼ inch.
3. Put a drop of glue into the hole in the horse's rump; insert the tail. When the glue is dry, trim the tail to the desired length.

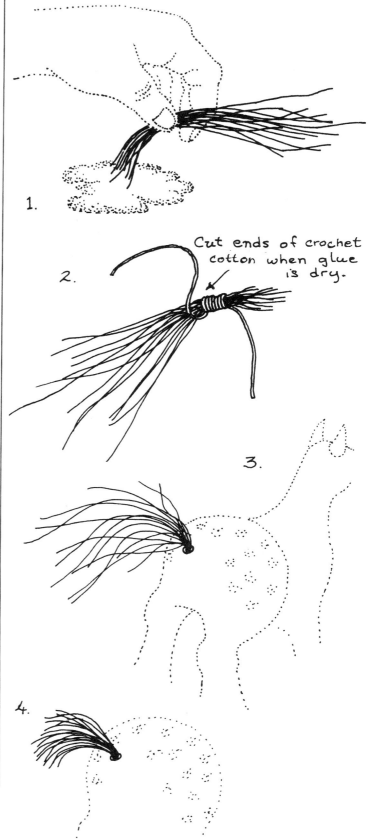

1.

2.

Cut ends of crochet cotton when glue is dry.

3.

4.

Whittling for Children

My husband, prevented in his youth from bearing toy arms, learned to whittle astonishingly realistic guns by the age of eleven. My children can manage wooden paddles. Assuming they better represent the average, I suggest you suggest wooden paddles, spoons, rolling pins. They can all be whittled from lengths of ⅜-inch dowel. The piece should be long enough to hold securely.

Resist the temptation to play safe with a dull blade. Because of the force a child has to use to push a dull blade through the wood, he's likely to get a worse cut than he would with a sharp blade.

All these shapes can be worked by holding the piece against the body and pushing the knife *away*. Only after some experience should a child try other, riskier whittling strokes.

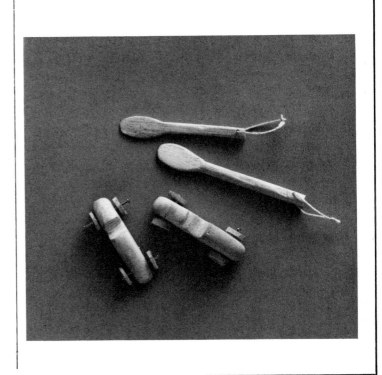

A Note on Knives

Pocketknives can be used for whittling if the blade is a high-quality steel but soft enough to hone to a much sharper edge than such knives usually have. One brand to try is a Buck Knife. The blade of any pocketknife has to be honed on a fine stone every few minutes.

A hobbyist's knife, sometimes called a slim blade knife, is an excellent tool. It is used with interchangeable razor-sharp blades. X-Acto and Stanley are two brands widely available. Buy the thick, not the thin, handle. The most useful blade is a rounded one, but there are other shapes to try. Buy plenty of blades as you will be changing them often.

Buy adhesive bandages too. I cut myself four times on this one rocking horse.

Enlarging and reducing. The photograph from which this pig was copied happens to be about 5 inches across. What if you don't want a 5-inch pig, but would prefer an 11-inch one or a 3-inch one? This grid method will help you enlarge or reduce a drawing to any size you want.

Before you begin Step 1 below, the original drawing must be superimposed on a grid pattern. It could be traced onto graph paper, as this one is, or you could draw a grid over it. The grid can be made up of 1-inch squares, ½-inch squares, or any dimension that divides your drawing into segments simple enough for you to copy later onto a smaller or larger grid.

Number the finished grid like a graph, beginning with zero. This drawing is 5 squares wide. It doesn't matter how many inches it is.

Now decide how big or small you want the drawing to become. Your decision does not have to be in inches, either. Make two marks on a piece of paper to represent how wide you want the enlargement or reduction to be. The decision here was to reduce the 5-inch pig to about 3 inches.

Step 1 on page 166 begins at this point, with a vertical line drawn through each of your two marks. Follow the steps carefully, using a triangle and a ruler. The triangle will give you true verticals, horizontals, and diagonals if you place it carefully in the positions shown for each step. The ruler is not used for measuring, but only to divide up the space between those first two lines into the same number of squares as your original grid. In this case, the number of squares across is 5, but you could use the same method to divide any space into any number of equal parts—all without measuring.

When you have finished the six steps shown here, you will have a grid of exactly the same number of squares as that on your original drawing. The squares will simply be larger or smaller than the original.

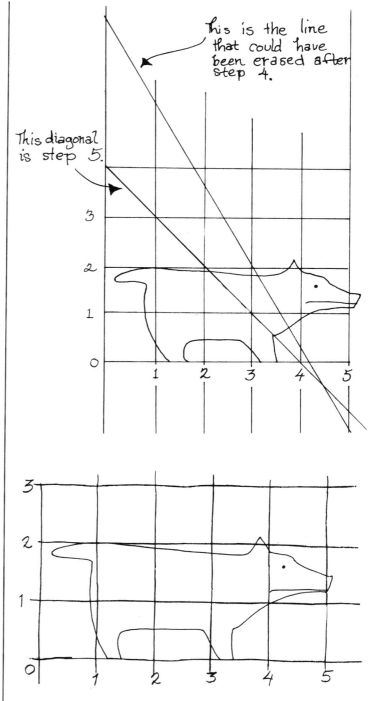

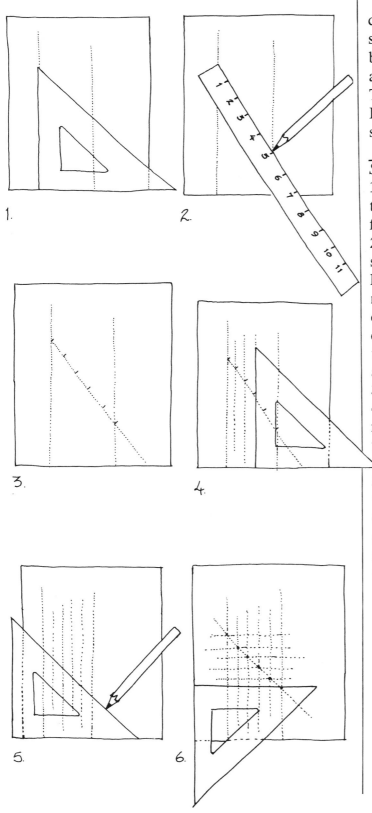

1.

2.

3.

4.

5.

6.

Now copy your drawing onto the new grid, doing one segment at a time, each in its proper square. Check your position by looking at the numbers so you don't get lost in the grid. Use a pencil, as you will need to correct your work as you go. This pig was my first attempt at the grid method, and I was pleased with the results. I did, of course, play safe with a simple shape.

Six steps in enlarging or reducing a drawing.
1. Draw two parallel lines. The distance between them should be about the width you want your finished drawing to be.
2. Place a ruler diagonally between the two lines so that the beginning of the ruler falls on the first line, and the numeral 5 (or 11, or 6, or however many squares there are across the grid on your original drawing) falls on the second line. It doesn't matter what angle the ruler is at. Draw the diagonal and make marks at 1-inch intervals along it.
3. This is what your drawing looks like so far.
4. Draw a vertical line at each of the marks you made on the diagonal. When you are finished with this step, erase the diagonal so you don't get confused at the next step.
5. Draw a true 45-degree diagonal across all your vertical lines.
6. Draw horizontal lines at each point where the diagonal intersects a vertical line. Number the resulting grid the same way you numbered the original one.

❦ Cigar Box Furniture ❧

This cigar-box method is not for those who wish perfect reproduction furniture. Because of their thick wood and boxy construction, the pieces cannot be copied from actual furniture. With its chunky knobs, oversize drawers, bulbous curves, and wild paint job, this chest is a caricature put together out of some fictional image built from dozens of actual Victorian chests. Yet something about caricature makes it realer than real. When you put this silly chest in a room next to correct scale reproductions, it is the reproductions that look wrong. The chest is invigorated by exaggeration. It is inviting. It is made to be played with.

And when that cigar-flavored cedar aroma emanates from the chest, it wins my heart. Other woods can certainly be used without changing design or building techniques, but they will never smell so good.

Wood

Much miniature furniture is made with bass wood, which is soft and easy to work as well as thin enough to be in proper scale. Bass wood is sold in hobby or model stores and by mail from miniature supply houses. Bass wood is not used in our dollhouse because I don't like it. Bass furniture has no heft; it is featherweight and smashable.

The best miniature furniture is made with such hard woods as maple and birch or softer woods like pine. Stock lumber must first be sliced to ⅛ inch or thinner by ripping with professional power saws or by power planing. Mills and model makers are equipped for this sort of work, but it is beyond the scope of the casual hobbyist. I have seen commercial dollhouse furniture made from very thin, apparently hardwood plywoods. I have not been able to find a source of supply.

The thicker woods I use are widely available. They are also easy to work, of a texture to take a good finish, yet sufficiently heavy and strong to withstand children's play. My favorite source, the cigar box, is still obtainable from smoking shops, and older ones can also be found in junk stores and thrift shops. The wood they are made of is cedar ¼ inch or 3/16 inch thick. Occasionally tops and bottoms of such boxes are made of thin plywood, which is useful for drawer bottoms and tabletops, where thicker stock might be too clumsy.

I also use a 3/16-inch white wood (poplar) veneer plywood. It is not sold in sheets, but is available in the form of decorative valance boards in lumberyards. The light-colored fine-grained veneer does not splinter like similarly thin mahogany veneered plywoods, and it takes a good finish. The valance comes in 8-foot lengths, in various patterns, and widths of between 4 and 9 inches. Select pieces for smoothness and lack of defects on both surfaces. A single board will last you a long time.

Clear pine lattice boards used as trim come as thin as ¼ inch and in board widths as wide as 2⅝ inches. This stock is nice to work with and can be bought in convenient 8-foot lengths.

If it becomes absolutely necessary to use ⅛-inch-thick wood, thin plywood is widely available, though the splintery surface of the veneer is annoying. The other frustrating fact is that, like all plywoods, minimum quantity is a 4-✕-8-foot sheet.

The Basics—Furniture Patterns

The method used to make cigar box furniture involves no measurements and few pattern pieces. The pattern pieces are derived directly from accurate profile, full, and top views of your design. There may be almost no difference between the design stage and the making of patterns. Those who can sketch in

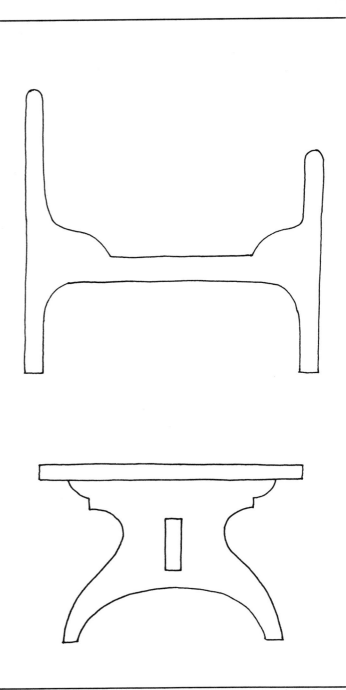

All these pieces have straight sides except for the cradle with slanted sides, *overleaf*. A rasp or file is used to bevel edges in slanted furniture.

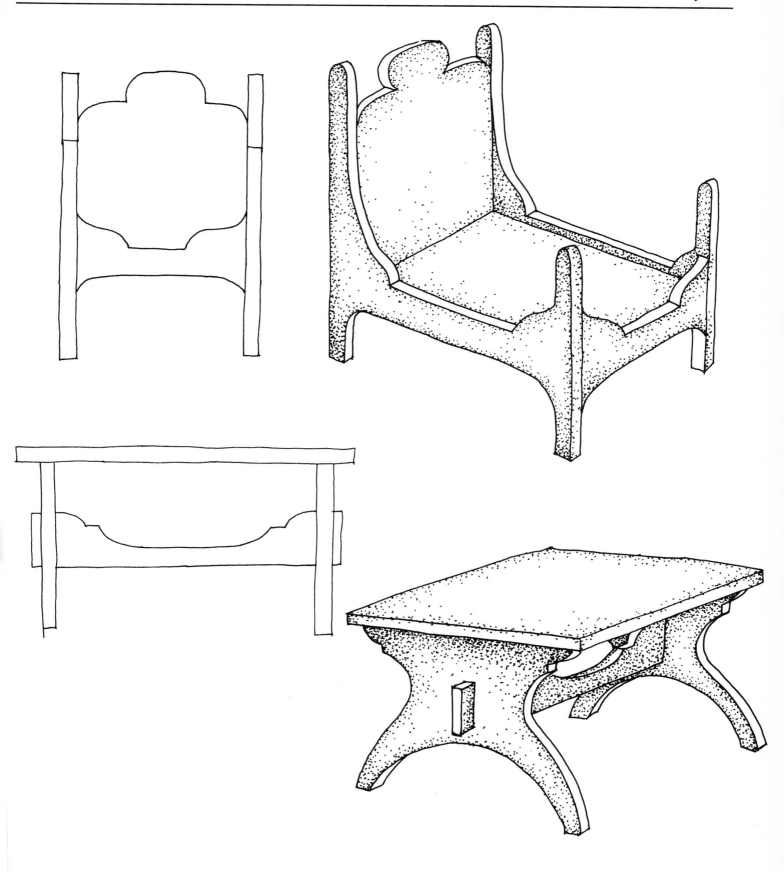

perspective may, of course, fool around on paper to arrive at a design, and then get down to the more formal work of making patterns. But I design in profile, full view, and top view, instead of in perspective (the perspectives are shown here only to help the reader visualize the finished piece). The drawings are at first inaccurate, but then, by following the method below, they are brought from vague to crisp and true and finally to actual pattern pieces.

Use a good quality Bristol drawing paper for all your work so that what starts as sketches can evolve into cutout pattern pieces heavy enough to trace around. Use a pencil so you can erase. As soon as you are beyond the sketch stage, always use a triangle to keep the sides parallel and the corners square (page 166). A French curve, available at art stores, will help you to get smooth curves. Keep at hand a small sample of the wood you will be using, as a guide to edge thickness in your drawing.

These stools and chest were made by a child for his frogs, Turk and Isabella, when he was twelve years old. A stool is the best first project for a child. The one here is composed of only three pieces: two sides, with a top glued across them.

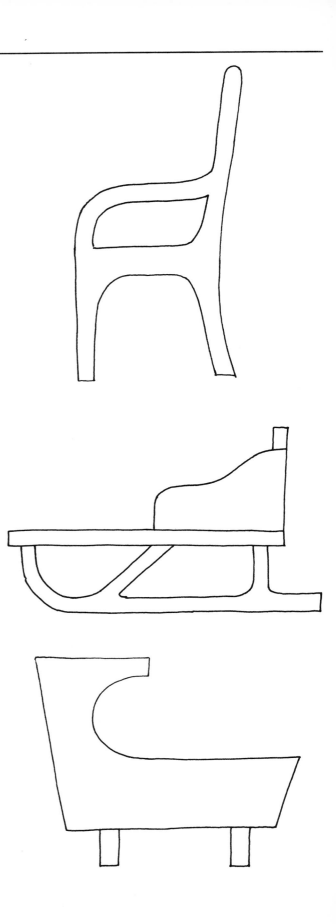

The profile view. Draw a profile, in the actual size you want, of the piece of furniture you have in mind. If you have difficulty picturing a piece of furniture in profile, practice by squatting down and viewing your own household furniture from the side. Chairs are particularly enlightening, and a good beginning project anyway. Another resource might be children's book illustration, particularly where the furniture is of the style of "Goldilocks and the Three Bears." Painted Mexican dollhouse furniture also uses strong profiles.

When your sketch pleases you, use a sharp pencil, a triangle, and possibly a French curve to clarify your lines and correct them so they are true. Erase the fuzzier original lines as you go along. Where a portion of your profile actually represents a separate piece of wood seen on edge, as for instance the top of this stool, use an actual piece of wood to determine the thickness your drawing should represent.

Cut the profile out carefully with sharp scissors. All or most of it will become a pattern piece. See the last step for how to cut out a symmetrical piece so it is even. If you are unsure of the size of your design, hold the profile up in the dollhouse to check the proportion. Now is the time to redraw and recut the profile if it is too large or too small.

The full view. The full view of your design can be from the front, as the table; from the rear, as the sled; or encompass a view of both the head and foot of a piece, as the bed. On a new sheet of paper, tape the profile down with its bottom edge against the bottom edge of the paper. This will automatically make its sides parallel to the side of the paper.

Draw a line parallel to the bottom edge of the paper to indicate the height of the profile. This line automatically indicates the height of the full view as well. Add other parallel lines to indicate where critical horizontal pieces, such as chest tops and chair seats, will abut. Use the wood scrap to gauge thickness. Using the height line as a guide, sketch in the full view of your design. Experiment with the

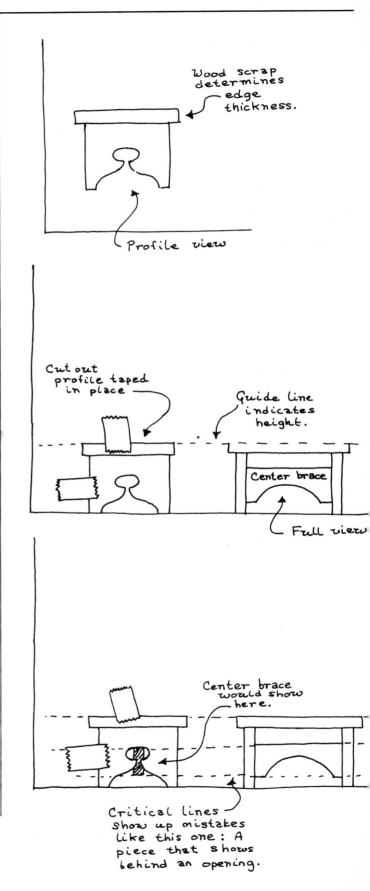

Wood scrap determines edge thickness.

Profile view

Cut out profile taped in place

Guide line indicates height.

Center brace

Full view

Center brace would show here.

Critical lines show up mistakes like this one: A piece that shows behind an opening.

number of drawers, with the difference in height between head and foot boards or with various slat designs for chair backs. As you sketch, check that you have not drawn something that fails to correspond to the profile. For instance, that you have not designed a drawer front that drops below the skirt line on the side of the chest, a mistake similar to the one in the illustration. Parallel lines at critical points as shown will help you to keep your full view in correspondence to your profile view.

When you are satisfied with the full view, clarify your lines as you did with the profile, and again, cut the view out carefully.

Do you need another view? Study the various designs shown here to decide whether or not the piece you are designing needs another view. The table does not require a third view unless its top is to be other than rectangular in shape. Similarly, no top view of the chair is necessary since the front view defines the width of the seat and the side view defines the depth of the seat. The sled, however, requires a third view. Neither the profile nor the full view of the back indicates the shape of the sled surface. Only a top view will provide the necessary pattern piece.

The top view. You will use both your cutout profile and your cutout full view as a reference for the top view. On a new sheet of paper, tape the profile down with its bottom edge along the *side* of the paper, near the center. Draw the cutout full view along the bottom of the paper, also near the center. Draw two horizontal lines and two vertical lines to indicate the general rectangular area within which the top will fall. Remember that furniture tops may project beyond the sides of the piece. If this is the case with your design, the top view will extend beyond your lines. If not, the top view will be drawn within the four lines. Proceed through the sketch stage to a finished accurate drawing, and cut out this view as you did the others.

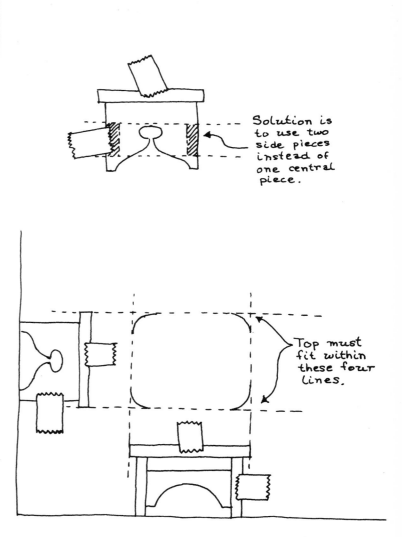

Solution is to use two side pieces instead of one central piece.

Top must fit within these four lines.

Which parts are the pattern pieces? Study the samples again. Only some portions of each view will become pattern pieces. In the chair the whole profile view is one pattern piece, but only the shaded portion of the full view is the second pattern piece. For a piece like the bed, the full view will have to be copied to get separate pattern pieces for both the headboard and footboard. Each pattern piece can be cut from your finished drawing with sharp scissors. All other pieces will be made as the furniture is assembled. But there are two steps to accomplish first.

Making a reference sketch. Since you will be cutting up your drawings, you may want to trace first onto a thinner paper each of the views for reference later. Assembling pieces of wood can be confusing without a drawing to jog your memory.

Making reference lines. Untape all your views from the pad. Lay them alongside one another and check to see where one piece of wood will abut another. Draw dotted lines to indicate these positions, using the scrap of wood as a guide to thickness. Later, identical lines will be transferred onto the cutout pieces of wood and will help you know exactly where to glue each piece. (Don't panic if this phase confuses you and you just can't figure it out. If worse comes to worst, you can put the guidelines onto the wood after the first pieces are glued together and you can better see what you are doing.)

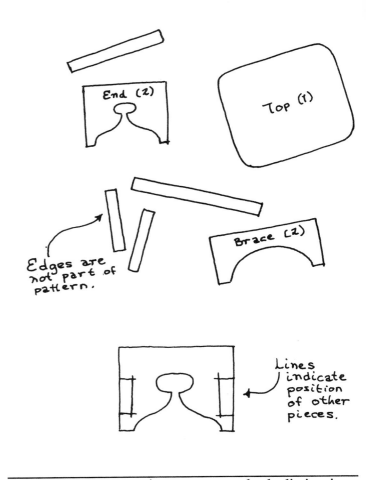

Since some pattern pieces may not look distinctive once the edges are cut off, it's a good idea to label them and to indicate how many of each piece to trace and cut.

Cutting out the patterns. Simply cut out nonsymmetrical portions of a pattern freehand. If a piece is symmetrical from one side to the other, such as the skirt of a chest of drawers, or the back of a chair, fold your drawing exactly in half, choose the side you feel you have drawn most pleasingly, and cut the folded paper through both layers along these lines. If the piece is symmetrical both from side to side and from top to bottom, as an oval mirror or a round-cornered tabletop, fold the drawing into quarters, choose the most pleasing portion, and cut through all four layers of paper along those lines. If a folded pattern won't lie flat after cutting, press with a warm iron before using.

You are now ready to make your piece of furniture.

Sandpaper Patterns

If you are going to be making many of one piece—a set of chairs, for instance—it is worthwhile to make your pattern pieces from sandpaper instead of drawing paper. Sandpaper patterns, when placed face down on the wood, do not slip as you trace around them. Use very fine sandpaper and draw the pattern on the back. Don't use your best scissors to cut the patterns out, as the gritty surface eventually damages scissor blades. If these patterns are to be used for any period of time, label each pattern piece with the name of the piece of furniture and the part represented.

Materials
Wood, 1/4 inch or 3/16 inch thick
White glue or carpenter's glue
Fine sandpaper

Tools
Hand coping saw or power scroll saw
Vise
Half round and triangular jeweler's files (from hardware store)
Wood rasp
Pencil
Furniture pattern pieces

Step by Step

Tracing pattern pieces onto wood. Lay each pattern piece in turn on the wood you are using, orienting it to get the most strength from the direction of the wood grain (see page 161). Trace around the outline with a very sharp pencil. Repeat for pieces you will need two of, reversing the pattern to its mirror image by turning it over if there is a "good" and a "bad" side to the wood.

Cutting the traced pieces. Whether you are using an electric or a handsaw, cut slowly, just to the outside of the line. Extra wood can always be filed off; more wood can't be added. Handsawing must be done in a vise. See page 160 for the way to cut out an interior space if you have one in your design.

Correcting the straightness of a cut. More often than not, straight lines will come out slanting, wavy, or crooked. Put the piece in a vise and, using the flat side of your rasp, run it along the edge, much as a carpenter would use a plane. The straightness of the rasp surface will automatically straighten out the edge of the wood. The rasp can be used both with and against the grain.

Correcting the shape of pairs of pieces. Where you have two pieces that are supposed to be identical, such as the two sides of a chair or chest, the shapes will have to be corrected after sawing. Neither of the saws suggested here is a precision tool, and no matter how careful you have been, no two pieces will come out the same.

Line up the two pieces as best you can, and insert them into the vise. Using small files and the larger wood rasp suggested, even out the two edges. Turn the pieces in the vise as necessary until all edges have been filed even.

The alternative, cutting two pieces at the same time, does not work well either. If you saw by hand, there is no way to keep the saw blade at right angles to the work. If you saw by machine, the problem of holding the two pieces of wood together is troublesome, and the clumsiness of the operation seems not worth the effort.

Correcting the size of opposite pieces. If among the pattern pieces you have cut there are two that are of different shapes but should have identical widths, as for instance the headboard and footboard of a bed, check that the widths actually match. If they don't, the difference would throw off the squareness of the finished piece of furniture. Hold the two together, insert them in the vise, and with the rasp even out first one side, then the other, until the pieces are of the same width.

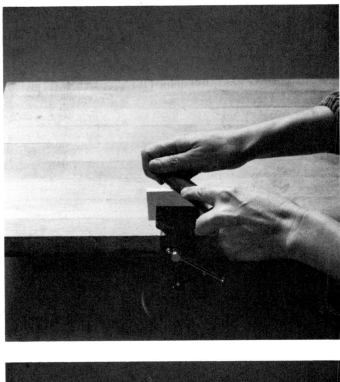

Transferring pattern lines onto the cut pieces. Before you start to glue anything together, transfer from the paper patterns onto the wood all the lines that indicate where other pieces will abut. These lines will guide you as you glue pieces in place. Without them, it is easy to get a whole piece out of kilter, with one leg off the floor or shelves that run downhill.

Assembling the frame. Assemble at least three parts of your piece of furniture to form a framework against which you can measure for other non-pattern pieces of your design. For instance, the two side pieces and the back of the chair, the two side pieces and the headboard and the footboard of the bed, the two ends of the table and the cross piece that runs between, the two sides and the back of the sled, or the two sides and the front skirt of the chest.

Spread glue evenly but thinly over both surfaces to be bonded, position them, using the lines you have transferred from the paper pattern, and press in place. Keep up the pressure for a few minutes. The suggested glues bond in less than five minutes, but other glues may differ.

Marking for non-pattern pieces. For each of these designs, at least one non-pattern piece is still to be cut. For the chair, only the seat is still needed. But for the chest of drawers shown in the illustration no fewer than five additional non-pattern pieces are needed, after all the pattern pieces are cut—and that's not counting the drawers. The illustrations for How to Make a Drawer show the technique by which pieces still to be cut are marked against the assembled frame to get the correct dimension. Only one cut is made at a time, checked and corrected. Each piece is glued in place before the next piece is marked and cut. An exception would be identical pieces such as slats or drawer sides which can be cut and assembled at one time. The work is tedious, but much less frustrating than if one were to cut out all the pieces and find that none fit properly.

Completing the assembly. One at a time, mark, cut, correct, and glue in place the other pieces of your design. The order in which you do this will differ from piece to piece. If you start with one or two simple practice pieces, the logic will become clear to you until eventually even the complexities of a chest of drawers will fall into a comprehensible sequence.

Filing and sanding. When the whole piece is assembled and the glue has dried, use the rasp and files to even joints, smooth out curves, or neaten up indentations. Sand the whole piece thoroughly with fine sandpaper.

Rasp and File

Because of the basic imprecision of both hand coping saw and power scroll saw, rasp and file are indispensable shaping and correcting tools. This photo shows four particularly useful shapes of small files:
1. Half-round
2. Round
3. Flat
4. Triangular

The round and half-round are used to smooth concave curves. The flat one is excellent for both convex curves and short straight areas. The triangular file is used to neaten up indentations.

The wood rasp (5) has both a rounded and a flat surface. The flat surface is used to plane down flat edges and to straighten uneven portions. The harsher grating surface is used where there is a good deal of wood to remove. The finer surface is used to remove smaller amounts of wood.

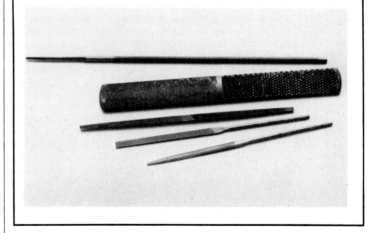

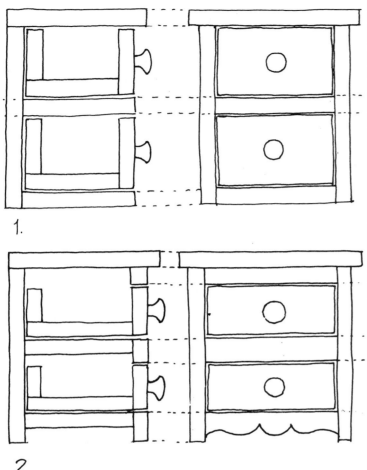

1.

2.

Above: Making a drawer is not particularly difficult, but before you even begin, the interior of the piece of furniture must be constructed to receive it. Shown here are:

1. The simplest arrangement, in which the height of the drawer is the same as the opening into which it fits.

2. A more complicated arrangement in which the height of the drawer need not correspond to the height of the opening. This second arrangement, though it requires several more pieces of wood, allows much more flexibility in design.

Finishing the piece. See Furniture Finishes, pages 186–189. Use any of the methods described, leaving out, of course, the step of removing the old finish.

How to Make a Drawer

1. Hold a piece of wood against the drawer opening and mark it for the proper width. This piece will be the drawer bottom.

Extend the mark into a line, using a triangle as shown to keep the angle true. Cut along the line. Insert the piece into the drawer opening to check the width. It should not be snug. If it is, correct with a rasp until, when it is inserted into the opening, there is a gap about the thickness of a shirt cardboard between the side edge of the drawer bottom and the side of the opening.

2. Using the drawer bottom as a guide, mark a piece of wood for the width of the drawer front. Extend the mark and cut along the line. Check the width against the drawer bottom and correct if necessary.

3. Mark the height of the drawer front against the drawer opening. Extend the mark and cut. Check the height of the piece against the drawer opening. It should not be snug. If it is, rasp the top down until there is a gap the thickness of a shirt cardboard between the top of the drawer front and the top of the opening.

4. Glue the drawer front to the edge of the drawer bottom. Allow the glue to dry for half an hour.

5. Insert the front and bottom assembly into the drawer opening *backwards* (drawer front to rear of opening). Mark under the projecting portion of the drawer bottom, using the edge of the opening as a guide. Cut along the line. Insert the assembly the correct way and check that the drawer front is now flush with the opening. Correct if necessary.

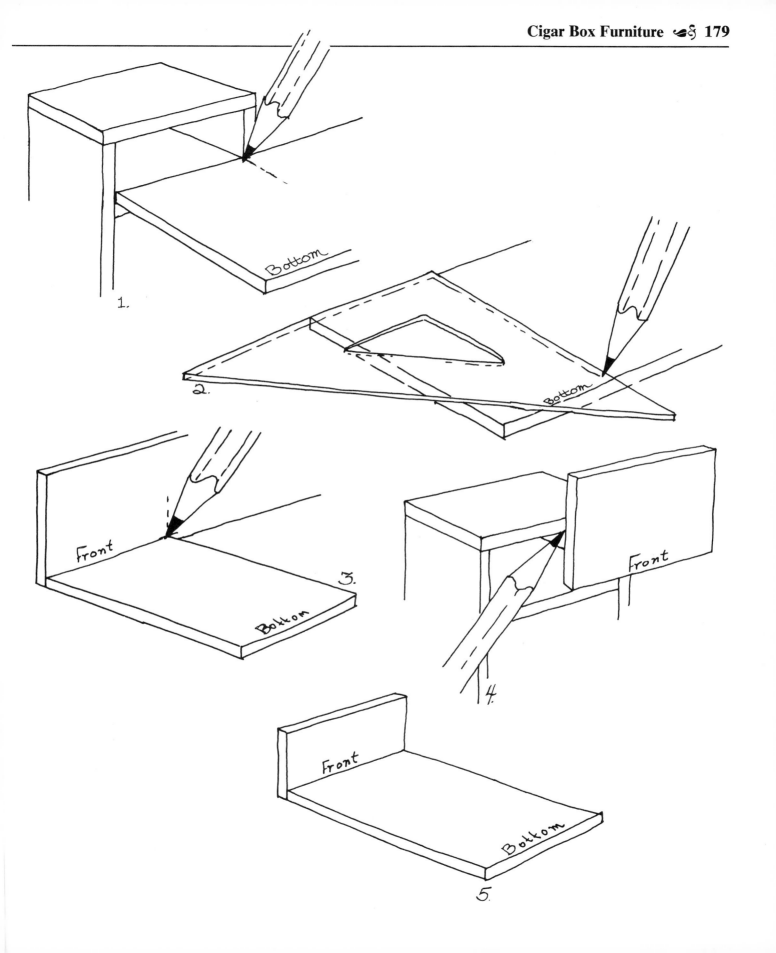

1.

2.

3.

4.

5.

6. The other three pieces of the drawer will be glued *on top of* the drawer bottom.

On a piece of wood slightly longer than the total of the remaining three sections, mark the height of the drawer sides and back, using the inside of the drawer front as a guide. Extend the line for the total distance and cut.

7. Using this strip, which is now of the proper height, mark first the length of the drawer back. Extend, cut, check, correct, and glue in position.

8. Mark the lengths of each of the sides, using the space between drawer front and back as a guide. Extend, cut, check, correct, and glue in position.

After the glue has dried for one hour, the drawer is ready for routine filing and sanding prior to finishing.

This excess is cut off.

Bottom

6.

7.

8. Side   Back   Front

9. Side   Back   Front

Knobs and Hinges

Other than the sources mentioned for routine miniature supplies, here are suggestions for making or devising simple hardware for your homemade furniture: The knobs on the chest of drawers in the photograph were shaped from ⅜-inch dowel. The tools and techniques are the same as for shaping clothespin dolls, pages 154–56. The finished knobs are glued in place.

Unshaped wood knobs could be made by cutting ⅛-inch dowel into short lengths. Other shapes could be formed of self-hardening clay (page 123) or firing clay (page 128). Hobby stores often carry very small wooden beads that could be nailed to the drawer with ¼-inch brads or brass escutcheon nails.

The smallest hinges I have been able to find in hardware stores measure ¾ inch high × ¼ inch wide (in closed position). The dimensions are workable for doors and shutters but are too large for furniture. Hobby shops may carry dollhouse-scale reproductions of antique hinges, which are also available from The Dollhouse Factory, Box 456, Lebanon, N.J. 08833 by mail order.

Small strips of leather can be glued in various positions to hinge doors and lids.

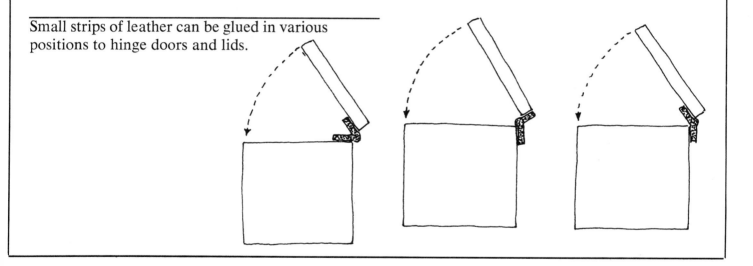

Mirrors

Pocket mirrors and mirrors from discarded compacts can, of course, be used in dollhouses. Other choices, if these are too thick or are of the wrong size and shape for your needs are: sheet aluminum (lumberyards and hardware stores sell it as rolls of flashing, but may consent to cut you a few inches), mica, silver paint covered with clear or tinted acrylic plastic (sold by the sheet in art stores, or robbed from a scrapbook or credit card cover).

❧ Paneling and Carving ❧

By using small chisels as well as a straight knife blade, you can achieve surface carving that resembles paneling or reproduces carved motifs. The knife blade is used for incising straight into the wood; the chisels are used to cut obliquely. The tools are not particularly hard to use, but the results in the hands of an amateur are somewhat crude. This corner cupboard is tucked safely away at the rear of a deep bedroom, where it looks perfectly handsome. Other items that could be made with this technique include wainscoting, doors, shutters, and mantelpieces.

Sources
Design ideas for paneling, cabinets, doors, carving for mantels: *A Treasury of Early American Homes*. Richard Pratt. New York: McGraw-Hill Book Company, 1949. *The American Fireplace*. Henry J. Kaufman. Nashville, Tenn.: Thomas Nelson, Inc., 1972.

Materials
Unassembled piece of furniture or other wood to be carved
Fine sandpaper
Drawing paper
Carbon paper

Tools
Pencil
Hobbyist's knife handle, thick type
Straight-edged cutting blades to fit handle
V-grooved, round, and flat chisel blades to fit handle
Flat, triangular, and half-round jeweler's files
Sharpening stone
Steel rule

Step by Step

Designing the pattern. Starting with the portion of furniture or other piece of wood you want to carve, trace around its shape on paper. Sketch the design you have in mind within the traced shape. Although the carving will be three-dimensional, you do not need to represent that on your drawing. The only lines you need are the outlines of the design, which represent the straight deep cuts of the carving. Compare the outline drawing (page 184) with the cupboard doors in the illustration to see how the lines correspond to the deepest cuts.

Transferring the design. Transfer the carving pattern onto the wood with carbon paper.

Making the straight cuts. Use the straight blade on your handle to incise the wood all the way around your outlines. Hold the piece down flat on a tabletop with one hand. Run the blade along the edge of a steel rule (page 100) for straight lines; cut by eye for curving lines, rotating the piece as needed. Be sure your cut lines meet at the corners. Don't press hard. If you make a mistake while pressing hard, you will have damaged the piece. Instead, use a light stroke, which will be easier to control. The shallow cut you make will be enough for your blade to follow on repeated strokes. Change knife blades frequently.

All the strokes to incise the outline should be cut straight down. How far down is up to you. Caution dictates starting with rather shallow cuts and doing some chisel work before cutting to the full depth you have in mind.

Making the oblique cuts. Oblique cuts are made with a chisel at an angle to the straight cuts. The result is a groove with one straight side and one slanted side. To make the oblique cut, use the straight chisel held at an angle to the incised outline. A chisel is pushed rather than pulled. Use the V-grooved or round chisel to shape the moldings further as you wish, running along the groove already started. Sharpen chisel blades frequently on a sharpening stone.

Correcting the cuts. If you find your cuts are less than crisp, you may want to use various shapes of small files to improve them. This is cheating, of course, but certainly helpful. The triangular file is particularly good for crisping a groove. Sharply creased sandpaper may be used, too.

Finishing the piece. When the carving is finished, sand the surface. If the piece is unassembled furniture, complete the assembly. See pages 187–89 for various finishes for wood.

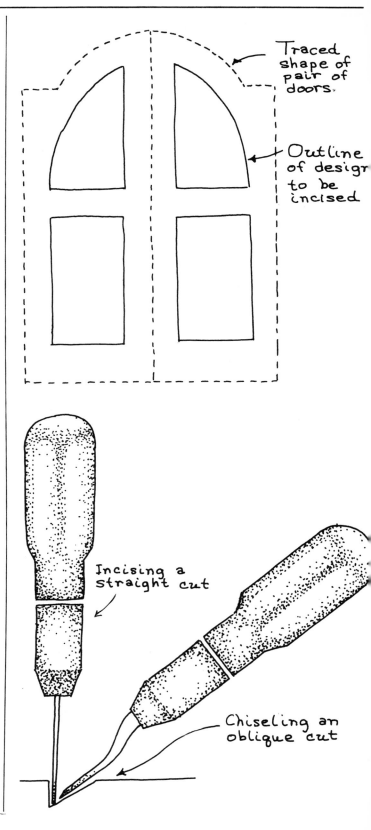

Traced shape of pair of doors.

Outline of design to be incised

Incising a straight cut

Chiseling an oblique cut

Stone Mantelpiece

Chisel blades can also be used to carve soapstone. Soapstone is an extremely soft stone that comes in a variety of colors and grainings, some of which are good mimics of marble. The stone is sold by the pound in chunks at sculpture supply houses.

Slice the stone to the thickness of the mantel with a handsaw. This mantel was made in two pieces—a thinner one for the facing, a thicker one for the shelf above. Use a soft pencil to draw the shape of the mantel on the surface of the slice. Cut around your line with a hand coping saw.

Draw the moldings or other motifs onto the stone. Carve out the design with knife and chisel blades. Go very slowly; the stone chips easily and requires very little pressure to cut. As you get toward the end of the job, merely scrape away excess stone with the edge of your blade instead of cutting down into it.

Smooth the piece with files, followed by fine sandpaper. To harden the surface somewhat after you are satisfied with the carving, varnish it with several coats of matte varnish and wax the surface two weeks later with a high-quality paste wax. The two parts of this mantelpiece were glued together with white glue, and the whole piece was then glued to the wall. The "brick" fireplace was molded from red, gritty firing clay, fired in a kiln, then glued into position on the floor of the dollhouse.

✐ Furniture Finishes ✐

This table is a modern commercial piece. The fact used to bother me considerably. It didn't have the charm of either antiques or homemade pieces, but the table worked well in the nursery. The solution was the one I learned in my twenties when I had to make do with secondhand furniture: refinishing. The various techniques suggested here can be used either on commercial furniture or on furniture you make yourself. It would be a pity to touch an antique or a fine handcrafted piece.

Sources

Design ideas: painted chests in *The Flowering of American Folk Art*. Jean Lipman and Alice Winchester. New York: The Viking Press, 1974. *American Painted Furniture*. Dean A. Fales. New York: E. P. Dutton & Co., 1972. Pennsylvania Dutch design motifs: *Pennsylvania Dutch American Folk Art*. Henry Kaufman. London and New York: Studio Books, 1946 (not in color, but the basic motifs are shown). *The Art of Painted Furniture*. Gisland M. Mitz. New York, Van Nostrand Reinhold Co., 1971.

Removing Old Finishes

Use a gel-type paint and varnish remover such as Zip Strip. The runny liquid ones are harder to use and don't work as efficiently. Follow the instructions on the label. The remover will raise the grain on the wood, making it rough to the touch. Sand with very fine sandpaper until the wood feels smooth again.

Staining

The common wood stain available at hardware or paint stores is an oil stain mixed with a turpentine or benzine solvent and sold in natural wood tones in quantities as small as ½-pint cans. Though very easy to apply, the effect is good only if the wood has been prepared properly. Any rough spots or scratches will be emphasized by oil staining. Edge grain will always show up darker than surface grain. Porous wood such as bass will tend to look opaque, and little if any grain will show up. The better the quality of wood used, the better the stain will look.

Preparing the wood. Sand with fanatic care (don't prime with shellac, as the stain won't penetrate through it). Choose the color of stain you want, or mix a different tone from two or more colors of stain. One good all-around brown is mixed from ⅔ Golden Oak, ⅓ Special Walnut. Test the color on the back or bottom of the piece before you use it. Once on, you can't get stain completely out of wood. Follow the instructions on the can to apply the stain. Let the stain dry for several weeks. Then wax for a lustrous finish.

Painting

Furniture can be given a painted finish with any of several sorts of paint. The finish can be a plain color, or the paint can be used for decorative designs or even pictures and for imitation wood graining or marbleizing. The great advantage of paint is that it covers up poor wood.

Preparing the wood for painting. Shellac the piece of furniture with one coat of white shellac. When dry, sand with very fine sandpaper until the surface is smooth and all slick areas are dulled.

Plain painting. You really do not have a very wide choice of color for furniture as most colors are simply not believable when applied to a chest of drawers or a bedstead. The most natural-looking colors are those used (because they were the only ones available) in the early history of America. They included a lime white, ochre, barn red, black, and a dark blue/green. All these are earthy, subtle colors. Brighter peasant colors can be found in some Mexican painted furniture; the clear blue, orange/red, and chrome yellow are cheery but refuse to look old.

No matter what kind of paint you use, a ¼-inch flat artist's sable brush does a smooth job.

Tempera paints, especially the artist's quality gouache that comes in tubes, can be mixed to subtle colors. Two coats are usually needed. The finish is not waterproof and must be followed by two coats of matte varnish to protect it.

Acrylic paints, which are waterproof, are not advised because of the garish colors and difficulty in applying the paint smoothly.

Interior flat wall paint makes an excellent surface, the only problem being that the wonderful colors you can get these days come in minimum quantities of a quart. The amount you need to paint a piece of dollhouse furniture is in comparison immeasurably small. However, it may be that you can use the paint for something else, or already have it left over from another job. Either water-based (latex) or oil-based (Alkyd) paint is fine. Allow the first coat to dry, sand it lightly, and then apply a second coat. In some cases a third coat may be needed, too. If the paint is later waxed, the result is a rich, glowing finish.

Decorative painting. Use interior flat wall paint as a base color for both imitation graining techniques and pictorial treatments. For pictorial painting, the design can be brushed on with oil paints or tempera paints over the base coat, using an 0 or 00 rounded artist's sable brush. You may get some spread of oil into the background with oil paints, but this darkening will be invisible when the whole piece of furniture is later darkened by waxing.

The method set forth here for imitation marble and wood graining is particularly good for the beginner. Neither artistry nor even much manual skill is required. The effects are achieved by coating the base color with shellac, then applying a thinned coat of oil paint, which recedes into itself to form streaked or mottled areas.

First paint the furniture with a base color of two or three coats of interior house paint, as described under Plain Painting. Color samples are shown on page 19.

Color formulas

Dark wood graining:
Barn red base color:* Dutch Boy Brown Touch, #106/G
Brown/black grain color: ½ Indian red, ¼ raw umber, ¼ Prussian blue

Light wood graining:
Ochre base color: Dutch Boy Pacer, #10/D
Red/Brown grain color: ⅓ cadmium-barium yellow deep, ⅓ raw umber, ⅓ Indian red

Dark marble:
Blue/green base color: Dutch Boy Sugar Grove, #151/G
Off-white grain color: titanium white slightly tinted with raw umber and Prussian blue

---

* All base colors will appear too light in the first stage. They darken when shellacked in the second step.

You can use your own imagination to paint a hope chest, or use design sources such as those listed on page 186.

Light marble:

Off-white base color: Dutch Boy Ibsen, #25/A

Gray grain color: ⅔ titanium white, ⅓ raw umber, slightly tinted with Prussian blue. (Both this color and the red/brown can be wiped on over the base color for a warmer marble.)

When the paint is dry, shellac the surface with one coat of white shellac. Allow to dry thoroughly.

Mix up about a teaspoonful of the second color of paint. It should be formulated from about ½ Damar varnish, and ½ artist's oil paints, in the formula given opposite or according to your own tastes. An even higher proportion of varnish will give you a more translucent effect.

Cover a portion of a table with newspaper. Set out on the newspaper a small bowl containing the varnish/oil paint mixture, another bowl containing a small amount of turpentine, and half a dozen three-inch squares of paper toweling (not the softest, mushiest types, but a firmer brand), each crumpled into a ball.

For wood graining wet down the first surface to be painted with a ball of paper toweling dipped in turpentine. Dip a second ball of paper into the paint mixture. Wipe the ball across the turpentined surface with a straight or slightly curved motion, or dab the paint on the wet surface, for a mottled tortoiseshell effect.

For marble, wipe paint over the surface first, then dab the turpentine-moistened ball of paper over the paint. With a dry ball of paper, dab at the surface again to remove some of the color.

Don't be alarmed if during the first seconds your work looks terrible. The secret of this method is that the slick shellacked surface somewhat repels the turpentine-thinned paint; the painted areas slowly retreat into themselves. The effects achieved are not exactly planned, but they are usually pleasing. If you don't care for a particular result, however, just wipe the paint off with turpentine and try again.

Allow each surface to dry before painting the next surface.

Waxing

Whether a piece of furniture is finished by painting or by staining, wax will further improve its looks. Wait until the surface is very dry—this will be anywhere from a day or less, for furniture painted in water-based (latex) house paint, to a month or more for oil paint. Use a hard paste wax, preferably one intended for fine antiques, like Goddard's. Spread the wax very thinly with a bit of rag, allow the wax to dry, and buff with a soft, clean cloth.

You may have noticed that none of the finishes suggested here ends with a coat of varnish. The reason is that the slick, superficial gloss of varnish is usually exactly what made a commercial piece of furniture look vaguely second-rate in the first place.

❧ Upholstered Furniture ❧

The method for upholstering given here is based on the furniture construction method outlined on pages 167–81. It is neither the simplest one could devise (gluing cloth over padding), nor the most authentic (what upholsterers do), but is somewhere in between: a padded and tufted surface that approximates Victorian upholstery and requires some dexterity and a great deal of patience. This project is not particularly fun to do. But there is enormous satisfaction in finally being able to have upholstered furniture that looks decent. Of all the commercial miniatures on the market, upholstered furniture seems to be the most disappointing—unless one can pay a devastating price.

Velveteen is a good choice of fabric. It is a cloth that seems to do as it is told, and it hides stitches well. The rich colors, plushy texture, and even printed patterns give the finished piece an air of luxury.

Materials
Polyester stuffing
Cotton velveteen, plain or printed
Silk buttonhole twist to match fabric
White glue
Rubber cement
Unassembled furniture
White paper

Tools
Pencil
Triangle
Ruler
Scissors
No. 10 "sharp" needle
Dremel Moto-Tool and stand, $\frac{1}{32}$-inch and $\frac{1}{16}$-inch drill bits
Flat toothpicks

Step by Step

Preparing the wood frame. Using the method described on pages 172–76, design your sofa or chair with a solid back and seat. Cut the side pieces from ¼-inch wood, but cut the seat and back from ⅛-inch wood. Check that the pieces fit together properly, but do not assemble. Sand and finish the side pieces by any of the methods suggested on pages 187–89. Put these aside and continue the upholstering process with the unfinished seat and back pieces.

Cutting down the seat. Cut ¼ inch off the front or rear edge of the seat. This is necessary because the padded upholstery will prevent you from gluing the seat up tight against the wood of the back. Since the upholstery will be about ¼ inch thick, the seat will have to be correspondingly shorter.

Making the tufting pattern. Trace the outline of seat and back with a pencil on white paper. Using ⅛-inch graph paper, lay out a pattern of dots and lines as shown, extending the pattern if necessary for a larger piece of furniture. Tape the graph paper over a bright windowpane, center your outline over it, and trace with a pencil those dots that fall within it. The dots will be for tufting the upholstery.

Top: Unassembled chair. The wood frame of an upholstered piece may be two sides, a back, and a seat.

Bottom: Paper drilling pattern. This upholstery method relies on holding the cloth to the seat and back by stitching right through drilled holes in the wood. A paper pattern is made first to use as a drilling template. This is the pattern used for the rocking chair in the photograph. It is temporarily glued to the chair back with rubber cement, and a hole is drilled through each penciled dot. The pattern is peeled off the wood before upholstering. A separate pattern is made for the seat and used the same way.

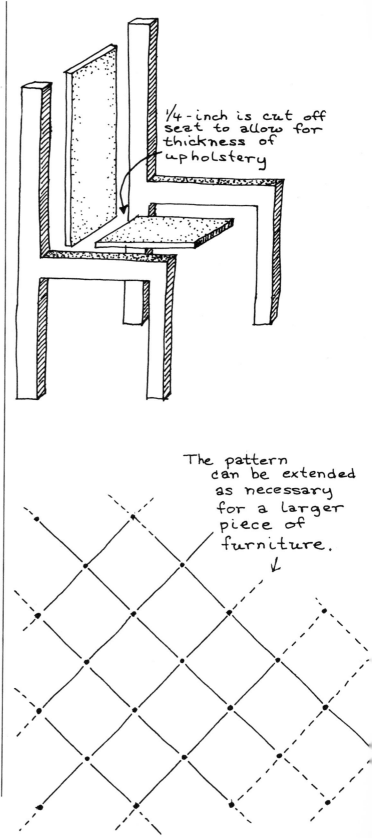

¼-inch is cut off seat to allow for thickness of upholstery

The pattern can be extended as necessary for a larger piece of furniture.

Draw a series of dots ⅛ inch apart around the perimeter of each piece. The row of dots should be about ⅛ inch in from the edge. These dots will be for edge-stitching the upholstery.

Affixing patterns to wood. Cut out the paper patterns. Spread the backs with rubber cement and press them immediately into place on the wood back and seat. The rubber cement will hold the patterns in place while you drill, yet it will be easy to peel them off before upholstering.

Drilling the holes. With the drill mounted in a stand to assure vertical holes, drill through each dot in the seat and the back. The perimeter holes for edge-stitching should be drilled with a $\frac{1}{32}$-inch bit. The holes for tufting should be drilled with a $\frac{1}{16}$-inch bit. Check that your holes are going all the way through the wood. When the drilling is finished, peel off the paper patterns to use as patterns for cutting the cloth.

Cutting the cloth. The piece of cloth that covers the padded front of back or seat must be cut larger than the piece of cloth that covers the unpadded back. Using the same paper patterns you used for drilling, trace the seat twice and the back twice onto the wrong side of the velveteen. The pattern should run along the straight grain of the fabric, and each piece should point in the same direction. Cut one of each shape with a ¼-inch margin, the other with a ½-inch margin. You will be using the larger pieces for the padded, tufted side of the upholstery.

The next three steps—padding, tufting, and edge-stitching—will be described for the seat of a chair or sofa. When you are finished, repeat the three steps for the back.

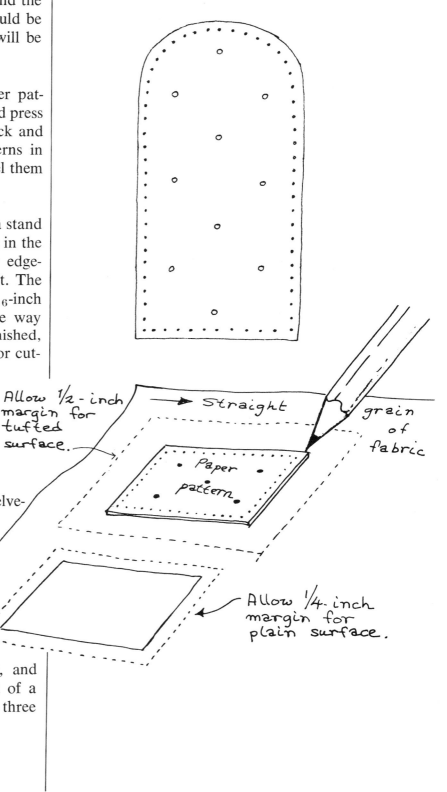

Allow ½-inch margin for tufted surface.

Straight grain of fabric

Paper pattern

Allow ¼-inch margin for plain surface.

Padding the surface. Lay stuffing out over the seat, pulling it with your fingers to smooth it evenly over the surface. It is impossible to tell you exactly how much stuffing to use. In its fluffy state, it should be at least ½ inch thick, which will compress to about ¼ inch after tufting. If you have too much, you can always pull some away as you work. If you have too little, you can poke more in with a knitting needle after the tufting is completed.

Hold the stuffing in place with your fingers and, using sharp scissors, trim the ragged edge off even with the perimeter holes all around.

Tufting the cloth. Thread your needle with a single piece of silk buttonhole twist 20 inches long. Make a large knot at one end. With the padded side toward you, push the needle down through a perimeter hole to catch the knot. The needle is now at the back of the work, ready to begin tufting. Place the larger piece of cloth cut to the seat pattern over the stuffing. Center it so the margins are even all around. Bring your needle straight up through the nearest tufting hole—right up through wood, stuffing, and cloth. Re-insert the needle into the cloth $\frac{1}{16}$ inch away from where it emerged, and push it back down through cloth, stuffing, and the same hole in the wood. Pull the thread taut. This single $\frac{1}{16}$-inch stitch is the first tuft.

Check that the cloth is still centered on the seat before taking the next stitch. When it is in position, bring your needle up through the next tufting hole, re-insert it $\frac{1}{16}$ inch away, and bring it back down through the hole again. Repeat until there is a tufting stitch at each hole; pull the thread taut each time. The thread that shows on the back between holes will be covered by fabric. When you are done, bring the needle up through the nearest perimeter hole and leave it in place while you prepare for edge-stitching.

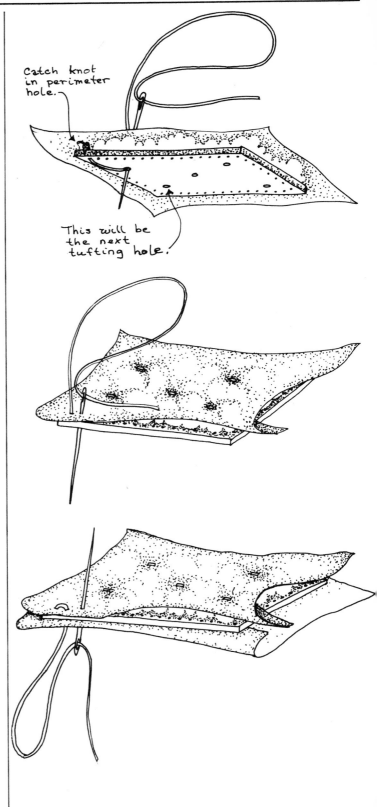

Catch knot in perimeter hole.

This will be the next tufting hole.

Edge-stitching. In edge-stitching, both the top and bottom pieces of cloth are turned under ¼ inch and sewed to the wooden seat through the perimeter holes. Unlike tufting, the needle goes down through one hole and up through the next one.

Before you begin stitching, check the amount of margin on the tufted piece of cloth. More than ¼ inch is clumsy to turn under. Trim away excess if necessary.

Starting where your thread is, turn in a ¼-inch margin on the tufted piece of cloth and bring the needle up through both thicknesses ⅛ inch in from the edge. Re-insert the needle ⅛ inch farther on and push it back down through both thicknesses of cloth and into the next hole. This first stitch will hold the top piece of cloth in place while you position the bottom piece.

Position the bottom piece of cloth evenly so the margin is the same all the way around, turn under the ¼-inch margin, and push the needle on through both thicknesses ⅛ inch from the edge. Push the needle back up through both thicknesses of the bottom cloth, through the next hole, and through both thicknesses of the top cloth. You have now completed the first two stitches of edge-stitching.

Continue to take these ⅛-inch stitches through the cloth and each perimeter hole in turn, folding under the ¼-inch margins as you work. The resulting stitches will be nearly invisible but will form a nicely finished raised edge similar to cording on a pillow. When the entire perimeter has been stitched in place, finish the thread by taking several tiny stitches in one unobtrusive spot.

Repeat the three steps of padding, tufting, and edge-stitching the back before continuing on the next step.

Assembling the pieces. The chair or sofa is assembled by gluing the side pieces to the back and seat along the exposed wood edges. Spread white glue sparingly, being careful not to get any of it on the upholstery. (If glue does get on the fabric, wipe it off immediately with a damp sponge.) Glue one side piece to both back and seat, allow it to dry, then glue the second side piece.

Covering the edges. After assembly there will still be two places where raw wood shows: the top edge of the back and the front edge of the seat. To cover them, cut strips of velveteen the width of the exposed edge and the length of the area to be covered. Spread glue over the back of the cloth strip with a toothpick and press the strip into place over the wood.

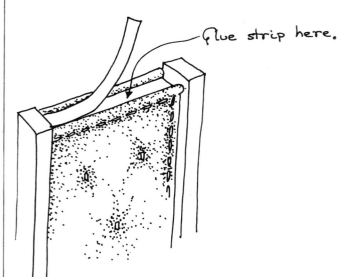

Glue strip here.

Upholstering arms. The arms of the chairs shown in the photograph are upholstered in the easiest way: by gluing a piece of cloth in place over a small bit of stuffing. Figure out first the length of the portion of arm you wish to cover. Cut two strips of cloth ½ inch wider than that dimension and several inches long. Turn the rear edge under ¼ inch and glue the strip to the arm as shown. After the glue is dry, poke a small amount of stuffing under the cloth with a toothpick. Turn in the front edge ¼ inch and glue it in place. Allow it to dry. Trim the ends of cloth that hang below the arm and push any stuffing that protrudes up out of the way. Spread glue along the inside of the cloth with a toothpick and press the bottom edges into place. Repeat with the other arm.

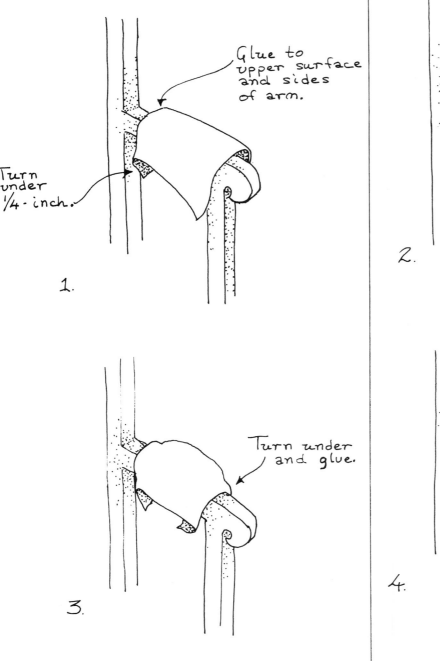

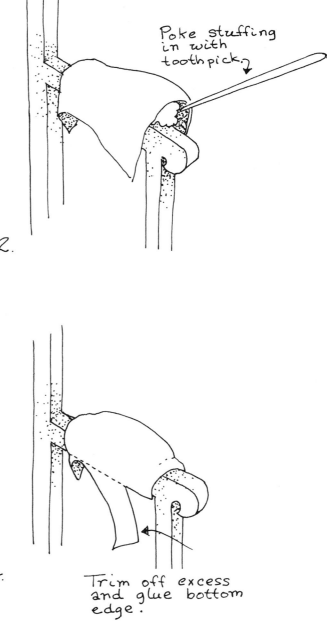

🙌 Copper Pots 🎀

This is the project I saved until last for the dollhouse because it felt so foreign to me. Solder, blowtorch, pickle, and flux—where does a woman learn of such things? The answer these days is in shop in high school, so I enlisted the aid of a high-school girl to see me through a weekend of broken saw blades, popped seams, and a persistent—though irrational—fear that the whooshing sound of a propane torch is a prelude to explosion. My inexperience may improve my attitude as a teacher. Heavens knows you have my sympathy. But the proof that a rank amateur can succeed is in this photograph of four pots, all completed between noon Saturday and supper Sunday.

The Basics—a Short Course in Soldering

One piece of copper can be fastened to another by melting solder—a mixture of lead and tin—into the joint between them. The surfaces to be joined are prepared by cleaning them with emery paper until they are shiny. Then flux is painted onto both surfaces to encourage the solder to flow and adhere. The pieces are placed in contact with one another in exactly the position desired, and are held in that position if necessary by restraints, such as a vise, C-clamps, a twist of wire, or simply pressure applied with a hand-held tool. Tiny bits of solder are placed at intervals along the joint, and the flame of a propane torch is applied to the pieces until the solder melts and joins them. The piece is then cooled and cleaned in pickling solution.

Since the flame of a propane torch is extremely hot, you cannot do your soldering on a wood surface. I used a steel vise to hold the pieces themselves, and also when it was closed, as a small flat surface to lay the pieces on.

Prepare the solder by hammering a portion of the wire flat and snipping off a dozen or so tiny pieces with scissors. A very little bit of solder goes a very long way, and putting on an excess will only result in the job of filing it off later.

Pickle may come as a bottle of premixed solution or as a dry powder to be mixed with water. In a wide-mouthed glass or ceramic container prepare one cup of pickle according to instructions. Pickle is a strong acid which removes burn marks from copper and restores its flexibility after heating. It also cools the piece so you can handle it. The acid can burn both skin and clothes, so use pliers to dunk and remove pieces from the container. Rinse the piece off in water after each dunking.

Set out the solder, pickle, flux, paintbrush, insulated needle-nosed pliers, matches, propane torch, and any of the restraints suggested in detail in Step by Step. All these should be within easy reach of the vise you will be using as a soldering station.

Clean the surfaces to be soldered with emery paper, spread flux on them with the brush, put them in position, and hold them in position with restraints (sometimes it is easier to spread the flux after the pieces are held). With fingers or pliers set bits of solder at half-inch intervals along the joint to be soldered. Light the propane torch and adjust it to medium flame. Direct the torch to the area to be soldered, moving the flame gently back and forth to heat the area evenly. Shortly, the flux will begin to bubble and turn white—a sign that the solder itself will melt within seconds. The solder melts suddenly and completely, flowing rapidly into seams and even up them. Continue to heat until you can see that all the solder has flowed into the joint to fill it completely. Remove the flame, but if you are hand-holding the pieces in position with pliers, don't let up the pressure yet. Before removing any restraints, let the solder cool for about one minute. Then put the torch out and, using a potholder or pliers, remove restraints and dunk the soldered piece into the pickle. Leave it there to soak for a few minutes before rinsing it.

Soldering a second joint in the same piece, as when you have already soldered the pot and the handle separately and now want to solder them together, is a little trickier. There is a risk that a previously soldered joint can spring open during reheating. Luckily, the temperature required to remelt solder is slightly higher than that required to melt it in the first place, so if you don't linger too long with the torch, chances are you'll get through all right. The professional way of solving the problem involves the use of three types of solder that melt at respectively higher and higher temperatures. The first soldering is done with the one that requires the highest temperature, the last with the solder that melts at the lowest temperature. These solders are available from jewelry supply houses.

Sources

Jeweler's rouge, pickle, and jeweler's saw: jewelry supply houses, occasionally hardware stores

Copper flashing: sold by the foot in lumberyards and plumbing supply houses. Get the narrowest available

Files, Moto-Tool, shears, solder, paste flux, propane torch, pliers, emery paper: hardware stores

Materials

Very fine emery paper
16-ounce* copper flashing

* The gauge of copper is given as weight in ounces per square foot.

Pickling solution
Jeweler's rouge or metal polish
Paste flux ("pipe sweating" compound)
Paper for making pattern of handle
Solder
Soft wire (not copper)

Tools

Small bottled propane torch
Light hammer, ball-peen hammer, or wood mallet
Insulated needle-nosed pliers
Steel vise
Glass or ceramic container for pickling solution
Small artist's brush
Copper coupling or other cylindrical object to bend
     pot side around
Scissors
Jeweler's saw and fine metal-cutting blades
Metal shears
Ruler
Pencil
Moto-Tool and $\frac{1}{16}$-inch drill bit, buffing wheel
Awl
Files: fine half-round jeweler's file, and small coarser
     flat file
Board for drilling into

Step by Step

Designing the pieces. Design is to some extent limited by what you can find to bend the sides of a copper pot around to shape it. The most useful object I located was the copper coupling suggested under Tools. This three-inch-long sixty-nine-cent item is intended for plumbers who are joining a ¾-inch pipe to a 1-inch one, so the piece has cylindrical ends of both those sizes. The frying pan was bent around a glass nose-drops bottle, as were the ends of the deep oval pot. Besides determining the size of the base by what you can find around (other possibilities are dowels, bottles, pipes, tool handles), the only other

aspect of design to consider is height in relation to the base, and the length and shape of the handle. These pot handles are designed to flare slightly at both ends as shown. The dotted line indicates where the handle is bent to form a flange that can be soldered to the pot. The various relationships between these dimensions for the three standard-type pots are as follows:

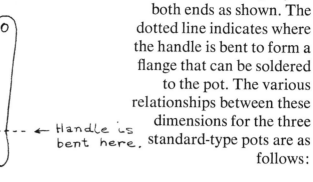

Handle is bent here.

	Diameter of base	Height	Length of handle*
Small saucepan	¾ inch	½ inch	1 inch
Large saucepan	1 inch	¾ inch	1⅛ inch
Frying pan	1½ inches	⅜ inch	1¼ inch

* This dimension is how far the handle projects from the pot. Add ¼ inch to allow for the bent portion that is soldered to the pot.

Making a pattern for the handle. Draw the handle as illustrated in the drawing or another shape of your choice. Refer to the chart above for length. Cut out the pattern with scissors.

Cutting the first layer of the handle. The handle is made of two layers of copper soldered together to give it sufficient strength. The first layer is cut, soldered to a second piece of copper, then the second layer is cut, following the shape of the first.

With shears, cut two rectangles of copper a bit larger than the pattern. On one of them trace the pattern with a pencil (a ball-point pen won't work on copper). Using a jeweler's saw and with the piece held in a vise, cut the shape to the outside of your pencil line.

Soldering the two layers of the handle. Flatten the second rectangle by gently tapping it with the hammer against your working surface. Flatten the cutout piece as well. Prepare both surfaces by cleaning and spreading flux. Clamp the pieces together with one or two C-clamps. Hold the whole assembly in the vise by tightening the vise around one of the clamps. The copper pieces should lie in a horizontal position. Lay bits of solder at ½-inch intervals all the way around the cutout piece. Heat with the torch until the solder melts into the joint. Pickle and rinse.

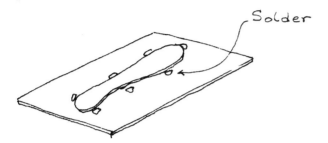

Solder

Cutting the second layer of the handle. Holding the soldered piece in the vise, saw through the second layer of the handle, following the shape of the first. Inaccuracy is okay as long as you don't cut away any metal beyond your original traced line.

Filing the handle. With the handle in the vise, file down both layers to conform to your original pencil line (retrace around the pattern if the pencil lines have smudged off by now). For most of the filing, the small, flat, relatively coarse file is best. You may want to switch to the finer half-round file when the shape is almost right. This file is also useful for removing any burr (rough edge) that may have been kicked up from the rougher file.

Drilling and bending the handle. If you wish to hang up the pot, you can drill a hole at the end of the handle. Clamp the handle flat to a board you can drill into. Use an awl and hammer to begin the hole at the right place, as otherwise the drill bit will spin across the surface instead of penetrating the metal. Drill through the awl mark, using $\frac{1}{16}$-inch bit in a Moto-Tool. Enlarge the hole slightly if you want by moving the bit in a circular motion after it has penetrated all the way through the copper.

Transfer your bend marking from pattern to handle. Insert the handle straight down into the vise, bottom first, to just before the bend line. Tap the handle lightly with a hammer to bend it over to the desired angle.

Cutting a strip for the side of the pot. Mark with a pencil and cut with a saw a strip of copper of the height you wish your pot to be and at least ¼ inch longer than the circumference of the object around which you wish to bend it.

The strip should be along the edge of the piece of flashing so that you can trust the straightness of at least one edge. To approximate the length of the strip, wrap the copper around the bottle, pipe, or whatever you will be using as a mold. Make a pencil mark where the strip meets itself and cut the length at that mark.

Bending the sides of the pot. Bend the strip around the mold with your fingers. Place strip and mold on the top surface of the closed vise and tap lightly all the way around it with the hammer until there are no obvious gaps between strip and mold. Holding the copper tightly in this position with your fingers, make a pencil mark where one end of the strip overlaps the other.

Straighten the piece, put it in the vise, and cut it just to the outside of your line. Bend it around the mold again and tap it with the hammer until it is circular.

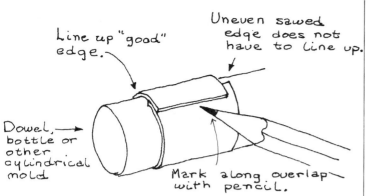

Line up "good" edge.

Uneven sawed edge does not have to line up.

Dowel, bottle or other cylindrical mold

Mark along overlap with pencil.

Hold the circular strip carefully so as not to distort its shape. With the flat file, file both edges of the side seam gently until you can see no light (or only a mere crack of light) through the seam when you hold the edges together. If the long edge you have sawed isn't straight, don't worry about it now. It's the other, bottom one that you will be soldering to the base.

Tap the strip around the mold again to be sure the curve is as evenly round as you can get it.

Soldering the side to the base. Cut a square of copper just big enough for the circular strip to rest on comfortably. Flatten the square with a hammer against the working surface. This square piece will be the bottom of the pot.

Hold the circular strip together so the seams meet, and wrap a piece of wire around the top of it, twisting it tight with pliers. This wire will hold the side seam together during soldering. Don't use copper wire as a restraint, since it could get soldered onto the pot by accident.

Clean the square with emery cloth. Place the wired circular strip "good" edge down in the middle of the square and hold the two together sideways in the vise. Affix two of the C-clamps so they are clamping the pot side to the pot bottom. Remove the assembly from the vise and affix a third clamp. Check to see that little or no light is showing through the seam around the bottom. If there is an area of light, you may have to apply another clamp or simply hold it tight with the pliers during soldering.

Hold the whole assembly level in the vise by tightening the vise on one of the clamps.

Brush flux around the circular seam both inside and outside the pot. Brush the flux up the vertical side seam, too, as it will be soldered at the same time.

Place bits of solder at ½-inch intervals on the square around the outside of the bottom seam. Be sure to place one of these pieces right against the side seam.

Light the propane torch, adjust the flame, and direct it around the base of the pot. As it melts, move on around the base until the whole circumference is soldered. The solder will of itself creep up the side seam, soldering at least most of it. If the top portion of the side seam lacks solder now, that will be taken care of when you solder on the handle.

Let the joint cool for a minute. Remove the clamps and wire with potholders and pliers, pickle the pot and rinse it.

Cutting the base. Put the rinsed pot back in the vise so you can saw off the square base close to the side of the pot. Again, great accuracy is not necessary.

Filing the base and evening the top edge. Keep the pot in the vise to file off the bottom even with the sides. The aim is to get rid of both edge and solder so the seam between sides and bottom can't be seen at all. Start with the flat file, but finish with the finer half-round file so you don't mar the pot sides.

To even the top edge of your pot, turn the pot upside down and rub it vigorously across sandpaper flat on the work surface. Use rough sandpaper if the top edge is very uneven, fine sandpaper if it is only slightly uneven. When the top edge is straight, you are ready to solder the handle on.

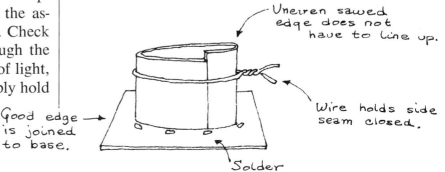

Uneven sawed edge does not have to line up.

Good edge is joined to base.

Wire holds side seam closed.

Solder

Soldering pot to handle. Place the pot firmly in the vise sideways with the side seam uppermost. Brush flux along the seam and along the inner side of the bent portion of the handle where it will be sealed to the pot. Light the torch. Hold the handle in position near the top of the seam with insulated needle-nosed pliers. Place bits of solder along the joint. Direct the torch to the area. Remove the flame the instant the solder melts, but continue to hold the handle in position for a minute. Pick the pot out of the vise with pliers, pickle and rinse it.

Polishing the pot. With the fine half-round file, file off any excess solder from the surface of the pot.

Begin the polishing by rubbing the pot with the finest emery paper. Rub it around and around inside and outside the pot. Rub along the handle and the edges. Rub back and forth along the bottom. Follow this preliminary polishing either with the buffing wheel of a Moto-Tool and jeweler's rouge or with any metal polish. The buffing wheel does a much better job, of course. To apply rouge to the wheel, hold the cake briefly against the wheel while it is spinning. Repeat often. The oil residue of the rouge on the pot after buffing can be washed off with soap and water.

Sawing Copper

Sawing copper is not hard, though the saw blades break rather often. Hold the piece of copper to be sawed firmly in a vise. Move it in the vise as often as necessary to keep the portion you are working on held securely. Use a jeweler's saw with a fine metal cutting blade. Tauten the blade in the saw as much as you can. Start sawing just to the outside of your pencil line (you can always file off any excess). Try a two-hand grip on the saw handle instead of the usual one-hand one. Continue sawing to the outside of your line, moving the piece around in the vise as you go without removing the saw, until the whole shape is cut out.

❧ Dollhouse ☙

Our dollhouse is not ordinary, and it is not easy to make. It is not ordinary because its simple painted surface, its drawers, and its moldings make it look like a piece of furniture. It is not easy to make because it is constructed like a piece of furniture. In fact, we didn't make it. A model maker, following plans my husband drew, built it for us—at considerable expense. A good finish carpenter or cabinetmaker equipped with table saw and router could also have built the dollhouse, also at considerable expense. What follows here, then, is a method for constructing a similar dollhouse based on methods I have used and can handle with the simpler tools available to me. The drawers beneath the house have been sacrificed but could be reinstated in the guise of an inexpensive unfinished case of drawers. The dollhouse could then be designed to fit on top of the drawer unit.

You need not copy the drawings for building your house. Dollhouses are fantasies, eccentric ones, private ones. Mine is a saltbox with a drawer. Perhaps yours is a townhouse with a turret or a mansion with veranda. Maybe you want it shingled or gingerbreaded. Don't be afraid to make what you really like. Forget both the rough dimensions and the detailing shown on these pages. Study the method for designing a model, for making a pattern, and for cutting and assembling a house. The methods will be the same no matter where your dreams wander.

Sources
Stairways, clapboards, shingles, doors, windows, shutters, flooring, and other details people might like to use to elaborate on any basic dollhouse design are available by mail order from Northeastern Scale Models, Inc., Box 425, Methuen, Massachusetts 01844.

Tools

Handsaw, circular saw, or table saw
Brace and bit
Square
90-degree triangle
Utility knife
Hammer
Screwdriver
Nailsink
24-inch steel rule
Rubber sanding block
Wood vise
Wood rasp
Hand coping saw or saber saw

Materials for model

Foam core board (art supply store)
Bristol board (art supply store)
White glue and freezer tape
Pencil
Dressmaker's pins or T-pins

Materials for house

⅜-inch plywood, birch veneer both sides
Various 1-inch moldings
⅜-inch birch veneer stripping
White glue
⅞-inch finishing nails
Putty
Fine sandpaper
White shellac

Step by Step

Building a model. Before putting saw to wood, work out shape and proportions of your dollhouse by building a foam-core model. Foam core is a stiff, featherlight board easily cut with a utility knife. It comes in 30-×-40-inch or 40-×-60-inch sheets at art supply stores.

Begin by making the rear wall of the model. Prop a piece of foam core against the wall. Roughly draw the outline of the house you have in mind. Cut out the shape with a utility knife.

Prop the cutout piece against the wall again and see if you like it. Change it or cut another piece as necessary until the shape is one that pleases you. You can add width or height by cutting strips of foam core and securing them to the original piece with freezer tape on both sides of the seam.

Measure and cut the side walls. (See pages 178–80 for the technique of "measuring" without rulers.) Begin by making the side walls about 16 inches from back to front, then cut them narrower if the house feels too deep to you. Attach the side walls to the rear wall with freezer tape.

Measure and cut the roof pieces. Tape them together at the ridge and lay the roof on top of the house.

With a pencil, mark where you think the floors should go inside the house. Measure and cut the floors. Pin each floor in place by sticking pins through the wall from the outside and into the edge

FIRST FLOOR PLAN

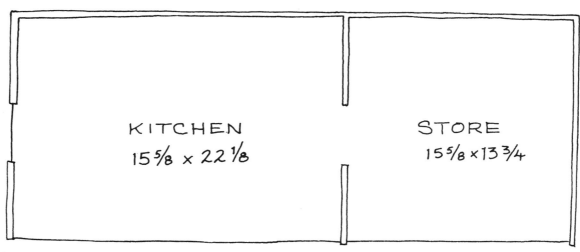

KITCHEN
15⅝ x 22⅛

STORE
15⅝ x 13¾

of the floor. Put some furniture in the model now and see if the space feels right to you. If you need more headroom, add to the height of the house with strips of foam core taped to the bottom. If the ceilings seem too high, cut the house at the bottom and adjust the floors accordingly.

Experiment with the position of partitions by using scraps of foam core. When you are satisfied, measure and cut the partitions. Secure them with pins and tape.

Mark with a pencil where you think doors and windows should go. Put some furniture in place again to see if the openings would work well. Make any changes, then cut out the windows and doors. Now look at the outside and see if the doors and windows are pleasing. If not, patch the holes and try again until openings look and function well both in and outside the house.

What you now have in front of you will be crude, probably lopsided, and patched here and there. But basically you have worked out the dimensions of your dollhouse.

Making a pattern for the rear wall. Using a large piece of Bristol board or other heavy paper, draw the outline of the rear wall of the house, using the measurements of your rough model as a guide. Use a square to be sure 90-degree angles are true, and a triangle to get the line of the peaked roof exact. The roof pitch of this dollhouse is 45 degrees. A shallower roof pitch is usually 30 degrees.

Draw lines parallel with the bottom edge to mark the top and bottom of doors and windows. Then measure for their width, using the model as a guide and a square to be sure openings are not cockeyed.

Draw two parallel lines ⅜ inch apart where each floor will abut the rear wall. Do the same to locate, where each partition will abut the rear wall. This double line corresponds to the ⅜-inch thickness of walls and floors.

With steel rule and utility knife (page 100) cut out the rear wall pattern, including the door and window openings. This is the only pattern piece you will need to begin the building of the actual dollhouse. All measuring for the other walls, floors, and partitions are done by the direct method of holding a piece to be cut against an already cut piece, marking the dimension, and extending the mark into a line to indicate where the new piece should be cut. Detailed instruction in this method will be found on pages 178–80.

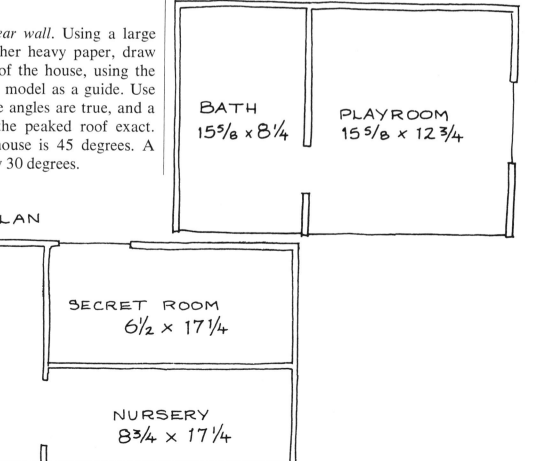

ATTIC PLAN

BATH
15⅝ x 8¼

PLAYROOM
15⅝ x 12¾

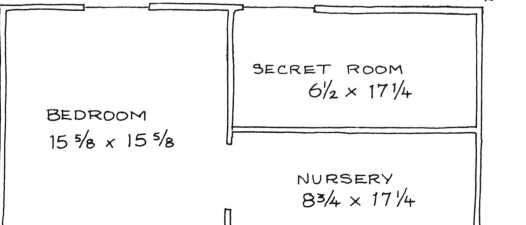

SECOND FLOOR PLAN

BEDROOM
15⅝ x 15⅝

SECRET ROOM
6½ x 17¼

NURSERY
8¾ x 17¼

FRONT OF DOLLHOUSE

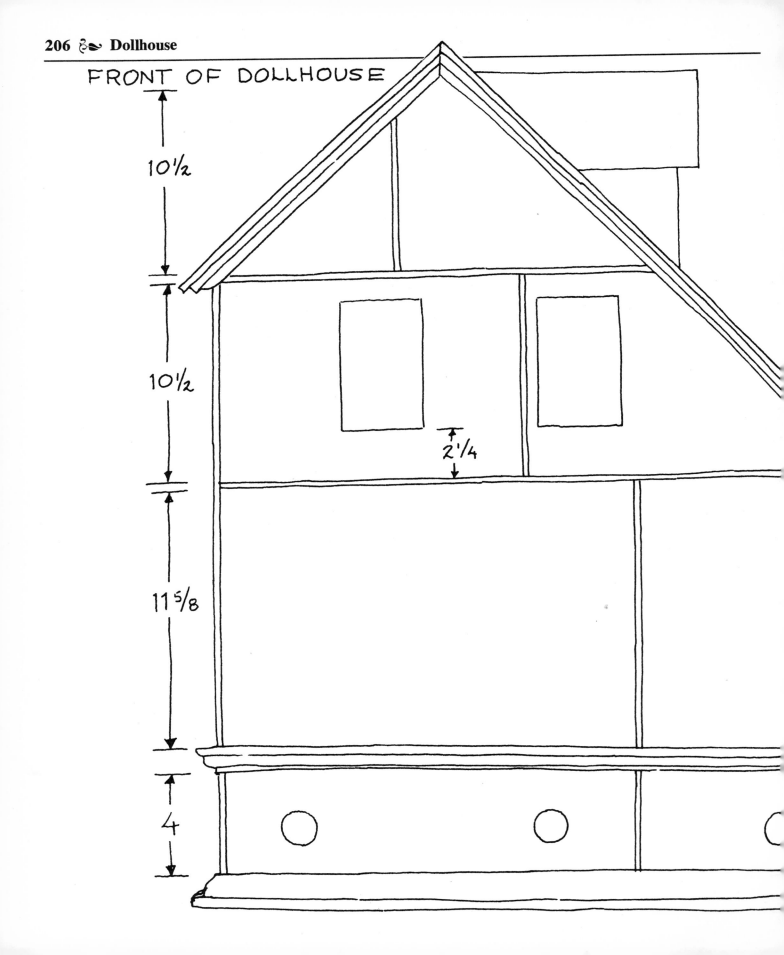

10½

10½

2¼

11⅝

4

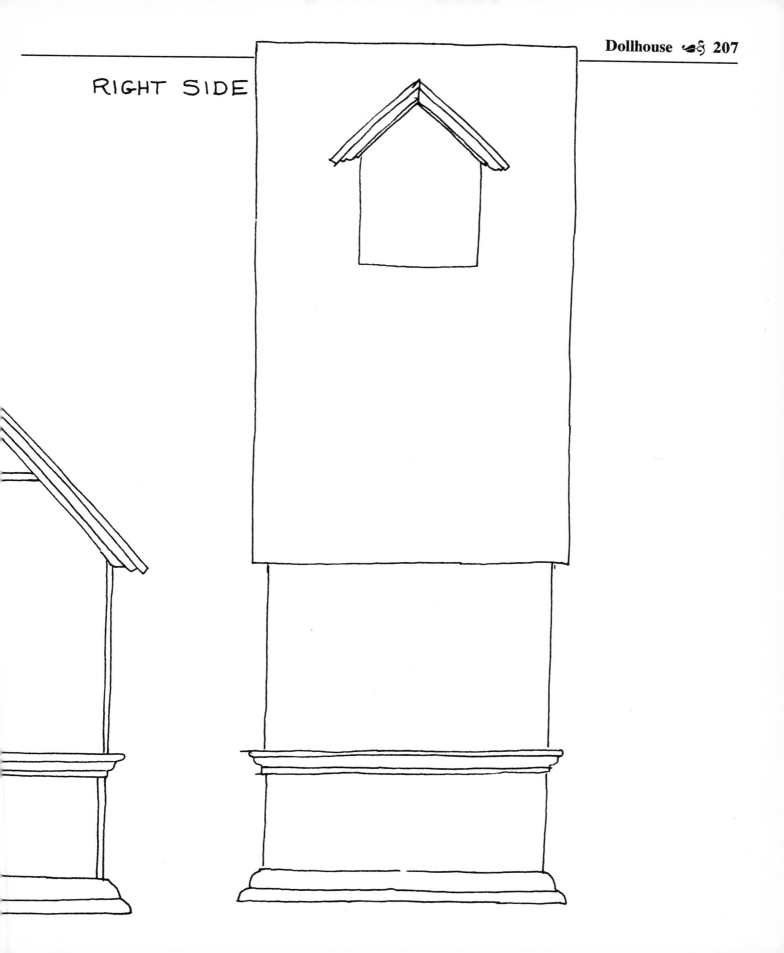

RIGHT SIDE

REAR OF DOLLHOUSE

9¾

7

←4¾→

14½

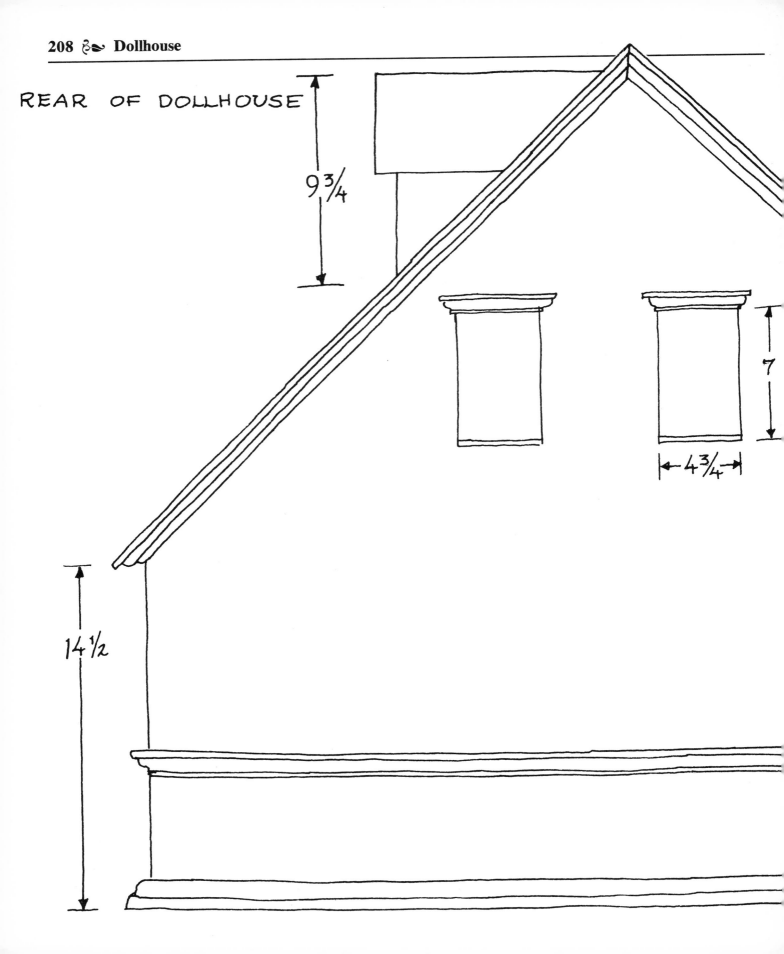

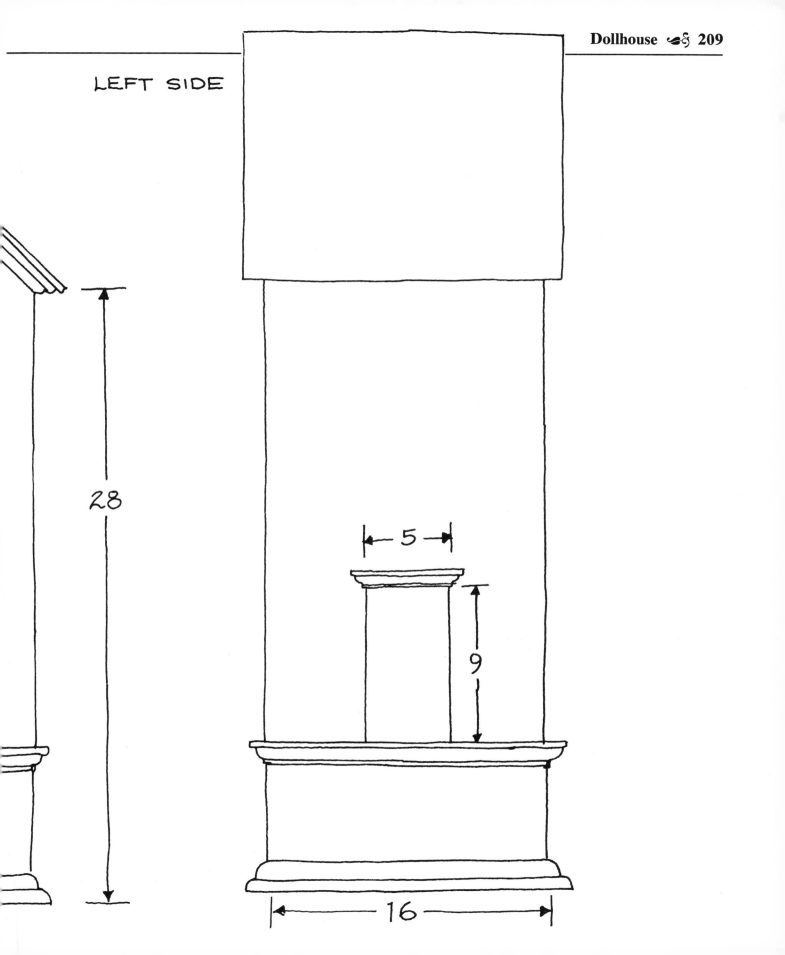

28

5

9

16

Transferring the pattern onto plywood. With a sharp pencil, trace the outline of the rear wall on ⅜-inch plywood. Trace the openings too. Transfer onto the plywood all the floor and partition lines.

Cutting out the rear wall. Cut the rear wall out with a handsaw, circular saw, or table saw. Don't cut the openings yet. Check the trueness and straightness of your cutting with a square, and recut or correct edges with a rasp (page 176) if necessary. This first cutout piece of the dollhouse will be the basis for measuring and marking the other pieces.

Measuring and cutting the side walls. Hold the plywood that will be a side wall in place against the rear wall. Mark where it meets the roof angle. Using a square, extend your mark into a line across the wood to indicate the height of the wall. Using the model as a reference, make a line to indicate the depth of the wall. Do the same for the opposite side of the house. Before you cut out the side walls, be sure to notice which edges need to be beveled where they will meet the roof. To cut a bevel, set table or circular saw to the same angle as the roof. It is very hard to cut a long beveled edge with a handsaw, but some people can do it. Cut the side walls, check, and correct.

Marking openings and floors on side walls. Lay the rear wall and the two side walls down on the floor with their sides together and their edges aligned. With the square and rule, extend the floor lines that are already drawn on the rear wall onto both side walls. If there are to be openings in the side walls of your dollhouse, extend the parallel lines that indicate tops and bottoms of doors and windows to both the side walls.

Use the model as a reference for locating the position of doors and windows. Unless you have a reason to vary the size, make side doors and windows the same widths as those on the rear wall.

Cutting doors and windows. Use a hand coping saw or a saber saw to cut openings. Drill a ½-inch hole near one corner of the opening. Insert one end of the saw blade through the hole, re-attach it to the saw, and cut along your lines, skirting the corners rather than trying to cut them square. When the piece opening is cut out, go back and cut into each corner from both sides until the cuts meet cleanly at the corner. Uneven edges can be straightened with a rasp.

Measuring and cutting the floors. Tack the side walls in place against the rear wall temporarily by hammering 1-inch brads partway in. With the side walls in place, mark the width of the floors. On a piece of plywood, extend your mark into a line and cut. Hold the piece of wood in place in the house and mark the depth of the floor. Extend the mark into a line and cut. Repeat these two steps of marking and cutting the width, then the depth, for each floor in the house. (If you have an attic floor that abuts a pitched roof, both sides will have to be beveled to fit against the roof snugly. You might wait until after the roof is in place before marking and cutting this floor.)

Measuring and cutting the partitions. Tack the floors in place with 1-inch brads. Extend the partition lines already drawn on the rear wall along the floor. Mark the height of each partition on a piece of plywood, extend the mark into a line, and cut. Partitions that abut a sloped roof will have to be beveled along their top edge to fit snugly. Hold the partition in place inside the house and mark its depth. Extend the mark into a line, and cut. Repeat these two steps of marking and cutting height and depth for each partition.

Using the model as a reference, and the height of any exterior doors as a guide to height, draw interior doors in the partitions. As these are accessible to the saw, you will not need to drill a hole for the saw blade. Use the same saw as for the other openings, and the same method for cutting clean corners.

Measuring and cutting the roof. The ridge of a peaked roof can be made by either overlapping one edge over the other or by beveling both pieces so they meet exactly at the center. Beveling is nicer; overlapping is easier. The amount of roof that projects beyond the walls, forming the eaves, is also a matter of choice. To accommodate the 1-inch molding used as trim under the eaves of our house, the roof projects 1⅛ inches.

Cut the rear edge of both roof pieces and the beveled or straight ridge. Both pieces should be both wider and longer than the roof will be.

With rear edges lined up, tack the two pieces together at the ridge line. Lay the roof assembly on the temporarily assembled house. Move the roof back and forth until the depth of eave at the rear edge of the roof pleases you or correctly accommodates any decorative molding you intend to use.

When the rear of the roof is exactly placed as you wish, trace a pencil line up under the eaves all the way around where roof meets walls.

Remove the roof pieces from one another and from the house. Using the correct rear eave as a guide, measure out the same distance from your traced line on front and side eaves, draw a line, and cut. Your eaves will now project equally on all sides of the house, and the traced line will serve as a guide for placing the roof on the house accurately during the final assembly.

Assembling the house. Assemble the house in whatever order seems most convenient to you. It will help if someone else is around to hold things in place while you work. Use both carpenter's glue and 1-inch brads to hold together everything except the partitions. Partitions can be attached with glue only. Don't try to assemble everything at once. Let the glue dry in the first few joints before continuing to the next.

Finishing the house. Countersink all nails (push the tops below the surface of the wood), using a nailsink and hammer. Fill nail holes and cracks with putty, using your fingers, a putty knife, or a small spatula. Sand the exposed plywood edges, or cover them with a ⅜-inch birch veneer strip, applying white glue to the edge a few inches at a time and unrolling the veneer as necessary. If the veneer doesn't adhere well, hold it in place until dry with very fine brads, nailed in only partway so you can remove them later.

Sand the house inside and out until smooth to the touch. Use a rubber sanding block for flat surfaces; do inside corners and moldings by hand.

If you want to add shingles, clapboards or other exterior embellishments, they should be glued onto the surface at this point. The same is true of stairs, built-in cupboards, ceiling beams, and similar add-ons on the inside of the house. When all trim has been applied, the house is ready for painting, staining, and papering.

Follow the directions on the can for oil-based stains or semigloss interior house paint. In general, the wall edges should be treated the same as the exterior walls. You may choose to treat the floors and floor edges the same also. If the interior walls are to be papered, ceilings will look better in a color that complements the paper.

If the interior walls are to be painted a different color from the floors, finish the floors first. When they are dry, protect them by laying strips of 1-inch-wide freezer tape all around their perimeters and covering the rest of each floor with newspaper while you paint the walls.

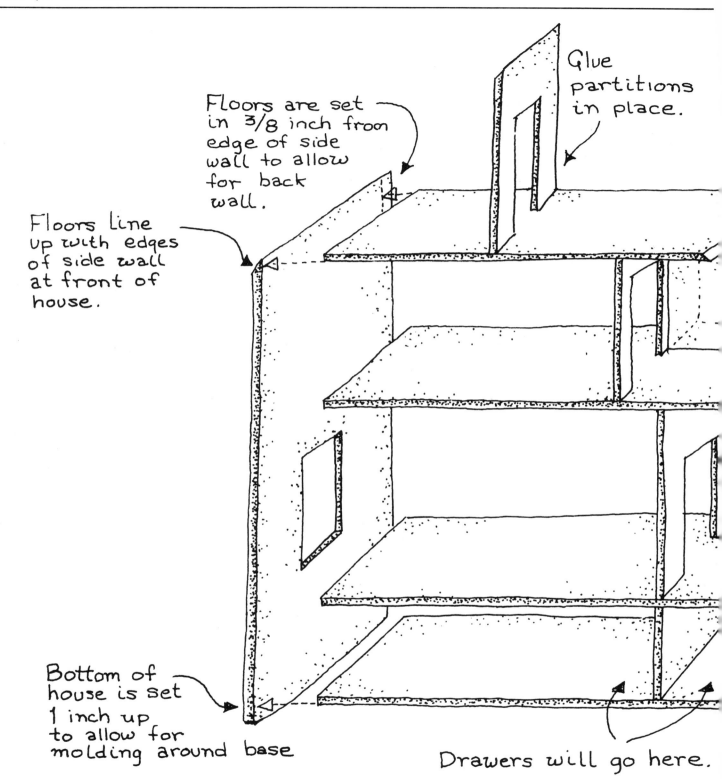

Floors are set in 3/8 inch from edge of side wall to allow for back wall.

Glue partitions in place.

Floors line up with edges of side wall at front of house.

Bottom of house is set 1 inch up to allow for molding around base

Drawers will go here.

CONSTRUCTION OF SIDE WALLS, FLOORS AND PARTITIONS

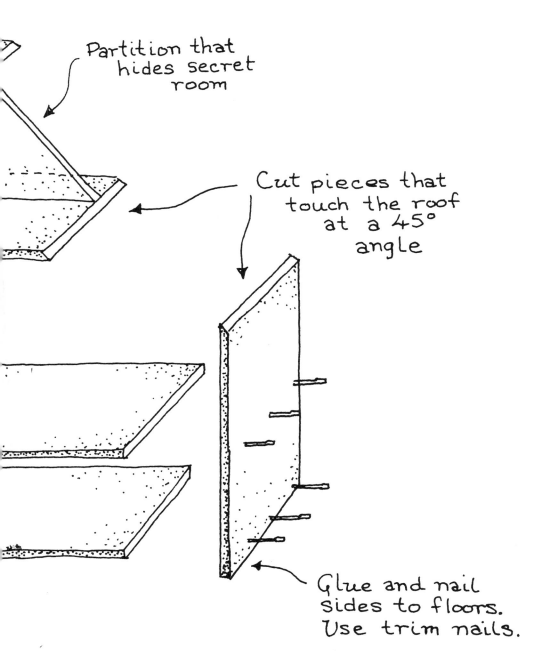

Partition that
hides secret
room

Cut pieces that
touch the roof
at a 45°
angle

Glue and nail
sides to floors.
Use trim nails.

~ FRONT VIEW

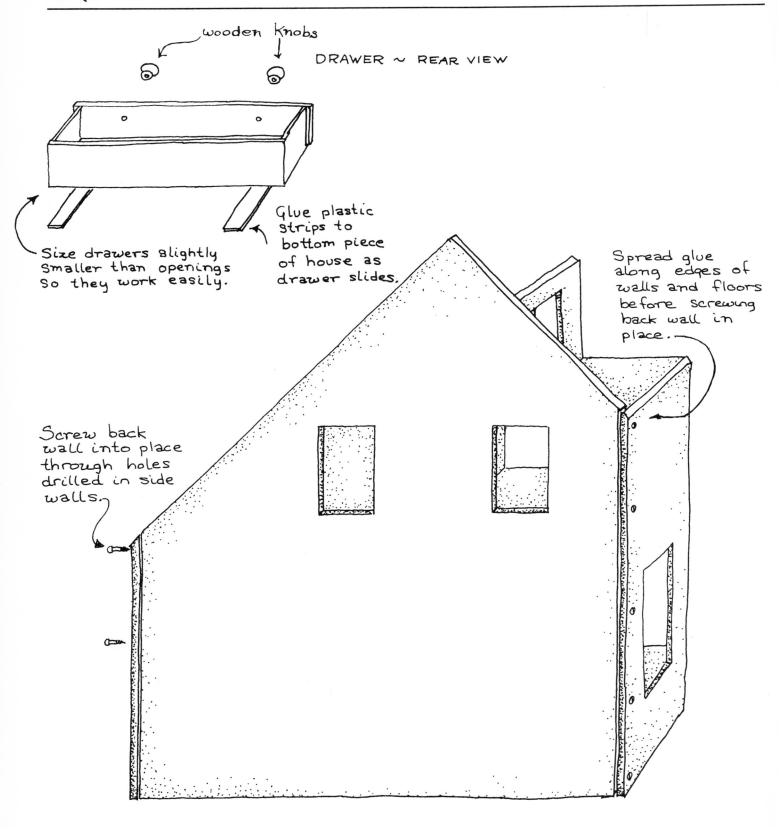

wooden Knobs

DRAWER ~ REAR VIEW

Size drawers slightly smaller than openings so they work easily.

Glue plastic strips to bottom piece of house as drawer slides.

Spread glue along edges of walls and floors before screwing back wall in place.

Screw back wall into place through holes drilled in side walls.

ATTACHMENT OF BACK WALL ~ REAR VIEW

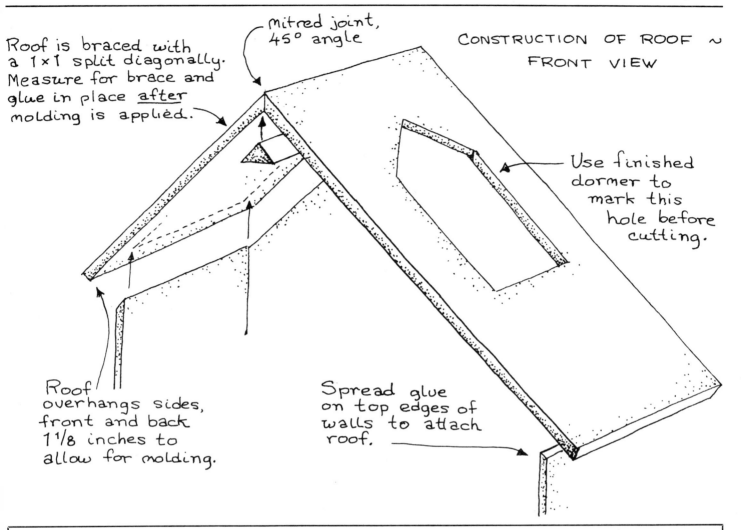

Roof is braced with a 1×1 split diagonally. Measure for brace and glue in place **after** molding is applied.

mitred joint, 45° angle

CONSTRUCTION OF ROOF ⁓ FRONT VIEW

Use finished dormer to mark this hole before cutting.

Roof overhangs sides, front and back 1⅛ inches to allow for molding.

Spread glue on top edges of walls to attach roof.

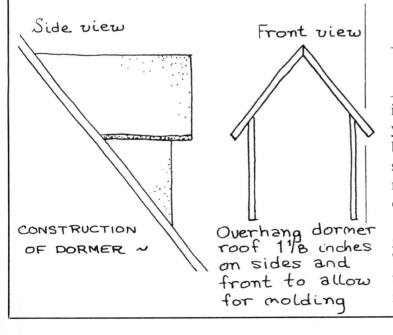

Side view

Front view

CONSTRUCTION OF DORMER ⁓

Overhang dormer roof 1⅛ inches on sides and front to allow for molding

Dormers

I f you want a dormer, build it of foam core first to get the proportions and angles right. Be sure you are aware of where the opening for the dormer will hit inside the house, so you don't end up with a window that extends below a floor or above a ceiling. Following the same procedures you used for other pieces, make accurate patterns, mark the wood, and cut the pieces.

Tack the dormer together and use it as a guide to mark the opening through the roof. The opening comes to the inside of the dormer walls, not to the outside. Cut the opening in the roof the same way you did the other windows.

Moldings

The moldings used on this house are of six different profiles. You may not be able to get exactly the same ones shown, but you can see from the drawings that different shapes give various effects. See what is available in your local lumberyards, and if possible bring home short samples to experiment with before you make final choices.

Mark a line indicating position for each piece of molding around the house. To measure for each piece of molding, hold the molding along the line, letting it project beyond both corners. Mark the inside of one corner, then cut it, beveling it outward (the outside of the molding will be *longer* than the inside). Hold up the piece against the line again with the cut edge in place and mark the inside of the other corner. Then bevel that corner. Continue with each piece, checking that they fit well against one another. Glue and nail the moldings in place.

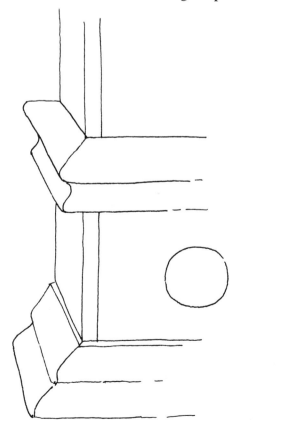

MOLDINGS ABOVE AND BELOW DRAWER

MOLDING UNDER
MAIN ROOF

MOLDING UNDER
DORMER ROOF

MOLDING ABOVE WINDOW,
AND SILL

Wallpapering

To wallpaper, measure the wall you want to paper. Cut the paper slightly larger than your measurement. Don't cut out doors or windows yet. Hold the paper in place against the wall and crease any excess. Remove the paper and cut along your crease lines. Check again that the paper fits well. Brush ordinary wallpaper paste over the back of the paper with a 1-inch paintbrush. Put the paper on the wall, sliding it into place. Smooth it from the center to the edges with a bunched-up piece of paper towel. Wipe any paste off the surface with a clean, damp sponge. Continue papering each wall, one at a time. When the wallpaper is dry, cut out the doors and windows with a utility or hobbyist's knife. Run a nail file along the edges to get them flush to the edge of the wood. A matte varnish can be brushed over the wallpaper the following day to make it washable (though not scrubbable).

Though special tiny-scale papers are sold to miniaturists, they may look too precious for this bold a dollhouse. Instead, try regular wallpaper in miniprints. The wallpaper sample books to look in at decorating stores are Stone Mill and Laura Ashley. If single rolls are not available (or cost too much), see if a decorator can order you a cutting (for which there is a small charge). These large samples are usually adequate for at least one good-size room.

🙐 Metric Chart 🙚

Inches convert to millimeters or centimeters, feet convert to centimeters or meters, and yards convert to meters:

To convert inches (″) to millimeters (mm.), multiply by 25 (1″ = 25 mm.).
To convert inches to centimeters (cm.), multiply by 2.5 (1″ = 2.5 cm.).
Below is a conversion table for fractions of inches:

1″ = 2.5 cm. = 25 mm.	⅜″ = 1 cm. = 10 mm.
¾″ = 2 cm. = 20 mm.	¼″ = .6 cm. = 6 mm.
⅝″ = 1.5 cm. = 15 mm.	$\frac{3}{16}$″ = .5 cm. = 5 mm.
½″ = 1.3 cm. = 13 mm.	⅛″ = .3 cm. = 3 mm.

1 foot (1′) = .31 meter (m.) (1 m. = 39″, or 3′ 3″)
1 yard (3′) = .91 m.

Teaspoons (t), tablespoons (T), and cups (C) convert to milliliters (ml.):
1 t = 5 ml. (thus 1 ml. = .02 t)
1 T = 15 ml. (1 ml. = .07 T)
1 C (= 16 T = 48 t) = 240 ml.

Ounces (oz.) and pounds (lb.) convert to grams (g.) and kilograms (kg.):
1 oz. = 28.4 g. (1 g. = .04 oz. or $\frac{1}{25}$ oz.)
1 lb. (16 oz.) = 454 g. = .45 kg. (1 kg. = 2.2 lb. or 2 lb. 3 oz.)

To convert Fahrenheit (F) to Centigrade (or Celsius—C):
Subtract 32 from the F temperature, multiply the result by 5, and divide by 9 (or multiply the result by .56).

To convert C to F, just reverse the process:
Multiply the C temperature by 9, divide by 5, and add 32 (or multiply by 1.8 before adding 32).